THE
HOLE
IN THE
FLAG

BOOKS BY ANDREI CODRESCU:

POETRY:

Belligerence (Coffee House Press, 1991)
Comrade Past and Mister Present (Coffee House Press, 1987)
Selected Poems: 1970–1980 (Sun Books, 1983)
Diapers on the Snow (Crow's Foot Press, 1981)
Necrocorrida (Panjandrum Press, 1980)
For the Love of a Coat (The Four Zoas, 1978)
The Lady Painter (The Four Zoas, 1977)
The Marriage of Insult and Injury (Cymric Press, 1977)
A Mote Suite for Jan and Anselm (Stone Post Art, 1976)
Grammar and Money (Arif Press, 1973)
A Serious Morning (Capra Press, 1973)
Secret Training (Grape Press, 1973)
the, here, what, where (Isthmus Press, 1972)
The History of the Growth of Heaven (George Braziller, 1971, 1973)
License to Carry a Gun (Big Table/Follett, 1970)

FICTION:

Monsieur Teste in America and Other Instances of Realism (Coffee House, 1987)
The Repentance of Lorraine (Pocket Books, 1976)
Why I Can't Talk on the Telephone (kingdom kum press, 1971)

MEMOIRS:

In America's Shoes (City Lights Books, 1983)
The Life and Times of an Involuntary Genius (George Braziller, 1975)

ESSAYS:

The Disappearance of the Outside (Addison-Wesley, 1990)
Raised by Puppets Only to Be Killed by Research (Addison-Wesley, 1989)
A Craving for Swan (Ohio State University Press, 1986, 1987)

TRANSLATION:

At the Court of Yearning: The Poems of Lucian Blaga (Ohio State University Press, 1989)
For Max Jacob (Tree Books, 1974)

WORKS EDITED:

American Poetry Since 1970: Up Late (Four Walls/Eight Windows, 1987)
The Stiffest of the Corpse: An Exquisite Corpse Reader (City Lights Books, 1988)
Exquisite Corpse: A Monthly Journal of Books and Ideas (est. January 1983. Published by Culture Shock Foundation)

THE
HOLE
IN THE
FLAG

A Romanian Exile's
Story of Return and
Revolution

Andrei Codrescu

WILLIAM MORROW AND COMPANY, INC.
New York

Parts of this book in slightly or substantially different forms were first broadcast on National Public Radio's *All Things Considered*. Other portions appeared in different shapes in *Harper's*, November 1990, *American Way*, November 15, 1990, and *Organica*, February 1990.

Library of Congress Cataloging-in-Publication Data

Codrescu, Andrei, 1946–
The hole in the flag : a Romanian exile's story of return and revolution / Andrei Codrescu.
p.   cm.
ISBN 0-688-08805-8
1. Romania—History—Revolution, 1989—Personal narratives.   2. Codrescu, Andrei,
1946–   . I. Title.
DR269.6.C63   1991
949.803—dc20   90-26046
                                                                                                        CIP

Printed in the United States of America

First Edition

1 2 3 4 5 6 7 8 9 10

BOOK DESIGN BY KATHRYN PARISE

For UNCLE RIHARD, an officer of the old Romanian Army, may his tormentors rot in hell, and for THE POETS, DISSENTERS, and STUDENTS who brought down the Ceauşescu tyranny with their unarmed bodies, and for ADRIAN, STOIE, ION, and ORY, friends of my childhood in whom bits of that childhood still live, and for ART SILVERMAN, MICHAEL SULLIVAN, and NOAH ADAMS of NPR whose hearts are bigger even than their mouths, and for ACTIVISTS as yet unknown to me who are making sure that the hole in the Romanian flag remains open to the winds of liberty. To all these, and to many others including my patient and long-suffering FAMILY and FRIENDS,

I am most grateful.

Contents

Workers of the World, We Apologize!
—*May 1, 1989, banner in Red Square, Moscow*

THE
HOLE
IN THE
FLAG

1

New Year's 1990
in Bucharest

Moments before the end of the decade I stood in the cold, ice-covered center of University Square in Bucharest, Romania, and said a brief prayer of thanks. The only light came from the small sea of candles burning in the snow at the martyrs' shrine before me. Bits of paper taped to a Christmas tree at the center of the shrine fluttered in the bitter wind. Penciled awkwardly on them: "Thank you, children, for dying so that we could be free!" "Your young lives ended here for us!" "You brought us Christmas!" "Good-bye, my child, you died for your country!" A few days before, dozens of young people had died here, murdered by machine-gun pistols firing point-blank into the unarmed crowd. There was still blood under the layers of ice and snow under my feet.

They had also died so that I could stand here for the first time, twenty-five years after leaving my homeland. This magical city of my youth, which I had once thought to conquer with my poetry, was both different and the same. The dome of the Athenaeum and some of the snow-covered church cupolas near the venerable music academy were just the way I'd kept them in memory. But other landmarks, including many churches, had fallen to the dictator's bulldozers. In their stead rose a forest of uniformly depressing apartment buildings. Beyond them, etched against the frozen sky, was a steel gray forest of cranes that would have built yet another layer of these ordered hives that had been Ceauşescu's vision of his gridded, controlled world. The dictator's architects had been poised to erase the country's past in order to transform it into a single cube of square cement in homage to their boss.

Over the two decades and a half of my exile I had nursed countless fantasies of return, all of them triumphant, involving Bucharest in late summer or fall. I saw myself at a sidewalk café, drinking the new wine, in animated conversation with the friends of my youth. Now and then a spray of linden flowers would descend gently from the trees above us to land in the wine and in our hair. The girls had deep black eyes and long raven black hair. We were, all of us, exactly the way I left us, in that faraway autumn of 1965 when I took the airplane to another world. There was Aurelia of the unruly hair and heart-shaped mouth, who held us spellbound with stories of mountains and bandits from the western Carpathians. There was Stoie, who burst into the drunken verses of François Villon—in his own translation—whenever the moon was full. Dumitru, a large and quiet boy, was partial to the thundering poetry of the revolutionary Soviet Mayakovsky whenever the spirit seized him. Kyra of the sparkling olive eyes bestowed her attention on whichever one of us could be more poetic and more fantastic. "If you ever write any prose," she once told me, "I will kill you."

I guess you'll have to kill me, Kyra. It is a quarter of a century later, and I'm writing the story of your revolution. But don't kill me too much; poetry is still my religion.

I came back countless times in my fantasy, not always modestly unannounced. Sometimes I pulled up to the famous Capşa Café in Bucharest, the meeting place of venerable writers for over a century, in a convertible white Cadillac with the poet's laurel crown at a jaunty angle on my long tresses. I could see the astonished faces of the venerable writers descended from the covers of books for just this occasion. "I've come to rejoin Romanian literature," I said casually, the ash from my expensive cigarette falling languorously on a gold ashtray held by one of my three top-hatted dwarfs.

Sometimes I came back for Aurelia, who had been waiting, leaning on an elbow at the fogged-in window of memory. Preserved in magic memory glass, she had not aged a bit. Aurelia and I parted under less than clear circumstances, trailing promises and adolescent tears. We had written to each other for a year or so after I left, long letters filled with the beating of our poetic hearts. After a while the hearts became mostly words and paper, and then there was silence. She married Max, the last Jew left in my hometown of Sibiu in Transylvania, the son of the tailor who made my high school graduation suit. They emigrated to Canada in the late seventies.

I had other, darker fantasies of return. I had to do something about Puiu, the man my mother married when I was ten years old, a railroad engineer, who now came to greet me with flowers. When he moved sufficiently close, I decked him. He didn't remember the time when he beat me for writing "Mailbox" on the homemade mailbox he made for our door. He was doubtlessly unaware also of the undying hatred I felt for him throughout my childhood. And surely he had no idea who it was that used to remove little pieces out of the amateur radios he liked to build. But now, as I decked him, a quarter of a century later, I had my own mailbox (several of them, in fact) and I owned three radios. And my voice sometimes came out of all three radios in my adopted land, mocking the primitive crystal sets he built to steal my mother's affection with. The adolescent heart is a funny beast. It's not to be trifled with.

All these different returns of the imagination ended eventually at the sidewalk café, with new wine under the lindens, drinking to return, reconciliation, harmony, and liberty. Gypsies played their violins; our passionate youth continued uninterrupted. . . . I never even considered the possibility of time altering either the features or the hearts of my friends. Whatever they had done to survive under the long dictatorship was washed from them by the waters of forgiveness. Whatever I had done in order to live was likewise erased. . . . Time for an exile has nothing in common with ordinary time. The past twenty-five years were a dream.

I stood in the fierce December cold, feeling happily warm. My personal triumph now did not involve only my person; it was the triumph of an entire people. I silently thanked the student martyrs of Bucharest, invoking a deity I rarely appealed to, because I, like the young people who died here, had been raised under communism to believe only in the material world. But the events of December that transformed Romania in the course of a few days were a miracle. The only appropriate response before a miracle is prayer. And the small tree blazing in the square was a Christmas tree, not a New Year's tree, as it had been euphemistically called for forty-five years. When I was six years old, my nanny, Kiva, taught me the Christians' Lord's Prayer, the words of which, in Romanian, I used only in cases of extreme emergency. After I left

Romania and came to live in America, I spoke less and less Romanian, and after many years my world was almost entirely in English. But there remained at the core of myself a little island of Romanian, at the center of which there lived this small prayer. These words surged out of me now like a bright shaft of childhood light spanning two languages and two worlds.

The silence was profound. The snow and ice-covered streets were deserted. The statue of Nicolae Bălcescu, hero of the Revolution of 1848, stood quietly in its coat of snow, deep in thought. The bullet-scarred walls of the University of Bucharest sported proudly their chalk and crayon graffiti, the first writings of post-Communist Romania. "Down with the tyrant!," "Down with the vampire!," "Down with the boot-maker!" read some of the simpler ones. Others were sheer poetry, written in feverish haste: "The bullets come/Invisible butterflies/returning into the bodies of those/who fed on our country's blood." Between two windows above another shrine, two-foot letters announced: "We fear no more!" In the next few days, rivers of people would flow in from every part of Bucharest and the surrounding country to view the handwriting of the young students of Bucharest who died here. In 1956, at the time of the Hungarian Revolution, when I was ten years old, I had written on a wall in a childish hand, "Long live the Hungarian Revolution!" Next day the sign had been washed away. But in 1989 these students had seen their graffiti inspire the streets and help topple the tyrant.

For now all was deeply quiet. I sensed that these moments before the end of the decade constituted symbolically the last silence before the country would explode into a frenzy of self-discovery and sudden awareness of liberty. Feelings held inside for forty-five years would come bounding to the surface with ferocious energy. This midnight marked the calm between two storms, the violent one that had just passed and the coming one that would involve everyone's conscience. The provisional government had asked people to spend the holiday home, to avoid firecrackers and loud noises. It was widely believed that units of Securitate hiding like rats in the vast maze of tunnels built by Ceaușescu under Bucharest would use this symbolic date to launch a murderous attack.

As the last second of the old age slipped out into history, the pop of the cork from our Hungarian champagne bottle shattered the silence and startled briefly the two militiamen in blue uniforms guarding the entrance to the metro. They briefly pointed their AK-47's in our direction. The metallic reflections of their weapons on the snow sent fugitive lights into the square. The moon was full. I walked toward them, with the bottle high in front of me, and together we toasted the New Year, 1990. *"La mulți ani!"* ("Many happy returns!"); *"Victorie!"*; *"Pace!"*

There was a gold leaf on the lapel of one of them, identifying him as an officer of Securitate. "Have you had friends who died?" I asked him.

"Yes," he said.

His name was Drăgan, Major Drăgan. His uniform was that of one of the world's most dreaded secret armies. In the past few days, thanks to worldwide TV coverage, the name Securitate had joined Tonton Macoute and SAVAK in the world's dictionary of dread. But only certain units of Securitate were said to have been involved in the massacres—namely, the notorious Section Five, led by General Neagoe, charged with the personal protection of the Ceaușescus; USLA (Special Unit for Antiterrorist Action), an elite force trained in urban guerrilla war, armed with nightscope rifles, led by Colonel Ardeleanu; and the Securitate School at Băneasa under the command of General Nicolae Andruță Ceaușescu, the dictator's brother.

I asked Major Drăgan what unit he belonged to.

"There are no more special units," he said. "We are with the people."

I looked at him closely. He was dark, tall, powerfully built. The well-tailored Securitate uniform fitted him well. He must have looked attractive to some of the young demonstrators on the streets of Bucharest.

"Did you fire on the students?" I asked him.

"No," he said, "none of us did. We are on the side of the people."

"Well, just who did?" I asked him.

"The terrorists," he said.

I lifted up the bottle. "To Free Romania!"

"We don't yet know how to be free," the major said, taking a swig of the proffered champagne, "but the first thing is for us to speak freely, without fear."

I drank to that. Until the previous week Romanian citizens had not been permitted to speak to foreigners. It had been Drăgan's job to arrest them for doing so. Now and then a desperate man or woman would dash to a foreigner on the street and quickly hand him a letter for Radio Free Europe or for a relative in the West. Even simple greetings were fraught with peril.

I offered the other militiaman a cigarette. He refused. He looked hard at his companion. Drăgan had not answered my question about his unit, and the other had not volunteered a single word. I didn't blame them. We were in the midst of an ongoing revolution. There was something indecent, and possibly premature, in our drinking expensive champagne to the revolution at the frozen center of the wounded city. Millions of people were uneasily celebrating New Year's behind darkened windows, not quite daring to give full vent to their feelings of euphoria. If they had been certain of victory, they would have undoubtedly streamed wildly into the streets to celebrate with Latin passion the end of an age of horror. But part of that horror still lurked invisibly in every part of the city with nightscope rifles trained to the street. The two officers seemed to be watching each other as much as the street. Was one of them USLA? The other a regular? Was one a "terrorist," the other a "revolutionary"?

The metro entrance gaped at our feet like a huge open mouth. We had read that the metro entrances of Bucharest were also entry points into Ceaușescu's maze of tunnels, a secret subterranean network constructed to outlast even nuclear war. There were reports of rooms stocked full of canned and frozen delicacies, armories containing missiles, communications centers gleaming with the latest technology. The underground network was reputed to be thousands of miles long, multilayered, a complicated nervous system whose exact shape and direction no one single person knew. Architects who had worked on portions of the system had been killed. When I told a poet friend that I could not think of anything similar in the modern world, he said: "I can . . . the Romanian mind after forty-five years of dictatorship."

Major Drăgan and his sullen comrade stood watch over something more than a dark metro entrance. They stood watch over a metaphor the terms of which reached far into a long and tragic history. If there were any terrorists within, they made no sound. Perhaps they were sleeping. Perhaps we were looking at them. There is a Romanian fairy tale about two brothers who separate at a crossroads. Before they go their different ways, they bury a knife in the ground. The one who returns finds that the knife has rusted, which means that the other is dead. Maybe Major Drăgan and I were the fabled brothers. He was the insider who stayed home and followed the rules, while I was the outsider. Our roads crossed over this metro entrance, but instead of a rusted knife we found each other. We both were much the worse for the wear but still brothers. I would have liked to hug the major, but even in my drunken happiness I realized that you do not hug an armed Securitate major on duty no matter what the circumstances. And perhaps I was altogether wrong, and the two officers were the only brothers who mattered. Maybe one of them was good, ready to shoot whatever reared its head from the tunnels, while the other was evil and would soon sink underground. Romanian history is rife with fratricide, and the land of Romania is combed with the tunnels of various ages. When I was a kid, I could get from my school to my house via an old tunnel that began just under the wall adjoining our chemistry lab. It was one of many built to serve as escape routes during a Turkish assault. It connected to older tunnels that honeycombed the city and ended in the mountains. We could sink under the city at the blink of an eye, and often did, when we skipped history, which was taught by a horrible man with an eye patch named Comrade Rana. But the tunnels existed precisely because history was one subject the Romanian people had been unable to skip. The world of daylight is only partially relevant to people who've had a rough past.

As I stood holding on to the nearly empty bottle of champagne before the martyrs' candles, I felt both euphoria and estrangement well up inside me. The dream motifs of magic and folklore have never lost their power here. "We are a dream in the mind of a madman," people said of the Ceauşescu years. The evil dreamer was gone, but journeying from his dream to the shores of reality was a dreamlike journey itself. The underground labyrinth below our feet was a fit image for the nightmare that the dictator had built for his people on earth. We stood on top of it, but inside our heads we were still looking for ways out.

Looming in monolithic ugliness behind us was the Hotel Inter-Continental, where our small news team from National Public Radio was quartered. The thirteenth floor of the hotel, which the elevator skipped entirely, had belonged to Securitate. Two days after Ceauşescu's downfall, in full view of the world's cameras, men came and carted away two trucks full of consoles, wires, headphones, and other, more obscure electronics. According to the former head of Romania's secret police, Ion Mihai Pacepa, there had been ten million microphones in a country of twenty-three million people. That would mean that nearly everyone had been listened to and then blackmailed into listening and reporting on others. A maze of psychic tunnels led from one person to another. The immediate effect of such perceived attention to the minutiae of everyone's life had been a dreadful intimacy, a lack of privacy equal to the shared living quarters in the block buildings of the cities. A feeling of claustrophobic oppression held everyone as if he or she were already living underground, in a place without heat and light, which was also actually true. Heat and electricity had been withheld for most of the 1980's so that Romania's foreign debt could be paid. People had been living in an increasingly cold darkness. But the dread and secrecy did not begin with Ceauşescu. I remember listening to Radio Free Europe in my childhood with the shades drawn, the lights off. If I walked down any darkened street of my hometown at that hour, I would have seen the lowered shades and the furtive dark in which glowed the soft dial of the radio. Everyone hid the obvious from everyone else. In the light of day we were forced to obscure ourselves. Thus, daylight was the time of the lie, while night held the truth. Everything had been thus twisted, reversed, made to stand on its head in the world the Communists made. This revolution, like all the others in Communist Europe, had to come in order to restore a sense of reality. But in Romania, unlike the other countries of Central and East Europe, this necessary change was made with the blood of children.

Looking at the massive hotel for foreigners, with its Stalinist facade set squarely against all human scale, I was not at all reassured about the removal of those listening devices. In Prague a few days before, an ABC news team had gone to the old secret police listening tower. Two workmen were going in to work. "We are custodians," they said, "the only ones left around here." Two hours later the newsmen returned only to find the two "custodians" ensconced in a soundproof room listening in to Václav Havel, the president of Czechoslovakia, just as they always had. The newsmen were able to enter because the policemen had left the door to the monitoring room unlocked. This wasn't typical carelessness. Either the two spies were too disheartened by everything to remember elementary security precautions, or else they were so cocksure of their former omnipotence that the idea of someone opening a door in a secret police building never occurred to them. (Vassily Axyonov, the Soviet novelist, illustrates the difference between the pre- and post-Gorbachev KGB by relating the story of a camera crew interviewing him before the KGB headquarters in Leningrad in 1989. When a KGB man came out to demand an explanation, the TV producer brazenly told him: "It's none of your fucking business!" That, said Axyonov, *is* the difference.) When the ABC newsmen in Prague told President Havel about the "custodians" in the tower, he just shook his head. "Apparently," explained the playwright-president, "no one had told them to *stop.* A job is a job." The Inter-Continental Hotel (and its counterparts in other cities) had been built for spies. "An intelligence factory," Pacepa called it. But even if by some miracle of virtue as yet unachieved by the Czechs and the Soviets, the Romanians had removed the real microphones, I knew that in the minds of millions of Romanians, secret policemen continued doing their job.

"It will be long," I told the major, "before the people get the police out of their head." I tapped the front of my fur hat.

"Somebody has to make sure you don't get too drunk," said the major, taking the last swig from the bottle. And then he saluted and smiled. He had crooked teeth and a funny face. With a smile on it, he was another man.

Major Drăgan, a militiaman, Securitate officer, and metro guard did not know that the very next day, on January 1, 1990, the militia, of which Securitate was part, by order of the provisional government— the National Salvation Front—would become the police, a highly significant semantic change. The militia had been the terror instrument of the Communist party. The police, which had its roots in *polis* ("community") would, it was hoped, function only to keep the peace.

In the next few days everything the Romanian people had learned to fear and hate for decades changed its name. Newly baptized newspapers would have been unrecognizable if not for similar typefaces. Ministries, factories, schools, local governments all renamed themselves. This festival of name changing was a vast act of symbolic New Year's magic by which the new leaders hoped to convince the people that not only Ceaușescu but the Communist party and its bureaucracy were also dead. In a country long ruled by Myth, Fable, Fiction, and Lies, the overthrow of rotten language was enthusiastically received. The next few days—given intensely and optimistically over to language— warmed, inspired, and put smiles on people's faces. The furtive looks, whispering, and dour expressions that used to mask everyone were laid aside and discarded.

As our small group of newsmen and the two guards huddled about the small flames of the shrine, some drunken Australian and Finnish journalists staggered toward us. They were in high spirits, full of rude sport, a self-congratulatory drunkenness that said, "Here we are, in a revolution! What amazing Boy Scouts we are!" One of them lit his cigarette from the shrine. It was a gesture of pure, stupid bravado, distasteful and thoughtless. Then they linked arms and sang "Auld Lang Syne," which echoed down the street and was lost over the snowy rooftops. One of my colleagues said, "We should punch them in the nose!" But Major Drăgan did not seem distressed. He smiled happily, as if to say, "One day we will feel free enough to act just as foolish as you!"

He was right, of course.

2

Death of a Dictator

"The Antichrist died on Christmas Day!" With these words the Romanian radio announcer let the nation and the world know that Nicolae and Elena Ceauşescu, the rulers of Romania for a quarter of a century, had been put to death by a firing squad after a summary trial by a military court.

On television Romanians saw the two crumpled bodies fallen away from each other on the frozen ground of a small, dingy courtyard. The two corpses filled the living rooms of billions of people all over the world, via satellite. Thousands of miles away, in New Orleans, I watched, fascinated and repelled. Few images conveyed as starkly the end of an era. I remembered seeing Ceauşescu on TV less than a week before, standing woodenly on the balcony of his palace with his arms extended, speaking to an obedient crowd of hundreds of thousands. When the sea of people began suddenly booing him, he stood there, his mouth open, his arms frozen in a useless gesture. His face white, he turned and was gone—forever. At that moment he had looked already dead. Paradoxically, in death Ceauşescu looked more alive than he had on his balcony, making his last speech.

The courtyard where the Ceauşescus lay dead was bleak and undistinguished, a sunless cement enclosure. It was smaller than the smallest bathroom in the new presidential palace. Every year the Ceauşescus had demanded more and more sumptuous spaces for themselves. The great

Andrei Codrescu

hall of their palace was built for the sole purpose of framing the two thrones on which the couple sat when receiving foreign dignitaries. This so-called Palace of the Republic—in reality a private residence—was built on the grandiose scale of the Nazi office Albert Speer had designed for Hitler. In the end, both were reduced to an ignominy of smallness that mocked their grandiose dreams, Hitler to a dingy bunker, Ceau-şescu to a dirty cement yard. Their humble beginnings matched their humble ends. But between beginnings and ends there stretched the misery of millions against which no megalomanic dream was an adequate defense. It was later reported that at the very last moment, when it became apparent that they would indeed be executed—a job for which the entire unit volunteered, though only three were chosen—the Ceau-şescus tried to run. Certainly, whether they tried to run or not, at the moment of their deaths the Ceauşescus must have tried desperately to find the entrance to their tunnels. But the ground didn't open, the gate stayed elusive. They were cut down in childish flight, recipients of some thirty bullets each. Soldiers, who are only people, kill with guns, but the spirit kills with irony. The spirits of those who perished in the regime's jails and undergrounds made sure the smallest possible death would tend their murderer. And yet the faces of the crumpled bodies on the ground are still disbelieving. We are not dead, they seem to say, because we cannot possibly die in such a tiny, dirty place. This expression is perhaps what makes them seem more alive than they were at the stone-faced apex of their power. Ceauşescu had been one of the last of his kind. I remembered the grim parade of Communist leaders standing woodenly on rostrums at official parades. Some of them, like Leonid Brezhnev, may have been actually dead up there. No one could tell the difference. By the end of 1989 these leaders and the ossified societies they managed crumbled like mummies exposed to sudden daylight. How long had the people of these countries been ruled by the dead? And how long will it take them to shake off the chill of the grave?

Anyone watching the events of December 1989 had to shake a disbelieving head at the speed of the events. Time had suddenly compressed and history sped up to where few people could keep track of it. "Someone pushed the fast forward button on history," a *New York Times* reporter later said. How true. Between Christmas Day 1989, when Romania's tyrants lay dead on the frozen cement, and November 24, 1989, when the dead man had been reelected—to enthusiastic and tumultuous acclaim—leader of the party and of Romania, only a month had elapsed. A single month. Even most of that month appeared unremarkable. It was only beginning in the second half of December that history exploded. Forty-five years of Communist rule were undone in eight days.

The eight Romanian days that shook the world began in Timişoara, a city of one million people in western Romania. There on Friday, December 15, 1989, three hundred Hungarians, Romanians, Serbs, and other minorities formed a human chain in front of the Reverend László Tökes's house, and began shouting, "We are not leaving!" The rumor had quickly spread through the city that Reverend Tökes, the Hungarian minister of the Reformed Lutheran church in Timişoara, was going to be evicted from his house. He had been ordered by his bishop to leave immediately for a small country seat in a remote part of Transylvania. Tökes had been preaching a series of homilies in favor of human rights, minority rights, and democracy. The Hungarians in Transylvania had become increasingly oppressed by the Ceauşescu regime, which intended to destroy their ethnic identity or to force them to emigrate. Hungarian villages were singled out for destruction, the Hungarian language was removed from school curricula, and nationalist Romanian sentiment was encouraged in its most militant forms. The Hungarians drawing around Reverend Tökes were attempting to organize themselves in a democratic forum that would resist their destruction. But the Hungarian preacher's sermons reached beyond his immediate constituency. His human rights position struck a deep chord in Romanians, Germans, Serbs, and Gypsies as well. Everyone, even the Romanian majority, felt traumatized and oppressed. Romanian villages were being bulldozed right alongside Hungarian ones. The upheavals going on in the rest of Soviet-dominated Europe had aroused hope. Timişoara's closeness to Yugoslavia and Hungary allowed news broadcasts from those countries to be seen and heard with relative ease. In addition to these, Radio Free Europe and the Voice of America brought in the news of neighboring countries with an increasing pitch of urgency and despair. The despair, deeply felt by all manner of people, from dissatisfied workers to angry intellectuals, was complemented by a sense of shame, a sense of being left behind while the rest of the world was waking up. When news of Reverend Tökes's eviction, and imminent arrest by Securitate, spread among his faithful, it was received like a call for action. The ferment of the year 1989 in the crumbling Communist world had found its Romanian pretext. The multiethnic human chain linked arms and waited.

When militia units started arriving on the scene, a young man shouted, "Down with Ceauşescu!" It was a single cry, followed by several seconds of stunned silence. It was as if people realized, for the first time, what the horrible thing locked in their throats and hearts was. It was the spark that ignited the revolt. By nightfall the news that the piercing cry of "Down with the dictator!" had been uttered and that the sky had not erupted with lightning brought thousands, then hundreds of thousands of people out into Maria Square. All through the night people came. An immense crowd has gathered by dawn on Saturday, the sixteenth. "Down with Ceauşescu!," "Good-bye to fear! Ceauşescu will fall!," "Freedom!," and "Dignity!" were the chants now being heard. The poetry of the revolution was being scanned loud enough to be heard everywhere.

Sunday, December 17, the crowds in Timişoara moved into the central squares. There was no more room in front of Reverend Tökes's house. The springlike temperature was 22 degrees Celsius, unusual both for the region and for the time of the year. At five o'clock that afternoon a helicopter appeared over the crowds. "Nobody leaves until the dictatorship gives!" People raised angry fists at the sky. Soon after, Army tanks took positions at strategic locations, and soldiers behind white shields blocked the streets leading to the main square. Still, no action had yet been taken against the demonstrators, and hope blossomed. What if it were possible to persuade by sheer force of numbers, by sheer force of feeling, just as the people had done already in Czechoslovakia and Hungary? People in the crowd called out to the soldiers to join their revolution. "You are our brothers!" More and more people came into the street, many of them bringing their children. The confidence and goodwill of the crowd grew in proportion to the numbers. Who could kill this many people? There was singing and sharing of food.

In the early evening a small armored carrier caught suddenly on fire. At the same time a newsstand was blown up. The sound of breaking glass was everywhere as store windows were being smashed. Several small fires broke out on side streets. The demonstrators, peaceful until now, were baffled. The mood of the demonstration had been consistently nonviolent, even festive. There were many shouts of "We are nonviolent! Peace!" People speaking to the young boys behind the shields and the guns of armored carriers, started to beg, "Come join us, brothers! You, too, are Romanians!" The anguish on some of the boy soldiers' faces is plainly visible in the hastily snapped photos seen later. They stand absolutely still. They could be thinking, What good are criminal orders? They were not given long to think.

A half hour later, in Liberty Square, they were ordered to open fire. Not all of them did. Some refused, throwing down their weapons. Those who refused were taken out of formation by political officers and executed on the spot. For the most part, the soldiers obeyed their orders. Some demonstrators were shouting, "Blanks!" in an effort to calm the crowd. But there was the glare of a red tracer rocket, and people started falling. The demonstrators carried out the wounded. What had begun as a complete assertion of people's will, a festival in fact, suddenly became deadly. Men and women with children on their shoulders stood helplessly before tanks and received fire directly. Some held their children up so that the soldiers could see them. "Brothers, don't shoot our children!" But the fusillade continued, backed by machine guns mounted on armored carriers and by nests mounted on balconies of surrounding buildings. Panicked, screaming people tried to run, tripping over the bodies of those in front of them, mothers, children, young students. . . . Some stood their ground, singing "Arise, Romanians!" and "Dance of Unity," national songs from the past, forbidden under Ceauşescu. Many fell singing. Others, wounded, screamed as they ran or fell, "Murderers! Down with Ceauşescu! Liberty!" The answer was bullets. The pavement was red with blood; people were slipping and falling on blood. The bodies of the demonstrators, as well as those of the mutineers shot in the head barely out of sight of the crowds, were loaded in anonymous vehicles, one of which, however, seemed to be an official ambulance from a local hospital. This ambulance collected several wounded people who were later found executed. They must have been killed inside the ambulance.

The initial news reports from Timişoara were filed by Yugoslav, Hungarian, and Soviet reporters who were the first on the scene. Hungarian radio broadcast a report from a young journalist surrounded by the sound of broken glass and machine-gun fire. There were five to ten thousand people killed, according to the Tanjug correspondent who witnessed the events in the square. A Hungarian report, filed from near the cathedral, put the figure at seventy-five hundred dead people.

The "spring" day of Sunday, the seventeenth, ended with an unusual meteorological phenomenon: a violent storm with heavy rain, thunder, and lightning. The blood was washed from the streets. On Monday the sky was clear, the sun was shining. In front of the cathedral the people came back. A woman stood on the highest step, waving the tricolor flag. Everyone was singing "Arise, Romanians! Arise!" Children lit candles for the dead. In the afternoon the tanks reappeared. This time, when the order to fire came, many soldiers came to the side of the people, bringing their weapons, while other soldiers fired into the air.

There were several bursts of machine-gun fire from nests on the rooftops of buildings around the square, but they did not seem directed at the crowd. There was some panic and screaming, but also the feeling that there was no turning back. The matter had become too serious. Many people later said that they were willing to die. They refused to tolerate a regime that murdered its own people. They would come back every day until either they all were dead, or the dictator quit.

The newscasts from Hungary and Yugoslavia and the Romanian-language stations from abroad kept the people of Timișoara apprised of their own situation. They were told that flatbed trucks carted off bodies to quickly dug, shallow mass graves. A Pole who reached Budapest from Timișoara on Wednesday, December 20—my birthday—said that he "saw them tossing dead into the river." The hospitals were full of the dead and the wounded, many of them lying in the halls with open wounds, bleeding to death. There wasn't enough medicine to treat them.

There was a worldwide gasp of horror. The international wave of protest against the massacre of unarmed protesters, resembling the earlier shock at the massacre in Tiananmen Square, came also, significantly and first, from all of Romania's neighbors, the Warsaw Pact states. Trucks full of relief supplies, medicine, and urgently needed blood began breaching the closed Romanian borders, with the help of willing border guards. Young Solidarity workers from several Polish cities drove in with trucks under cover of night and were fired on. Some of them didn't make it. The official gestures of European chancelleries were just as immediate, but mostly symbolic. Ambassadors were recalled. The queen of England took back the knighthood she had bestowed on Ceaușescu only months before. Norway took back its highest honor, the Grand Cross of St. Olaf, which it had given both Ceaușescus. These same Ceaușescus, now mightily condemned by the world, had been the darlings of the West in the not so distant past and had enjoyed the admiration of American and British leaders for reasons of political expediency.

In the early seventies Ceauşescu had helped bring about the meeting of Richard Nixon and Mao Zedong. Presidents Nixon and Ford, who posed with the dictator on the terror-ruled streets of Bucharest, had never looked past their own interests into the bloody nightmare their errand boy had made for his people.

In the face of this debacle and international scandal, the country's president and supreme commander of the Army decided to make a state visit to Iran to pay his respects to Ayatollah Khomeini. With the country on the verge of exploding, Ceauşescu left home. Is it possible that by this time Ceauşescu was so out of touch with the country that he had no idea of the real magnitude of the disaster? Such contempt and self-assurance could hardly be justified. In any case, something of the gravity of the situation must have become evident while he broke pita with the ayatollah.

On December 20 a furious Ceauşescu returned from his state visit to Iran and called an emergency council of the party's Central Committee to discuss the events in Timişoara. Fuming with rage, the supreme commander berated the generals of the Army and of the Securitate forces for not using live ammunition against the demonstrators. Apparently either he had not yet heard of the body counts reported around the world, or he did not believe them. He insisted that they had used blanks. He threatened his underlings with the firing squad. Shooting blanks, he said, "is like a rain shower." His wife interjected that the demonstrators should never again be allowed "to see the light of day." Curiously enough, while calling for live ammo, Ceauşescu did not order the demonstrators killed. Real bullets should be used, yes, but first warning shots should be fired; then the demonstrators ought to be "shot in the legs," he commanded. If no one had been killed, one might understand this strange order. But what was the point if a civil war was already raging? In what seems like an eerily dated version of recent history, Ceauşescu went on as if the Timişoara revolt were still only a matter of demonstrators defending a priest. At the same time he accused his chief generals of treason. Defense Minister Vasile Milea and Securitate Chief Iulian Vlad had been unconscionably lax in their duties. They had not suppressed the revolt. Generals Milea and Vlad also seemed to share in Ceauşescu's belief that nothing had yet been done to put down the revolt in Timişoara. They attempted to argue with their commander in chief about the use of fire. That only added new fuel to the surreal discussion. "A few hooligans," screamed Ceauşescu, "want to destroy socialism, and you make it child's play for them! You do not quiet an enemy by talking with him like a priest, but by burning him!"

"You are cowards!" Elena Ceauşescu told the generals.

The twenty-five Central Committee members present at the secret meeting agreed with the Ceauşescus without the slightest hint of dissent. The reaction of Parliament President Manea Manescu was typical: "I agree with you, and all your measures." Hours later it was announced that Defense Minister Milea had committed suicide. He could not bring himself to order troops to fire on demonstrators. What happened to General Milea? According to his personal bodyguard, following the meeting the defense minister walked into a small office adjoining the great hall. He told his bodyguard to explain to his wife and children that he was unable to follow Ceauşescu's criminal orders. He borrowed the officer's pistol, closed the door to the small office, and put a bullet through his heart. Milea's suicide, announced by Ceauşescu hours later, was widely thought to be murder. Emil Bobu testified at his own trial that Milea was assassinated on orders from the dictator. That had to be the right explanation. General Milea must have known that the Army had *already* fired on demonstrators in Timişoara. Why would he commit suicide for refusing orders to do something that had already been done? Would anyone kill himself to maintain a fiction?

Defense Minister Milea's death, according to the provisional government, was instrumental in the Army's later decision (on December 22) to abandon Ceauşescu and to defend the revolution. The Army, however, on orders from people no one has yet been able to identify, *did* fire on demonstrators in Timişoara, killing hundreds, *and* on demonstrators elsewhere on December 22. But to this day the Army denies that it fired on anybody. The "heroic" version of General Vasile Milea's death led to his instant glorification after the revolution. A major highway in my hometown, Sibiu, was "spontaneously" renamed Gen. Vasile Milea Boulevard.

Monday, Tuesday, and Wednesday, December 18–20, were working days in Timişoara, but one after another the factories went on strike. Timişoara Electric went out first, followed by all the major industries. The workers began shouting, "Ceauşescu is guilty! Give us back our dead! Death! Death! Death!" The workers marched back to the center of the city on December 20. The revolution had gone on for three days, the loss of lives was reportedly staggering, but no one gave up. On this day the soldiers didn't just throw away their weapons. They came to the side of the people armed, some of them bringing their tanks. An extraordinary wave of joy went through the crowd, and the shout that would, for the next few days, shake the country was heard for the first time: "THE ARMY IS WITH US!"

It certainly looked like it that day. The soldiers who had now joined the people en masse turned their guns against the invisible machine-gun nests of Securitate. The tide of the revolution had turned. Some feared that this would be the beginning of a bloody civil war, but almost everyone knew that there was no turning back now that the Army had joined their fight against Ceauşescu and his inhuman Securitate. Securitate resistance had been mounting, and its invisible armies were said to attempt to hold on to the very end. Securitate was said to be better armed than the Army, which Ceauşescu had purposefully neglected. Securitate had also been trained by foreign terrorists and had ultramodern weapons. It was going to be a long struggle. Demonstrators climbed on the tanks waving tricolor flags and fraternized with the defecting soldiers.

The news from Timişoara electrified the citizens of Bucharest. In the capital they had been waiting for something to set off their own revolt. Students in the university had been secretly teaching themselves techniques of street action. Wall posters appeared, calling for solidarity with the people of Timişoara. Romanian radio, television, and newspapers in Bucharest reported Ceauşescu's comments that a "gang of bandits, Hungarian spies, and traitors are creating civil disturbances in Timişoara" and that their demands for reform will be granted "when the poplars have pears." Next day big pears cut out of paper hung from all the poplars of Bucharest.

Telephonic links to Timişoara were cut. The Romanian people stayed informed by Radio Free Europe, the Voice of America, and the BBC about the extraordinary events happening in their own country. Soviet and Bulgarian TV, which could be seen in the capital, relayed the chilling Yugoslav and Hungarian reports. Young men from all over Romania took trains to Timişoara to form patriotic guards in defense of the city. Workers occupied their factories. Block committees kept civic order and organized defense units against Securitate, taking positions on the roofs of their apartment buildings. By December 21 Timişoara was a revolutionary commune. It was said that special Army and Securitate units loyal to the dictator, many of them mercenary Arabs, were being flown in from secret camps in the Carpathian Mountains. The surrounded city awaited its fate. But there was only sporadic gunfire, on side streets. Orders to attack, if they had been given, were not being obeyed or were being countermanded at high levels.

Following the suicide (or murder) of his defense minister, Ceau-şescu called a huge meeting in Republic Square through regular party channels, which mobilized their members in Bucharest factories with banners kept in storage for such events. This was Ceauşescu's greatest (and last) mistake. It was a desperate gamble by a cornered man who still believed, however, that he had popular support. He was going directly to the "people." They showed up, his people, but other people of Bucharest also showed up, hundreds of thousands of them. When Ceauşescu began attacking the demonstrators in Timişoara, calling them "hooligans" and "CIA spies," the crowd erupted with shouts of "Murderer! Give us back our dead!" Astonished for a moment, the dictator stood there with his mouth open in mid-speech. It was the open mouth of a man who did not know how deeply hated he was. Had he known, he would have never appeared before the people on the balcony of the Communist party headquarters. But there he was, in his fur hat, protected so long from honest opinion that he lived fully in his delusions.

This was the balcony from which he had made dozens of hours-long speeches before adoring crowds with smiling children waving his portrait before him. He'd stood there only a month before, on November 24, after being unanimously reelected supreme commander amid the well-rehearsed chants linking his name to Romania. In a "tumultuously applauded speech," interrupted only by waves of perfectly timed rhythmic chants of his name, Ceauşescu had then condemned reform in Eastern Europe and vowed to defend socialism "to the end."

It is probably next to impossible for a Westerner to understand the weird feeling of being in such a gathering and having to shout in unison with thousands of people. During May First parades in my hometown we pioneers were obliged to perform this kind of rhythmic chanting. One of our chants was: "*Ura partidul!*" ("Long live the party!") Now the word *ura* in Romanian is ambiguous because, with stress on the last letter, it means "hated." Some of us, in daring contretemps would shout, "Hate the party!" instead of "Long live!" That was the kind of thing that landed one in prison. During this same November congress, Nicu Ceauşescu, the son of the "Maximum Leader," extolled his father as the "brilliant genius of the nation." This, too, received its portion of ovations. Besides "brilliant genius," Ceauşescu was called the "conductor" and the "genius of the Carpathians." In jokes and in normal conversation, the premier couple was referred to as He and She. The Ceauşescus believed that they *were* Romania.

So how could the rally of December 21 be different from every other rally of the past twenty-five years? It was not conceivable. This, like other rallies, was going to be a well-managed affair attended by people who knew what side their bread was buttered on. (Except that the bread was stale and butter wasn't on anybody's plate.) Here were his handpicked party members who had been quietly called out of their offices and workshops. What had come over them?

An architect from the Architecture Institute in Bucharest told me what happened: "When we saw the party people leaving, some of us started going from office to office, and we began discussing the situation. We decided that we would *all* attend the rally. Spontaneously, all over Bucharest, office workers and students stopped work and began forming groups. We started walking toward the square behind the party members. They expected the original crowd to be a few thousand . . . but it swelled to hundreds of thousands of people. After Ceauşescu blamed the events in Timişoara on 'fascists, hooligans, and Hungarians,' an electric current shot through us. . . . Every single person knew that tens of thousands of children and women in Timişoara were massacred by Securitate! It was first a ripple, then a huge wave. . . . We shouted 'Death! Death! Death!' and then 'Give us back our dead! Give us back our dead!' and then again 'Death! Death! Death!' And then 'Down with Ceauşescu!,' 'Down with the dictator!,' 'Down with the bootmaker!' I had chills up and down my spine. I will never forget this as long as I live!"

Ceauşescu, his mouth open, stood within the sea of hostile sound like a small piece of driftwood in a tidal wave. A few moments later both he and his wife left the balcony. The Romanian Revolution had begun.

On radio and television the speech, which was being carried live, was drowned by the furious jeering of the crowd. Too late the jeering was replaced with canned applause and then with patriotic music. It was Ceauşescu's last live appearance on the airwaves he had saturated with his face and voice for two long hours every night for decades of oppressive darkness. The next time the Romanian people saw him he was a well-dressed corpse lying on a dirty patch of cement.

Moments after Ceauşescu's hasty departure, students and workers surged into the Central Committee building. Seconds later thousands of Ceauşescu's books were thrown off the dictator's balcony. The woodenly written tons of party blather went up in flames. The people, tears streaming down their faces, danced for joy around the bonfires. Groups of demonstrators headed for the television and radio station. The Army and Securitate troops ringing the streets of Bucharest stood by doing nothing. People spoke to the soldiers, kissed them, and asked them to join the revolution. Unsure of their orders, most of them stood by, though some did join in the celebration. Two poets, Mircea Dinescu and Ana Blandiana, were recognized by demonstrators (Romanians have a great love for poetry) and carried on shoulders to the television and radio station. Dinescu had the great honor of announcing to the nation that the dictator had fallen, while Blandiana announced the news on the radio.

Inside the Central Committee building chaos reigned. Groups of demonstrators and government officials found themselves side by side. Discussion groups and civic committees were formed. At this point, it is said, the leaders of the National Salvation Front appeared spontaneously and began addressing the crowds from the balcony. Among them were Ion Iliescu, Petre Roman, Dumitru Mazilu, Silviu Brucan. After addressing the crowds, they were taken by armored Army vehicles to the television station to be presented to the country.

For six delirious hours various people made anti-Ceauşescu as well as anti-Communist speeches from the balcony. In addition to the well-spoken Iliescu and Roman, students and ordinary people spoke, quite movingly, about their suffering and now their happiness. Caught in the immense spotlights that used to light up Ceauşescu's night parades, these speakers were easy targets for the "terrorists" who, it was said, honeycombed the buildings surrounding the CC headquarters. But for a number of hours they held their fire.

The shooting began during the night of December 21. The unarmed crowds on the street, which had swollen to a million, were suddenly under heavy fire. In the Square of the Republic heavy artillery was heard. The library of the University of Bucharest went up in flames. Scores of other buildings were shelled.

The Battle of Bucharest raged for the next three days. The crowds surged on government buildings, which had civil defense armories, and received weapons from sympathetic military personnel inside. A special edition of the party newspaper, *Scînteia* ("Spark"), now called *People's*

Scînteia, appeared with a call to arms splattered in twelve-point type on the front page: CITIZENS, MEMBERS OF PATRIOTIC GUARDS! ANYONE WHO CAN USE A WEAPON, TO ARMS! DEFEAT THE ENEMIES AND TRAITORS OF THE COUNTRY, KILLERS AND VANDALS! The same newspaper announced the formation of the National Salvation Front, a broad coalition of dissidents, ranging from disgruntled Communists to still-jailed anti-Communists. Ion Iliescu, not yet officially the president of the front, issued an urgent proclamation on television, calling for the "quick liquidation of the terrorists of the former dictator, and the servants of his clan." To the people, overtaken by events and astounded by the flight of the dictator, it seemed that the provisional government was born on television. This is where they first saw Iliescu, at the height of the battle, at a long table, crowded in by students, TV personnel, Army generals. The situation looked chaotic.

The historic scenes of the war for Romania were shown live by Romanian television, using both the studio inside the Central Committee and the studios at the television station. One of the fiercest battles to be telecast was that for the television station itself, which reported its own situation in dramatic bulletins. Terrorists hidden in air vents had wounded six people inside the station. Gunfire had been heard in every part of the building. Army units that had come to the side of the revolution were defending the station, now ringed by several tanks. Throughout the fighting the TV never went off the air. The "terrorists" were unable, it seems, to knock out the tower or otherwise cut the electrical supply. The most dramatic miracle in Romanian history took place before everyone's eyes. Images of street-to-street combat were interspersed with the freedom proclamations of newly emerging revolutionary leaders. Some of the greatest decisions of the revolutionary front, which would affect the country forever, were made seemingly on the spot inside the television studios, with bullets flying around. On the street one saw children carrying supplies and bullets to fighters, while inside, a group of sleepless activists drafted the future. A man with a bagful of apples was distributing them to fighters. A man with a wound in his leg took an apple. Apples and bullets. We saw children, especially Gypsy ragamuffins, carrying water and food under fire exchanges to soldiers. People crept with Molotov cocktails alongside buildings and tossed them into the entrances to the tunnels. The Romanian tricolor, red, blue, and gold, with the Communist emblem cut out of the middle was mounted on top of tanks. The same flag, emblem cut out, was draped over the wall of the TV studio, and the words "FREE ROMANIAN TELE-VISION" were handwritten on a banner that became the new logo of Romanian TV. Most of all, here in living color were the faces, outside and inside, the beautiful, illuminated faces of citizens riding triumphantly on top of tanks, their arms extended in the victory sign or scribbling new constitutional freedoms at scarred tables, their sleepless eyes big and not quite believing that the end of the dictatorship had come. The face of Ion Iliescu, smiling a tired but kind smile, having close by his side the dashing Petre Roman, was imprinted forever on the minds of Romanians.

The National Salvation Front, as it emerged on television, was a broad-based coalition of "dissidents" against the old regime as well as "new faces" like Roman. Among the old hands was Silviu Brucan, former ambassador to the United States, an urbane and sophisticated man who had been among a handful of Communist party dissenters to draft a letter of protest against Ceauşescu the previous year. The letter of the six, as it was known, received wide distribution abroad. One of its signatories was the cofounder of the Romanian Communist party, Gheorghe Apostol. Other members were decidedly not Communists: Doina Cornea, a French professor from Cluj, was a pro-European, Francophile liberal; Mircea Dinescu and Ana Blandiana were poets known for their passionate opposition in verse to the tyrant, who had had both of them put under house arrest and enjoined from publishing; the Reverend László Tökes had sparked the revolt. The front had almost a hundred members. Its executive committee was another matter. There a smaller group held sway. Among them, in addition to Iliescu, Roman, and Brucan, one found General Nicolae Militaru, new commander of all the armed forces, and General Victor Stănculescu, who had been Ceauşescu's liaison between the Army and Securitate. (Today he is Romania's minister of defense.)

The television station served also as military operation center. Working around the clock inside to monitor and direct the military situation were General Ştefan Guşa, head of the Army—the first man in uniform to appear on TV to announce that the Army was indeed with the people—and General Vlad, head of Securitate, who claimed to have also joined the revolution. General Vlad issued several calls to his men to stop fighting—but to no avail. Standing right next to General Guşa, General Vlad, who was constantly on the telephone, heard everything that went on. The fighting forces of the Securitate seemed to know every move the Army made.

At a given moment the tide of the battle began to run against the people. It looked as if Securitate were gaining the upper hand. On the evening of December 23 it was announced that morale was very low among members of the National Salvation Front. An urgent meeting to discuss the situation was called. It was attended by three leaders of the NSF and ten generals, including Guşa and Vlad. At this meeting, at the urging of Silviu Brucan, General Vlad was placed under arrest. Brucan accused him of passing information to Securitate from the TV war room.

Vlad, according to his accusers, had been relaying all the orders given to the Army back to his Securitate men. Why did Brucan and the others wait so long to arrest him? During the two days Vlad commanded his invisible troops, hundreds of lives were lost. After the arrest of General Vlad the situation began to calm. Nicu Ceauşescu, the son of the dictator, was brought bruised and beaten before the cameras.

The situation on the streets was still chaotic. Armed revolutionary guards with tricolor armbands stopped all cars and directed the Army to places where sudden gunfire was erupting. Bucharest became the scene of one of the largest demonstrations in history, millions of people celebrating the fall of the dictatorship. At the same time pockets of resistance sprang suddenly into action, and young people, mainly students, were killed. The terrorists' base of operation was said to be the network of well-stocked tunnels under the streets of Bucharest. Hysterical witnesses saw Securitate gunmen popping out of subway entrances that communicated with their tunnels. They unloaded their weapons into anyone within range. They came out of fake gravestones in cemeteries and fired on mourners burying the newly dead. A doctor in a hospital who treated Cornel Popu, a wounded "terrorist," said: "He was uncommonly strong. He screamed: 'I'm dying for Ceauşescu! We will kill you all!' We injected him with liquid phenobarbitol and diazepam to calm him down. It had no effect. Four men tied him to a stretcher, but he was so strong he bent the stretcher! He was screaming: 'My mission is to kill! I will kill your children!' The blood tests showed that he had been given an extremely potent amphetamine."

Others reported seeing thousands of Palestinian and Libyan fighters armed with ultramodern weapons, including shoulder-fired missiles, fighting alongside the Ceauşescu forces. The many Arab students at the University of Bucharest who were studying to become engineers and doctors went into hiding. Gruesome scenes were seen and then told and retold. My driver, Petre, told me that an ABC crew he was driving came upon a wheel with spikes coming out of it into which had been inserted the heads, hands, and body parts of several men killed by a furious mob. The grisly discovery was never used by ABC. "It was one of the scariest things I ever saw," Petre confessed, "and I've seen plenty of bodies these few days." He had used his taxi at one point to blockade an intersection against militia units and then later transported wounded and dead to the hospitals. "Our cabdrivers are heroes," he told me. "We all helped the revolution."

Sixty to eighty thousand people were being reported to have been killed in the bloodiest uprising against a Communist regime in history. The street battles, as we saw them, over and over, on television, looked like the heaviest fighting in Europe since World War II. Direct from Romanian television, via satellite, especially from CNN, the glorious and terrifying sounds and sights of the Romanian Revolution stunned the world.

On December 24 Ion Iliescu announced the arrest of Nicolae and Elena Ceauşescu. Iliescu also announced the arrests of the dictator's daughter Zoia and of the entire membership of the former executive Central Committee, including Emil Bobu, the man who ran the country in the absence of his master. Iliescu promised speedy trials and called on the population to form civil guards, man checkpoints, and be vigilant.

After fleeing the Communist party headquarters balcony in the middle of his ill-fated speech, the dictator and his wife, Elena, clambered aboard a waiting helicopter on the roof of the Central Committee building. There were several others inside: Bobu, Ceauşescu's most loyal minister; General Neagoe, the chief of the presidential guards; and two bodyguards. With the pilot and the copilot, the flying machine was dangerously overcrowded. It lurched and listed even as the first demonstrators in the Square of the Republic scaled the building, reached the roof and started making for the helipad. The passengers could hear the shouts of the demonstrators: "Assassins! Get them!" The couple perched on each other's laps, squeezed between their subordinates. They flew to Snagov—where Dracula is buried—and there the two state ministers disembarked. Snagov, a monastery island built by Dracula to serve as a place of refuge, was also the site of a well-guarded Ceauşescu sum-mer palace. From there the chopper took off again, this time in the direction of Otopeni International Airport, which was reportedly in the hands of Ceauşescu loyalists. Somewhere on the way to Otopeni, Vasile Măluţan, the pilot, opened a secret frequency and had a brief conver-sation in code. "Listen to Radio Bucharest!" he was told. At that point Radio Bucharest was broadcasting the story of the tyrants' flight in a helicopter. "Is there anyone aboard?" the tower asked. "Yes," replied the pilot. He was then denied permission to land and told that if he headed for the airport, he would be intercepted and shot down. After a few moments he was given instructions to take his charges several kilo-meters from Otopeni to a certain highway near Boteni. A radio operator at the airport listened in on the secret frequency and, after decoding the message, broke in and tried to warn the passengers. But the couple remained unaware that their pilot was betraying them. The pilot told the Ceauşescus that Otopeni was unsafe and that they needed to refuel. He then landed on the Bucharest–Piteşti National Highway.

An argument followed as to the best next direction. The Securitate bodyguards disagreed with General Neagoe, who wanted to return to Bucharest. Meanwhile, three young workers from a chicken farm near the road approached, attracted by the helicopter. One of them, Radu Georgescu, looked in at the passengers and recognized Elena. "Go back to work!" she told him. Everyone got out to discuss the situation. When the couple and their two bodyguards were safely on the ground, the chopper took off, leaving them without a means of escape. The Com-munist king and queen of Romania were thus abandoned unceremo-niously with their servants in the middle of the highway. There was apparently some traffic because a car was approaching. The Ceauşescus hid in the bushes while the bodyguards stuck out their thumbs. The red Dacia stopped. The driver rolled down his window and asked the men where they were going.

"Give me your keys!" demanded General Neagoe. When the driver refused, the general simply opened the door and motioned to the cou-ple. "We have two precious charges," he said, "He and She . . ." After the Ceauşescus had climbed into the back seat, General Neagoe ordered the driver to step on the accelerator. The driver quickly rolled up his window and sped off. Left behind were the two bodyguards, one of whom had a black briefcase chained to his wrist. It contained the Ceau-şescus' financial records, which, although nobody saw them, were allegedly used as evidence at the trial. The two men apparently walked to a police station and gave themselves up.

The driver's name was Dr. Nicolae Deca. In his rearview mirror he could see his country's most powerful people huddling in fear next to each other. He could also see the barrel of the small machine gun pistol Neagoe was pointing to his head.

"Do you know what's going on?" the dictator asked him.

"No," lied Deca. "I've been on duty at the hospital."

"There's been a coup," Ceauşescu said. "Are you willing to come with us to help organize the resistance?"

"I can't. I have a family. Two children. I'm fifty-nine years old. I'm old. And sick. I don't know how to fight. Besides . . . I'm not a member of the party. . . ."

Dr. Deca later recalled the fear he felt and the incomprehensible urge to scream in the dictator's face that both his brother and his sister were living in the United States and that he himself couldn't wait to leave Romania! He ran out of gas instead in Văcăreşti, a village near Tîrgovişte.

Nicolae Petrişor was washing his black Dacia in front of the bicycle shop on the main street. Dr. Deca leaned out of the car and asked him, "Do you have any gas?"

Petrişor was happy to oblige. While siphoning gas from his car into a canister, he glanced inside the other car. "It's Ceauşescu," he shouted. "Viorica!" he called to his wife, who appeared in the doorway and clapped her hand over her mouth. The party in the car came out and moved into Petrişor's car.

General Neagoe shoved Petrişor: "Get in."

Petrişor started the car. He was trembling violently and crying.

"What's the matter with you?" asked Elena. "Are you drunk?"

"No," said Petrişor. "I'm a Seventh-day Adventist." Seventh-day Adventists had been jailed, persecuted, and tortured under the Communist regime (as had Buddhists, transcendental meditators, and yoga practitioners).

"Don't worry," said Elena. "Keep driving, and we won't kill you."

Petrişor drove to the center of Tîrgovişte, where a group of people was gathered, discussing, no doubt, the events of the past twenty-four hours. Petrişor jumped out. "I've captured the tyrant!" he screamed, gesturing wildly. The crowd gathered around the car, but just as quickly several men appeared and seized the passengers. They were plainclothes

Securitate men. In another version of the same story, Petrişor drove to a factory where he claimed he knew the night watchman who might be willing to hide the couple. He went instead to the factory club, where workers on break were watching television. At the very moment that Petrişor ran breathlessly in, Romanian television was announcing that the Ceauşescus had been captured.

"I have them in the car!" screamed Petrişor. No one believed him. After all, they had just heard the news on TV. At long last Petrişor's hysterical behavior convinced some of the workers to go outside and look. Sure enough. Soldiers appeared at this point and took the couple away.

They were driven to an Army base and made to climb inside a tank. On the way to their makeshift prison Elena offered the men who arrested them one million dollars to help them escape. The proud soldiers refused, even though, as one of them explained later, "she was talking real dollars."

Were these the Ceauşescus who commanded blind allegiance (ostensibly even postmortem) from their faithful? Here they were, alone, a tired old couple who had been aimlessly hitchhiking around the country they'd ruled with an iron fist for a quarter of a century. No one would hide them; no one would come to their rescue. What was going on here? Certainly, no one loved them—not even their children—but they were greatly feared. All those millions of microphones listening in and terrorizing the population had for their final aim the ears of these two old people. Where was the much talked-about Praetorian Guard whose job was to die for its leaders? Where were those children allegedly chosen from orphanages and raised by Elena and Nicolae to believe blindly in their "parents" after being trained by the PLO in all the killing arts? Where was Securitate? Where was that dreaded force that employed one of three Romanians in its network of spies, armed to the teeth with the latest technology and fearsome weapons? Was it possible that everyone had betrayed them? And if it was true that everyone had, who were the so-called loyalists and terrorists who kept fighting even after the dead Ceauşescus had been shown on television?

The prisoners inside the tank demanded fresh food. Given the stale bread that the soldiers ate, Elena exploded: "They are feeding us bricks now!" Ceauşescu demanded a new suit. He had been in the habit of wearing a new suit every day for fear of being poisoned with viruses hidden in the fabric. His food had been tested, his calories counted, his

Andrei Codrescu

blood carefully analyzed. Understandably he was indignant. Elena was understandably disgusted by the soldiers' fare. Here is one of the Ceau-şescu family's menus, dated August 23, 1989, at a time of general starvation: APPETIZERS: eggplant au gratin, pickled mushrooms, green pepper salad, cucumbers with yogurt and dill, rolled ham; FISH: stuffed salmon, trout with tomatoes, grilled carp; ENTRÉES: stuffed Parisian melons, lamb chops, veal medallions, chicken fillets, goose liver, stuffed cabbage; ASSORTED GRILLADE: filet mignon, roast pork, grilled Cornish hens; GARNISHES: mixed vegetables, peasant rice, potatoes au gratin; DESSERT: fruitcake, crepes with fruit and cheese, assorted ice creams, petits fours; DRINKS: brandy, vodka, beer, cabernet sauvignon, assorted liqueurs.

During the critical hours after their arrest the Ceauşescus were said to have been driven constantly in two tanks around the Tîrgovişte Army base in order not to arouse suspicion. Whenever the prison carrier stopped, a soldier would scrub it to make it appear that nothing unusual was going on. Two rescue efforts were attempted, according to Major Lupoi, but the locator device on the dictator's watch, which was supposed to alert his would-be rescuers to his position, failed to work properly inside the tanks. These "rescue attempts" were never described in any great detail. The capture by the Army was kept secret for two days, but the announcement was made before the capture. Army spokesmen explained that the reason for the secrecy had been to gain time to assemble a tribunal for a court-martial. No one explained the premature announcement.

The Tîrgovişte Army base claimed to have been fired on, and its commander wired his superiors that the prisoners could not be held very long. He received a reply from Gelu Voiculescu-Voican, vice-president of the National Salvation Front: "Hold them well. I am on the way with a military tribunal." The Battle of Bucharest was raging at the time, but it was unclear who was shooting at whom. According to Romanian television, where the new provisional government was working, it appeared that Securitate units fighting the Army were beginning to gain the upper hand. In Bucharest Voican assembled a court. He found a judge, Major Georgică Popa; a prosecutor, Colonel Virgil Magureanu; three assessors; a defense attorney; and a court reporter. Together with a cameraman and the Army's public relations spokesman, the group headed in three jeeps via a circuitous route toward Tîrgovişte. No one had been told his true mission by Voican. They believed that they were going to try two high-ranking officers of Securitate. When they saw the accused, the hastily assembled court could barely conceal its joy.

The court-martial was first shown on Romanian television in a truncated version, which was later supplemented by a longer tape. It is an extraordinary exhibit.

Before the "trial" a doctor takes the dictator's blood pressure and pronounces, "Sixty, seventy," then asks, "Can you tell me about your state of health?"

Ceauşescu does not answer.

The doctor next asks Elena, "Have you been ill? Do you need any medicines?"

Elena replies, "I don't need anything."

Standing behind what looks like a school desk, the couple faces the prosecutors (invisible in the edited version; in the unedited version the prosecutors are visible). To the charge of genocide, the dictator responds with angry derision. "This is nothing but a coup d'état!" He is clearly contemptuous of the tribunal whose authority he does not recognize. "A coup d'état organized by a foreign power!" he adds pointedly. No one asks him what foreign power.

"Who gave the genocidal order in Timişoara?"

Silence.

"Who ordered shooting the people in Bucharest? Who are the fanatics who keep shooting?"

Ceauşescu: "I refuse to answer. Nobody shot anyone in the Palace Square; no one was killed."

The prosecution continues: "Today there are sixty-four thousand victims in our cities. You reduced the people to misery. There are great scholars who are leaving the country to escape from you. Who are the foreign mercenaries who are shooting? Who asked them to come?"

Elena says: "It's a provocation!"

Asked about secret Swiss accounts, Elena looks astonished. "What accounts?"

The defender appointed by the court often takes the side of the prosecution. There is a painful feeling on the part of all concerned that they are participants in a hastily and very badly written play. But there is a sense of urgency, too, a rush to get the inevitable thing done.

Throughout the long hours of the "trial," an angry Nicolae Ceau-şescu keeps glancing repeatedly at his watch, as if to say, "How long is this charade going to continue?" Some have interpreted the gesture to mean that he was waiting to be rescued, and that he was simply impatient with his rescuers because this was the first time in twenty-five years that anybody had kept him waiting. Others have speculated that this was no ordinary watch, but a sophisticated locator or communicator, a Dick Tracy device. But looking at the well-groomed, silver-haired, lean man sitting at the schoolroom table with an expression of supreme contempt on his face, I believe that he was simply annoyed. It is not time he was glancing at when he looked at his wristwatch. His watch measured not time but his own patience. For twenty-five years in Romania time was only his own capacity for tolerance. Here was a man who for a quarter of a century *was* time, the incarnation of an age. He had himself chosen the name of his epoch: the golden era. Toward the end, when electricity was rationed and people actually began to live in the dark, the "golden era" became a standard joke. But not to the Ceauşescus. In their palace the bathroom fixtures were made of solid gold.

"I am the supreme commander of the state, and the leader of the party and I will accept only the judgment of the People's Congress," insists the dictator. At one point he throws his pointed fur hat on the table in a gesture of frustration, as if he were putting an end to an infinitely boring and long-winded speech. . . . He's had enough. He cannot understand why he is being made to endure this.

Elena Ceauşescu looks, by turns, angry and frightened. Only she appears to suspect that the proceedings may not end well. The "great scientist," whose "brilliant mind" was praised almost daily in Romania's newspapers, whose name was inscribed in flowing forged script on numerous bogus "scientific" awards and diplomas, may still have had a peasant girl's common sense about her, though it was a peasant girl who had to repeat fifth grade. Later, in the official biographies, that failed fifth grade became the time when she was first "persecuted for revolutionary activities." In fact, like her husband, she was undereducated, a capricious woman who rewrote not only her own life history but that of others if they didn't suit her. Her ascension to power was directly proportional to her husband's isolation. She trusted no one and ruled whimsically, to protect him. She had more than a touch of the instinctually treacherous and cruel politics of her land's former Byzantine, Turkish, and Phanariot rulers. During the proceedings a shrewd look often breaks on her face, as if an infinitely complicated and satisfying way to get out of this situation had just occurred to her. But there isn't any. There are little gestures of affection between them, touching of hands. . . . It is easy to forget briefly who they are and see only a tired, aging couple being teased on their imminent way to death.

The military tribunal charges them with the following: genocide; subversion of the state by ordering the massacre of unarmed civilians; destruction of communal property; subversion of the economy; attempt to escape from the country, having amassed and hidden more than one billion dollars in foreign banks.

They are found guilty of each charge, an outcome met by grimaces, shaking heads in disbelief, a burst of short, derisive laughter. There is a disturbing familiarity between the accused and their accusers. In spite of the grave accusations and the tragic outcome, they seem to be speaking the same language, a shorthand honed in secret meetings, a half language that reeks of shared assumptions.

"Do you know who is holding you?" asks one of the invisible prosecutors.

"Yes," answers Ceauşescu, "Securitate."

There is no follow-up. The protagonists know each other. At one point Elena Ceauşescu says: "I was like a mother to you." The edited version gives the impression that she is speaking to the Romanian nation. Watching the unedited version, we know. Her remark is directed reproachfully at her intimates, Securitate officers, her "children."

The sentence: death and confiscation of private property.

According to one account, the sentence was carried out immediately by soliders under the command of Major Mihai Lupoi, a rather sinister man, who spoke to Ted Koppel in January 1990 about his job with unconcealed pleasure. "Elena was worried about being tied up for shooting . . . she thought her hands would break . . . as if it mattered if your hands are broken if you're going to die in five minutes. . . ." Three soldiers were chosen, according to Lupoi, but the rest couldn't wait, and they all started shooting at once. But it now appears—according to interviews with other members of the military tribunal—that the hasty soldiers were actually beaten to it by two members of the tribunal who used their revolvers to kill them first. The two men were Colonel Virgil Măgureanu, a philosophy professor at the Securitate Academy, and Gelu Voiculescu-Voican, a geologist and amateur astrologer. Măgureanu is now the head of the "new" Romanian secret services, while Voican is vice-minister to Prime Minister Petre Roman and continues in a Rasputin-like function to advise the government. His long white beard can be seen flashing in and out of important offices in the Parliament building.

During the trial Ceauşescu kept staring fixedly at Voican, the only civilian in the group, possibly hoping that Voican was the one in a position to save him. Throughout the proceedings Voican kept looking repeatedly at his watch, just like Ceauşescu. A silent communication was established between the two men based on the rhythm of their repeated glances at their wristwatches. When the Ceauşescus were taken out the door to be executed, Voican looked at his watch one more time and grinned. Ceauşescu must have understood: his final moment was at hand. His fellow watch gazer was death itself, a figure like the one marking midnight in the medieval clock tower of Prague. The execution, according to Voican, took place so swiftly—because of either the enthusiasm of the soldiers or Voican's and Măgureanu's fast draws—that the cameraman had no time to record the historical event. One wonders.

The videotape of the court-martial was not shown on Romanian television until December 26, a full day after the Ceauşescus had been officially executed or two full days if they were executed on December 24. Why wasn't the tape released immediately if, as the new leaders claimed, battles raged murderously in the entire country and people were dying for their leader who they believed was directing the resistance from a Carpathian bunker? The tape showing their indubitably stiff corpses might have stopped some of the fire. *After* the tape was shown, members of the provisional government claimed that it did indeed stem the fighting because the Ceauşescu loyalists—the "terrorists" had nothing left to fight for. Who were these Ceauşescu loyalists? To this day it is still the unanswered question in Romania. The official explanation about the delay in showing the tape was that a great debate raged for two days between the young revolutionaries (students and workers), backed by the soldiers occupying the station building, and members of the old Ceauşescu administration of Romanian television. The old broadcasters and technicians, who had been kept around to operate the equipment, attempted to make a last stand against any truthful use of the medium. Some of them thought that it was "in bad taste," an astonishing aesthetic criterion to hold in the middle of a revolution. It is unclear who edited the "trial" tape in the way it was edited, removing the faces of the Ceauşescu tribunal. It was a bad job that left a sour taste in the mouth, no matter that those watching had little sympathy for the dead dictator. The official reason was that faces had been erased to protect the prosecutors from retaliation. But it could be equally surmised that someone(s) did not want the prosecutors to become heroes. One might also surmise with equally good cause that the makeshift trial and quick execution had taken place in order to protect people who might have been incriminated in a public trial. The dead bodies of the dictator and his wife were shown on Romanian television on December 26, but it was not until March 2, 1990, when a group of Securitate men was put on trial in Timişoara, that the three-hour tape was released unedited on Romanian television.

On the day of its release, the head of the military tribunal that condemned Nicolae and Elena Ceauşescu to death, Major General Georgică Popa, committed suicide. He shot himself in the head with his standard-issue Makharov pistol. He left a note in which he explained that he had been living in terror since December 25. "I could not find any other solution to free myself from the fear and dread that make the rest of my life unbearable. I desire neither flowers nor memorials from my colleagues. I am an only child. I have nothing to reproach anyone for, I have forgotten everyone. Help me, God, to cross this difficult passage. Let my wife know gently." The Ceauşescus claimed their accuser from beyond the grave. The embarrassed government, through the mouth of former Justice Minister Theofil Pop, claimed that "he'd been depressed, because of family problems, for ten years." But one of General Popa's best friends, Lieutenant Colonel Coriolan Voinea, rejected that explanation indignantly. In an interview published on March 4 in *România Liberă*, he says that the presiding judge at the tyrants' "trial" was being pushed aside by the new government, left out of important decisions concerning military justice after the revolution, and generally shunned by the very men whose gratitude he ought to have earned. Finding himself not a hero, as might be expected, but a pariah, General Popa attempted on several occasions to take refuge with his family in the American Embassy, hoping to leave the country. In the vast gap between these two explanations lies a secret only Major General Popa knew. And between the suicide (or murder) of General Milea and the suicide of General Popa lies a story as ambiguous as it is extraordinary.

Christmas Day 1989 was an unusually warm day in Romania. Believers in churches all over the country thanked God for the weather, which had been instrumental to the success of their revolution. The spring-in-winter had made it possible for millions of people to take to the streets to press for their freedom. And the Antichrist was dead. Whoever had killed him, and for whatever reason, had earned the gratitude of the nation. Only slowly, in meditative prayer, could people begin to piece together the week that shook their country and the world. The Romanian Revolution had changed the face of the country forever, and everyone hoped that communism was, for all practical purposes, dead. Everyone hoped that an age of human suffering at the hands of a bloody utopia that had unfolded between the two great parentheses of the Bolshevik Revolution of 1917 and the Romanian Revolution of 1989, had come to an end. The blazing candles in memory of the young dead of the revolution in University Square seemed to guarantee that hope.

3

The Long Road Back

Thousands of miles from Romania, my heart beat like a hammer before CNN Cable Channels 29 and 33, linking the world to the Romanian Revolution. "I have been dancing since the moment I first heard the news!" I told Noah Adams on National Public Radio when he called me for comment. "The old proverb is true: Dawn comes even after the longest night! Last night, December twenty-first, was the longest night of the year, and it looked for a while, on the blood-spattered streets of Romania, that dawn would never come. But it did come, and the Romanian people had given themselves the greatest present in a half century of bloody history: freedom. For me, personally, it is more than a Christmas gift because my birthday fell on December twentieth. Nobody has ever given me a better birthday present. I know that I have to go see the revolution for myself." Grand words, but truly felt. Those of us who had watched with increasing despair the fall of all the other tyrants in Eastern Europe hardly believed that our turn to rejoice had come.

I heard a member of the National Salvation Front say on television that the word "comrade" was dead in Romania, that henceforth people could address one another in a new and more dignified way. Like all other Orwellian speech of the soon-to-be-dust tyrants of the world, "comrade" had meant exactly its opposite for forty-five years. For twenty-five of those years I had felt the sorrow of Romania deeply. Few things

51

are certain in this life, but good things are even less certain than the few that are. During the next few critical weeks the Romanian Revolution needed all the help it could muster, as well as the goodwill and support of the world. I had something to offer—namely, understanding of the language of a people I hoped to be able to explain to Americans. I felt at least half American myself since I had spent nearly the same number of years in the United States as I had in Romania, so in a sense I wanted to explain the revolution to myself as well. Beyond that, I simply wanted to go back, to the place of my childhood, to look around. In a way I'd had my bag packed for a quarter of a century.

The spring weather had come to an abrupt end in Romania the day after Christmas. The temperature dropped, and an extraordinary snowstorm dumped over twenty inches on the capital. It snowed fiercely in Transylvania and in Timişoara, the cradle of the Romanian Revolution. An unusual cold spell descended on the country after the snow, lowering temperatures to well below zero. The snow froze, and most roads became treacherous sheets of ice. Movement became nearly impossible, and the newly liberated country came to a standstill. But for the first time in many years the Romanians had heat for their homes and the liberty of the word. The believers thanked God for this also.

Art Silverman, my friend and producer at NPR's *All Things Considered*, called every day after the events began. On December 22 he asked me if I wanted to go.

"Go?" I said. "Man, I want to fly the nearest duck!" (old Romanian proverb).

"What will your family say if I take you away from them for Christmas?"

"It's for my son's homework," I told him. "I've got to get news for his sixth-grade report!"

At the beginning of November 1989 my son Tristan's sixth-grade teacher assigned Eastern Europe to her students. Events in those countries had been filling the pages of newspapers at an astonishing rate. Poland voted in its first non-Communist government. Czechoslovakia announced free elections. Václav Havel, a dissident playwright in jail only three months before, was poised to become its president. Political parties in Hungary called for venture capitalism. Yugoslavian republics in turmoil began moves toward independence. Bulgaria's party boss was under house arrest. And these were just some of the biggies. The Berlin wall was yet to fall. Tristan's schoolmates each chose a country to follow in the news from November 1 to December 15. Tristan chose Romania. But there was no news about Romania.

"I'll tell you all about Romania," I told him.

"Aw, Dad!" he said, annoyed. "We're supposed to cut out things from the paper or tape stuff on TV and radio about it." Apparently he did not consider me—yet—a great source of news. In fact, I wasn't. The recurrent theme of my conversations with Romanian friends had been the extraordinary immobility of Romania in these dramatic times. In the midst of epochal changes in Eastern Europe Romania seemed to go its own way, a cruelly ruled slave ship unmoored from its neighbors and sanity. The state of dissent in the country was roughly that of Poland a full year before Solidarity. Appeals and protests were launched by intellectuals and even old party members. The signatories of these documents were "disappeared," put in prison, or—if known in the West— placed under house arrest. As Ceauşescu's paranoia about his neighbors increased, the disappearances multiplied.

Even the jokes, which had helped people weather past suffering, became grimmer. "Is it true," a reporter asks Ceauşescu, "that your people are freezing from lack of heat?" "Yes," Ceauşescu replies, "but nobody died from that." "Is it true," insists the reporter, "that there is no food and everyone is starving?" "It is true," Ceauşescu says, "but nobody ever died from it." The astonished interviewer throws up his hands. "Have you tried cyanide?" he asks. In another joke it appears that at long last a citizen obtains a gun and tries to kill the dictator at a mass rally. But he misses. "How could you possibly miss?" asks the colonel in charge of torturing him. "It was the crowd," the man says, "they kept shoving me this and that way: Shoot him, shoot her. . . ."

This was possibly the last joke told about the Ceauşescu family. It was as if even the jokes had run out of anything but the crude fantasy of revenge. In the end Ceauşescu did try cyanide on his own people— his security forces were said to have poisoned the water in Sibiu—and he would have taken the country with him if he'd been able to occupy the country's only nuclear plant. And the citizen assassin, who in November had been only a character in a joke, became only too real in December, when he, and his friends, pumped a great number of bullets into the tyrants' bodies. Those "invisible butterflies" invoked by a student on the wall of the University of Bucharest came home.

No one could have imagined the magnificent explosion of popular sentiment that overthrew the dictator. It was said that Romanians had

had their spirit broken by the dictatorship, that one in three worked for Securitate, that the national character was infinitely bendable, that the legacy of years of subjugation to Romans, Turks, and Russians showed, and so on. . . . But now look . . . Of course, it would have been good to have a revolution without martyrs, but these martyrs were going to ensure a fierce regard for liberty. Democracy won this way was irreversible. Or so I wanted most desperately to believe.

After I had told them about my country for so long, stories both true and imagined, my family and friends wanted to hear for themselves what the new story was. One day, I told everyone, we all will go to Romania to eat plums from apple trees, pears from poplars, honey from streams. Romania was more fairy tale than real place to them; but now a miracle had taken place, and the fairy tale had sprung to life.

My two traveling bags were loaded to the maximum portable weight with chocolates, cigarettes, New Orleans coffee, and Knorr soups obtained by my wife, Alice, in a thorough raid of the corner drugstore (a single K&B drugstore would probably feed Romanians for a year. Too bad I didn't have a shrinking wand so I could take this K&B, the A&P down the street, and maybe the Schweggman's store in Metairie with me). These few items I knew were an essential medium of exchange. Coffee and oranges hadn't been seen in Romania for years. Ironically, the day I arrived, the government freed the secret stashes of the party and put oranges and coffee into stores. Nonetheless, it all came in handy, and New Orleans coffee is the best anyway. I also packed copies of my books to give Romanian friends. I was not traveling light, but I was taking in more things than I had taken out when I left in 1965. Back then I had been allowed only one suitcase, for clothes. No manuscripts, photographs, or books were permitted to leave. I had to abandon my poems in Romania, where they still were, in the safe keeping of a friend. I felt no great loss about my photographs, though leaving them had been my mother's great regret. She was a photographer, and over the years she had taken enough pictures of me to fill a seagoing trunk. But I didn't care for my old images when I left Romania. I intended to be a new me, and that included my face. I was now bringing in my new American poems and photographs of my family and friends to trade, perhaps, for my old ones. Still, I refused to take a camera, believing in the greater accuracy of my inner eye. This, I believe, was one of my sanest insights into a world plunged into uncritical delirium by images.

There was still fighting, but the Hungarian and Yugoslav borders were reportedly open. Several newsmen had been killed and wounded. Relief convoys had been attacked. The situation changed from hour to hour, but on December 26 it appeared to stabilize. The revolution had gained the upper hand. For a day or so before that it had appeared that a civil war was taking place. There was talk of international assistance for Romania's embattled revolution. The French proposed the formation of international brigades and were the first to offer fighters. Thousands of young men signed up and gave blood at the same time. There was also talk of Soviet intervention, an idea so appalling to Romanians that they might have preferred the old dictatorship to another Soviet occupation. The United States had just invaded Panama. Romania shared the spotlight with Panama. The difference between the two wars was painfully evident, and painfully embarrassing to me. "Look," I told everyone, "lip service is being paid to the Romanian Revolution while a crude occupation of a small country goes on. Romanian television's broadcasting scenes of euphoria, optimism, and spontaneity, while Panamanian television is in the smooth hands of the professional propaganda machine of the U.S. Army!" One shocking event of that time still remains utterly mysterious. Secretary of State James Baker appeared on *Meet the Press*, at the height of the crisis, and invited Soviet troops into Romania. No, he said in answer to a question, we would not object to Soviet intervention in Romania. It seemed to me that a peak of insensitivity was reached at that point in the habitual callousness of the big powers evident since the Yalta agreements after World War II. It occurred to me that Romania was alone. Not only was Romania alone, but so was Eastern Europe, lip service from the West notwithstanding. The fall of communism was upsetting especially to anti-Communists of the old right. Still, delivering Romania blithely into the arms of the Soviets was insane. No matter what deal had been cut, it couldn't have been as crude as "Hey, boys, take this country over here!" And yet how else was one to interpret Secretary Baker's invitation to the Soviets? There was no seemingly reasonable explanation, and like so many of my media confreres, I preferred to exult in the sunny certainties rather than muck about the depths.

The day after Christmas I arrived at Washington's National Airport. My Pan Am flight to Budapest was scheduled for later that evening. In the afternoon I stopped by the offices of NPR on M Street to say my good-byes and to speak about my upcoming trip with Linda Wertheimer for that evening's news. "Are you nervous about going back to Romania?" Linda asked me.

"My hands aren't shaking," I told her, "but I have many mixed emotions, mixed in a variety of ways." I told her that I couldn't wait to revisit my childhood, which had been frozen in my mind for decades, that I wanted to see if things were the way I remembered them, because I had been told many times that buildings and places shrink when an adult revisits them. I wanted to revisit Sibiu, hoping the fighting that had been reported there had not damaged the old buildings I once dreamed in. I wanted to see my high school friends. I had not gone to our twentieth-year reunion, but I knew that this reunion—in a free country—would be many times better.

Linda asked me if I had any fears about going back since I had been so outspoken about Ceauşescu.

I confessed some apprehensions to her and said that I was hoping that the people who had been in charge of keeping the lists of their enemies in the dank basements of torture palaces were gone by now. I had felt their bad breath several times during my exile. At one point secret agents had been dispatched to the West to kill dissident writers. After the first attempts—against novelists Paul Goma and Virgil Tănase—failed miserably in Paris, Ceauşescu scaled down the program to beatings and intimidation. In any case, I did not believe that I was important enough to kill at a time when these agents were probably just fighting for their lives. On the other hand, I had heard that members of the new government and famous dissidents were still being targeted. I heard that Silviu Brucan was being ferried by armored carrier from one safe house to another and did not sleep in the same place twice. Other reports, however, spoke of the great joy and elation of people freed from the tyranny, roaming the streets in spontaneous groups, lighting candles to the dead, singing. I felt, even though I had not yet left North America, that a great feeling of relief had been felt by the whole world, as if a darkness had lifted from the psychic body of the planet. Finally, I confessed that I did not know what to expect. Twenty-five years is a long time to be away from a place. Neither places nor people would be the same. My adolescent memory may have been holding only the shadow of a place that was no more.

I arrived in Budapest, Hungary, on December 27. Noah Adams, my traveling companion, carried a briefcase full of important-looking position papers on Romania. I read a long history of the Romanian Communist party by Vladimir Tismăneanu, but my mind was elsewhere, ahead of myself in the world of my beginnings.

We were not sure how best to go to revolutionary Romania. The BBC was reporting fighting at Otopeni International Airport in Bucharest. No planes were landing there, and the few international relief agencies that had attempted landings had come under heavy fire. Some of the land routes were open. We heard that Michael Sullivan and Rich Rarey, our colleagues from National Public Radio, had reached Timişoara from Yugoslavia in a rented car. It was possible also to hire a taxi in Sofia for a four-hour drive to Bucharest. I was hoping that the *Orient Express* route from Budapest to Istanbul, which went through Romania, would soon start running again.

Meanwhile, I looked at the palaces and monuments of Budapest across the Danube River and inhaled deeply the decay of old Europe, with its peeling walls and diesel fumes. I was back, no doubt about it, in that Habsburg Europe that is still, for all practical purposes, a chain of related kingdoms steeped in absurdity, elegance, revolution, manners, Sacher tortes, puff pastries, and a kind of subterranean intensity that belies all those things.

It all looked familiar: the lettering on the shops; the style of the nineteenth-century facades; even the murmur of the streets. I found the sound of the Hungarian language reassuring. My people on my mother's side are Transylvanian Hungarian Jews, and Hungarian was the language of my babyhood. I fell asleep to its sounds in my grandmother's house in Alba Iulia. I felt, too, the insistent mystery of my Jewishness in this Hungary, where there were once hundreds of thousands of Jews, including my two great-aunts, who lived here and then were taken to Auschwitz and were no more.

I walked the streets of Budapest, looking into the narrow windows of shops full of hats, shoes, haberdashery, all the small trades of medieval Europe still in practical use. I went into old bookstores with door chimes and looked at pictures in atlases and art books. I took a taxi to nowhere and watched the cold river mist swirl about us. The wide boulevards teemed with life, but as evening approached and the lights of little cafés came on, another, ghostly city emerged. Three decades before on these same boulevards there were Soviet tanks. I remember seeing the photos of street fighters with berets and those old-fashioned Soviet machine guns with the round magazines, standing before a captured tank looking old-fashioned also. But for all that, the young fighters didn't look that different from the young Romanians whose faces I had been watching intently on television for the past week: the same open-eyed, hopeful look of naive strength, the same squint for the camera, the same sexy swagger that said, "Death is nothing to me!" And unhappily, death had come to many of those young Hungarian fighters, probably not long after those pictures had been taken. They had gone out just like that, smiling, sexy, young, full of swagger. Tragically also, they lost their revolution. In thirty long years the Hungarians had found another way to endure, one that forsook liberty for the basics of food and consumer goods. János Kádar's "goulash communism" had filled the shops on Váci Utca with fashionable goods and the plates of Hungarians with goulash. But watching over the table at which the Hungarian people were having their relatively plentiful meal were eighty thousand Soviet soldiers standing, machine guns at the ready, just in case some of the diners got up and went inexplicably insane. There was no sign of soldiers as I got out of the taxi. The sign over a coffee shop had attracted me. Inside, seated at small tables, were young students and perhaps intellectuals, drinking red wine, coffee, and cherry liqueurs. Some of the men were bearded and bespectacled, serious-looking, emanating a palpable air of seriousness and idealism. The women were lithe, pretty, alert, and they laughed easily. The banter and flirtatiousness were what one would expect in any Western European café, from Paris to Milan, but "This is Hungary!" I kept reminding myself. "This is Eastern, not Western, Europe, no matter that young people look like young people everywhere in their jeans, leather jackets, and beards." The difference was that even at this late date, with elections coming up, and the Communist party undergoing a face-lift, there were still Soviet soldiers hereabouts. And the ghosts of the Hungarian Revolution had not entirely receded into history. Neither had my two great-aunts nor my Jewishness.

As it turned out, I had not been far wrong to get out at this spot. When I left the café, buzzing slightly from two espressos and a schnapps, I found myself looking at a vast dark building so powerful even the streetlights were dim around it. The old synagogue of Budapest was a forbidding fortress in an advanced state of disrepair. There were marble slabs lying about the immense deserted yard in which stood a partially hidden sculpture dedicated to the survivors of the Holocaust. Profuse ivy grew in wild neglect on the high Moorish facade. As I strolled past peeling columns, peering into the winter dark at Hebrew letters on the rows of graves in the old Jewish cemetery inside, I had the feeling that I had been here before. I felt the chill—and it was not the December cold—of a once-full world that was now empty, a deserted center that was also somehow at the center of my being. Something lost, gone, irretrievable.

I ran my fingers over a frozen memorial plaque that said, "To the martyrs of 1940–1945," and there was such a profound darkness in those words, I started wondering why I had come back at all.

As I circled the building, I came to a small side door. A round man in a threadbare coat with the look of a holy simpleton spotted me and waved me closer. "Come, come," he said. I followed him into a narrow hall with a high ceiling, and there were people here, a small cluster of voices in the semidark. Someone took my coat, handed me a yarmulke, and guided me in. It felt like a dream. I walked past rows of dark galleries. We entered a smaller hall to the side, and for a moment I was blinded by the bright light. Lo and behold, a service was in progress!

It was the last day of Hanukkah. I couldn't believe my luck. I was standing here among the tattered remains of Hungarian Jewry, with a Hebrew book in my hand. Many of the men were old, but there were some bright-eyed young children in front. One of them was looking at me with open curiosity, and when I was unable to find my place in the book, he showed me his. I turned to the page.

The young rabbi looked at me. I saw also some of my features in others in the room. It was a strange homecoming—to a place I knew nothing obvious about: not the language or the service. But intimately and deep down, I was connected to these people in ways that criss-crossed history like underground rivers.

The young boy who had shown me his book was now asked by the rabbi to lead the service, and he began in a voice so confident and so pure it brought tears to my eyes. What's more, he sang about miracles, verses so appropriate to the extraordinary times I was living through, I henceforth dismissed all notions of concidence. In Hebrew the song of "M'oh Tsur" ("Rock of Ages"), a triumphant hymn that proclaims, "The time is nearing/which will see all men free, / tyrants disappearing."

I stood here in Budapest, in Europe's largest synagogue, sharing Hanukkah bread with my mother's people. Strange, I was on my way to revolutionary Romania, where—as in Hungary and elsewhere—Jews are, once more, at the center of issues. Most of the founders of Hungary's and Romania's Communist parties were Jews. In Romania anti-Semitism had a resurgence under Ceauşescu. But the new Salvation Front prime minister, Petre Roman, is a Jew, the son of an old Communist and descended, it is said, from a long line of rabbis. As the new Europe takes shape, being a Jew again becomes significant. I am keenly aware that far from being spent, the Jews of former Austria-Hungary are still playing out an as yet unknown destiny. But the voice of the young boy repeating the age-old words was giving me hope, It was the voice of an irrepressible spirit, born out of the ashes again and again.

I spent the next day visiting the statues of poets and revolutionaries, an abundance of which distinguishes this part of the world. I paid my respects to Sándor Petöfi, whose verses inspired the rebels of 1956, and to Lajos Kossuth, who led the revolt against the Habsburgs in 1848. I also looked at people, who, in truth, interested me more than statues. They wore warm fur hats over lively, interested eyes. Shopping with gusto, drinking in bars, restaurants, and arcades, they did not seem overly concerned with the past. Signs of the present were everywhere; a startlingly simple poster on AIDS consisted of those initials with the *I*, made to look like a penis, covered by a condom. The full restaurants gave off clouds of paprika steam, and little bursts of music came out whenever their doors opened.

But I was impatient to get on with my journey. Watching two French women gossip over coffee in a little café, I had the feeling that I was still in the West, that there were two Eastern borders, and that I had not, in fact, yet crossed the real one. Finally, on December 28, we got the word that tickets for the *Orient Express* to Bucharest were available. The train was running.

Early the next morning, on the twenty-ninth, Noah bought round-trip tickets for both of us. We were to meet at the Northern Station at six that evening. Noah went to the offices of the Hungarian radio station to prepare a story for that evening's broadcast on National Public Radio. I got our bags—two of mine and three of his (filled, for the most part, with tape recorders, reel-to-reel tapes, and other electronic gadgetry)—and checked them in at the station around four. The train station is a high Victorian building with soaring steel arches, built in the grand manner of an empire that never foresaw its end. One wonders at the optimist arrogance of such grandeur just moments before the world fell apart. The top-hatted gentlemen of industry and their corseted women must have surely had hints of doom. But you could not fathom those in Budapest's grand Northern Station, imperial eagle affixed to the clouds . . . even as the Russian Revolution and World War I come thundering in. Black marketeers, their pockets bulging full of Hungarian forints, accosted me in droves. "Dollars! Dollars! Deutsche marks!" The street exchange for those currencies is eight times the official rate. Policemen in pairs walked by stiffly, ignoring the brisk trade. It was a strange scene, this bustling, semilegal market, now tolerated in all Eastern European countries as a way to obtain hard currency. I thought of Hemingway's story "Inflation and the German Market," about the young French couples after the First World War who cross the border to Germany to gorge themselves on rich pastries worth almost nothing in worthless German currency. Well, that is no longer the case. German marks are the black marketeers' first choice.

I went hunting for sandwiches and mineral water for our sixteen-hour journey to Budapest. We had been told that there would be no food on the train. I contemplated briefly the dried-up finger-size sausages hanging pathetically out of tiny buns in the dusty window of the cart next to the station. A sign expressly calling these things "sandwiches" hung uselessly in front of them. I did not have the heart to explore the window display any further, so I headed down the boulevard for the promising lights in the distance. I was not optimistic. Hungary, like most of Europe, opens its restaurants at noon and closes them at four. Innovations like "food to go" are still exotic and American, sole province of the lone Budapest McDonald's. But that was far from where I was. After a long search in darkened arcades I was able to buy four wrinkled oranges from a man who looked as if he'd traded his children for them and four heavy bottles of mineral water, whose tops were locked in steel caps that would no doubt require the services of an industrial-strength opener. I also found a pastry shop stocked with mostly cream-topped fragile-looking things that would surely disintegrate in my arms before I even got back to the train station. The only sturdy confections were hardened muffins with a three-inch layer of yellow matter in between. This stuff turned out, eventually, to be nothing but butter as both I and a Danish journalist ascertained later on the train, after taking simultaneous bites. The sandwich problem was still more complex, but I solved it, I thought, when I walked into a bar and bought the whole tray of frozen croque-monsieur–like open-faced sandwiches on the counter. The hardened yellow cheese on the ancient toast was sprinkled with paprika and fragments of hard-boiled egg. I laid all these open-faced croque-monsieurs down on top of one another in order to produce portable sandwiches, a procedure that shocked the proprietress so much she nearly refused to sell. At long last, arms laden with the above—all were, by the way, wrapped in shredding paper, not inside a bag—I made my way back to the Northern Station, where I unchecked our luggage. I settled on Platform 12 to wait. This was where, I was told, the Bucharest train would, in due time, arrive.

At 5:55 P.M. seeing trace of neither train nor Noah, I had the fleeting thought that a misunderstanding of great proportions had occurred. In fact, it had. The 6:00 o'clock train left from the *Eastern* Station. At 6:10 I found this out from an engineer on the Moscow-bound train who said to me, "You must be crazy to go to Romania now! Why don't you come to Moscow?"

"I'd be crazy to go to Moscow," I told him, "after waiting for twenty-five years to go to a Moscow-free Romania."

While I stood there, cloaked in gloom, with five pieces of barely movable pieces of luggage about me, a young Danish man with wind-whipped hair burst onto the platform, looking as distressed as I. "I just missed the six o'clock to Bucharest at the Eastern Station," he said, "but there is a nine o'clock leaving from here!" Noah, who had no doubt left on the six o'clock, had my ticket, but that was a small matter. Hope revived, I rechecked the bags, and Mark Vedel and I positioned ourselves in a seemingly endless line at the international ticket window. There were Poles, Czechs, and Russians in line, loaded like beasts of burden with Hungarian goods rare in their countries. I hoped that they'd had better luck in their purchases than I had; the thought of those croque-monsieurs chilled my blood. Some hours later, not long before the long black *Orient Express* train pulled in, we had our tickets, second class, the only tickets available. I did not look forward to a second-class Eastern European train compartment. I remembered them only too well from my childhood. I once took a train from Sibiu to Bucharest squished between a peasant with an open gallon jug of brandy on his lap and his two daughters, who balanced an immense wheel of cheese on both their heads. I slid under the roof of that cheese as well as I could, but as the train began rocking into the night and the swaying family began nodding out, I found myself at various junctions holding that heavy cheese all by myself, a smelly roof whose sole support I was. Peasants holding live chickens and cardboard boxes full of eggs boarded the train at small stops as well and positioned themselves in every available pocket of air. That, of course, was in the days when such things as cheese and eggs were available in Romania. These days, sadly, there might be too much room. We were saved from second class, however, by a Russian named Misha, who sold us six sleeping compartments. We would have preferred two, but he was offering them en bloc. Since there were no sleeping compartments on the train at all, we were allowed to trade our six sleepers for first class, an arrangement that convinced me that alas, I really was in Eastern Europe. Mark and I commandeered one such compartment, and I noticed right away the letters *CFR* stamped on the windows. They stood for Căile Ferate Române ("Romanian State Railway"). My journey home had begun.

4

On the Budapest–
Istanbul *Orient*
Express

The sturdy square box lined in faded blue felt was vintage forties. It smelled like the trains of my childhood, all of them prewar monsters imbued with the bitter essence of Eastern Europe, a smell of soldiers, munitions, prisoners, bodies destroyed or marked for destruction, but also of sentiment, scented handkerchiefs, tears, Karenina, and copies of Tolstoy. I ran my fingers over the grain of the scarred wooden paneling, the heavy steel window latch, the stretched net of the luggage rack. . . . Even in America, where trains signify different (though not necessarily happier) things, there still pertains this black European melancholy.

I met a scary old Romanian man once on an American train, on the all-nighter from Chicago to New York. He had a deep wound in his forehead and only two fingers on his right hand. He'd been wounded by Yugoslav partisans toward the end of the war, he said, while commanding a train full of loot from Romania destined for a hollow mountain in Austria that held all the stolen treasures of Europe. A member of the Iron Guard, the Fascist party, he'd fled Romania for Germany after an unsuccessful rebellion against General Ion Antonescu, the too-liberal leader of the rightist government. In Germany he joined the SS and became part of an elite unit noted for its cruelty. I asked him about the rebellion against Antonescu, thinking how odd our encounter was thousands of miles from the Old World and ages removed from that war. "It was about getting rid of the lying Jews!" he exclaimed, as rabidly full of hatred in 1983 as he must have been in 1942. As chills traveled up my spine, he began ranting about how the Jews had invented the Holocaust to justify their killing of his people and how they were still taking over . . . and all this time he looked straight into my eyes, as if knowing full well that I was a Jew. I felt fascinated and paralyzed, as if I were looking into the eyes of a snake. I had choices: I could have put out my hand to choke his thin, wrinkled neck. I chose instead to listen to his story until I heard it all. I shuddered the whole time. Even more astonishing was the fact that he was going to New York to take an airplane back to Ceauşescu's Romania, to see his old country before he died. I became convinced that he was dying and pulling home like an old elephant. He even told me his name, defiantly, and I thought I recognized it; he'd been one of the worst monsters of the Iron Guard, a known war criminal. When I got home, I told a friend about my encounter, and he urged me to call the Romanian Embassy to tell them that a war criminal was on his way back. I didn't do it. I remember thinking that he was an old man who would soon die, and I felt that his time was gone and buried. Today, after hearing so much about the resurgence of fascism in Europe, I regret it. Old or not, he was still poisonous. I knew also, even then, that the Ceauşescu regime had been letting old guardists out of prisons and using them to help the dictator run his nationalist campaigns.

If the train I was on now was the same train escaping American bombs at the end of the war, the traces had been well hidden. There was no hint in the blackened windowsill or the worn felt that SS officers, supervising attached cattle wagons, had once played cards in here, on their way to death camps. All that was old stuff now. But there was no denying the melancholy. Even after the war trains separated lovers. You cannot wave a white handkerchief at an airplane while the face of a loved one recedes in the distance. You cannot wave that handkerchief the way Aurelia did when I left Sibiu, and her, for good.

Yes, this was a different train. Headed for revolutionary Romania, it was full of journalists, adventurers, and a handful of exiles. Somewhere out there in the cold winter night was the Romanian border, a line that divided one world from another. As the lights of the little

Hungarian villages flashed by, my fellow passengers walked up and down the aisle, exchanging gossip, suppositions, fears.

"Three months ago," an elderly Romanian gentleman told me, "the border guards ripped open my luggage, read my personal letters, kept me here for four hours. . . ." He was a renowned pianist who had, until now, been allowed grudgingly out of the country for well-paid concerts. The government had pocketed his fees. His intelligent face was deeply lined. "Ceauşescu was a genius of evil," he said.

A Finnish photographer, swinging a half-empty bottle of vodka, told me that last year in Bucharest he had brought his own lock for his hotel room because he was afraid that the Securitate, which followed everybody, was going to shoot him in the head.

A French journalist said that three days ago he'd gone to the funeral of a young man in Timişoara who *had* been shot through the head. "And only two days ago," he added, "three German tourists traveling by car were killed at a roadblock."

"There's been shooting right around here, just on the other side of the border," said the Finn.

German *tourists?* Revolutionary tourists? But through all this talk I felt the presence of something else, a tender but passionate belief and not-yet-real feeling of something radically new and miraculous.

While the Romanian pianist told me that he thought that the tunnels built by Ceauşescu under Bucharest were a reproduction of his insane mind, the train came to a halt. We were somewhere in the nowhere land between Hungary and Romania. I could see nothing but a vast field out the window. Moonlit telegraph poles marched over the dark earth into nothingness. My Danish friend stuck his camera out of the window but pulled it quickly back, frightened. He saw a flare followed by a burst of gunfire. "It is dangerous," he said, lowering the window. *I've come all this way,* I thought, *to die in a frozen field between two parts of Europe that have already seen more blood than I care to imagine.* But no, we were moving again, and, suddenly there, under the cold moon, there it was, the Romanian flag with the socialist emblem cut right out of the middle. It fluttered over a square brick building marking the frontier. *It's through that hole,* I thought, *that I am returning to my birthplace.*

The Romanian border guards boarded the train. They were wearing militia uniforms with tricolored armbands. The door to our compartment opened, and one of them came in, saluting. He was a sturdy, bullish man with the rocky, square jaw of a policeman, the kind of face that haunts the dreams of former prisoners. I could see him standing over me, rubber truncheon in hand, small mustache glistening in dim, bare bulb light, screaming, "All their names! Every single one!" Another day, a week ago perhaps, he might have. But not now. "Passports, please!" I handed him my American passport. He opened it to my Romanian name and smiled widely. "Are you coming back?"

"Yes," I said, not quite reassured.

"Welcome to Free Romania!" He shook my hand, then flashed the victory sign. Another guard appeared behind his back. The one holding my passport turned to him. "See, my friend, I told you. The patriots are coming home."

Amazing. A week ago I'd been a traitor. Now I was a patriot. We shook hands all around. No luggage check, no body search. He returned my passport briskly. Taking a sidelong glance down the hall, to make sure no one overheard him, he whispered: "He was a monster! He kept us in chains!" I nodded my head in agreement, wondering how seamlessly, in a single gesture, he had fused the old and the new world, the still-fearful glance tenuously joined to free speech. Here was a man caught between two eras, a creature metamorphosing before my eyes. The half of him that only a few days ago had ripped open suitcases and read private mail was being supplanted, no doubt, by a new, decent creature. (It is amazing how quickly one's faith in human beings increases the closer one gets to utopia! Or, as someone cruder might put it, it's amazing how stupid one gets for the sake of ideas.) It was going to be a long time before the deep roots of fear in him and in everyone else came to the surface. These roots, woven in every gesture, began in historical soils that transcended the dizzy individuals of these heady days. They came twisted right through the evil tunnels of Bucharest from a long history of fear and repression. A policeman's physiognomy wasn't made in a day. The smile floating over those hard-wrought features was fragile, a lily on a black pond.

The date on my Romanian visa now read, "December 31, 1989." Soldiers with machine guns patrolled the platform. I waved to them. They flashed V signs. My compartment mate, Mark, walked off the train and handed the soldiers cigarettes. I followed him and gave them chocolates. We shook hands. Everyone on the train now, moved by a generous impulse toward these young boys who at a critical moment had turned to defend the revolution, came streaming toward them with small gifts. Happy New Year! *La mulți ani!* I realized that I was standing on Romanian soil for the first time in twenty-five years, and I was not afraid. Quite the contrary. My heart was full of gratitude.

"You know the extraordinary thing," the Romanian pianist said, "there are no portraits of the tyrant on the walls of the border station . . . no slogans! This station looks . . . normal." He stopped, amazed himself at the paradoxical truth of his words. Guards that don't rip everything open, a little train station with clean walls . . . In Romania this was indeed extraordinary. Normality was a miracle in this place where the simple civilized gestures of human beings had been outlawed for so long. As the train pulled out, I caught a last glimpse of the extraordinary little border town of Curtici, an outpost of revolutionary decency in the middle of Europe. These European borders had marked nothing but suffering and despair for centuries. And in one short month the Berlin wall had come down, the Hungarian-Austrian border had been dismantled, the Czech borders were being rolled up, the Romanian border was open! Truly this was an age of wonders!

I fell asleep for an hour or so, a peaceful sleep all the more remarkable in that it was taking place in the country of my worst nightmares for the past twenty-five years. I used to wake up screaming from dreams of men in boots dragging me over wet cement floors toward electric straps on the wall. When I woke up this time, I found myself in a different kind of dream. Outside the windows were endless snowfields going up into the hills of the sub-Carpathians. They looked like clean white sheets under moonlight, the very opposite of Ceaușescu's filthy underground world. Romania was once, and will no doubt be again, a clean country with spotless peasant cottages, embroidered towels, clothes washed in mountain streams.

We were near Timișoara now, the cradle of the revolution, and Romanians were getting on the train. It was my first encounter with the civilians of new Romania. A family of five, a young couple with two elementary school-age children and the husband's younger brother, came into our compartment. They were in a sleepless, exalted state, eyes burning brightly, full of a kind of heartfelt excitement that was characteristic of almost everyone I was going to meet in the next few days. They all were talking at once. They offered us homemade wine from a bottle they were passing around. It was good, a light Tîrnave from local grapes that brought back the taste of fall in the Carpathian villages. This was the wine my friends and I drank at the end of summer, before going back to school. I heard, for the first time, the story of what happened, from participants. Or at least from natives. As I was going to discover in the next few days, everyone had been a participant. It was hard to meet a citizen who had not somehow been at the very center of events, particularly those events that were the most likely to strike a familiar chord with a stranger who had seen them on TV, heard them on the radio, and read them in the papers. The revolution, I soon found, was a collective story belonging to every single Romanian. Whatever was added to it, from whatever source, was immediately incorporated in the larger tale. Romanians are a great, imaginative people. The tale of the Timişoara family was spoken at once by several voices—even the children had many details to add—and there was barely any chronology. In fact, they argued about what happened when as if they were relating a dream. Mixed in with the facts were jokes, sad stories, snatches of song.

"Only a week before Christmas," said Maria, the mother, "these journalists came to our children's school. . . . Isn't that right, kids?" The children nodded expectantly; they knew what was coming. "They come to the school, see, and they ask the kids who their father is. They all say at once. 'Ceauşescu!' and then they ask them who their mother is, and they all say, 'Elena Ceauşescu!' And then they ask them what they want for Christmas, and every child but one says, 'Nothing. We have everything from our parents!' But this one is crying all by himself in a corner. 'What do you want for Christmas?' the journalists ask him. 'I want to be an orphan!,' he says."

"And now he is!" shouted her husband happily.

"Yup." The brother nodded. "They shot him on Christmas Day." "Amen!"

"We have a saying," said Maria. "Do you want to hear it?"

"Yes." I nodded, taking another long swig of Tîrnave.

"Uncle Nicu's gone, Saint Nicholas has come!"

I could see that Ceauşescu had already become a creature of legend, a monster of the past, linked to other figures of dread in a history rich in them. Maria's husband, Dinu, said that Ceauşescu often needed blood transfusions. To this purpose he selected healthy young boys from villages, had blood taken from them, and then had them killed. It's a good symbolic reflection of Ceauşescu's policy of destroying villages and removing peasants to sterile urban dumps. When he destroyed their villages, he drained their blood by severing their roots. In Bucharest and other cities the demonstrators shouted, "Down with the vampire!"

"And you heard about the blood banks?" one of the children, a twelve-year-old boy, asked gravely. I had, but I let him tell it anyway. "Ceauşescu ordered his men to smash the blood banks during the fighting so that the wounded would not get emergency aid," the boy said.

"They poisoned the water!" added Maria.

"He's Dracula!" they said, almost at once.

They compared Vlad Dracula, the Wallachian prince, and Ceauşescu for a long time. "Dracula was better. He was a just man who helped the peasants!" They agreed that Dracula was by far the better man. They crossed themselves. There was a momentary silence in which I heard the train rattling across snowy fields. I was afraid to look out the window for fear of seeing that river of blood that runs out of Romanian history, connecting the people and their tyrants.

Again and again the family from Timişoara puzzled over the story of the tunnels. One thing scared them more than all the others. During the days of the heaviest fighting, when the terrorists emerged from secret subway entrances and popped out of fake gravestones in cemeteries to empty their machine guns into people, the Salvation Front called on all the engineers and architects who had worked on the tunnels to come forth. But none came. "That was because Ceauşescu had them all killed," the younger brother said, and they all crossed themselves again.

"Like the Egyptian pharaohs!" exclaimed the pianist. "The builders of the pyramids died with the king."

They all were shocked by the continuous revelations of the Ceauşescus' opulent life conducted amid sacrifices by the people. Maria put her arms around her children. "I had no milk for them for three years! It was so cold I slept with them every night."

"They took baths in Perrier water!" said the husband.

Water and blood are common in Romanian folklore. Countess Báthory, the so-called Blood Countess of Transylvania, once killed virgin girls and bathed in their blood in order to maintain her youth. Rejuvenating water and cures for old age are characteristic Romanian legends. The water of life are said to be located somewhere in the Carpathians. Romania's most famous product for the last two decades was Gerovital, a rejuvenation drug as yet unapproved by the FDA in the United States, but widely used by aging movie stars. Dr. Ana Sălăjan, who invented Gerovital, also runs world-famous rejuvenation clinics. The Ceauşescus had food tasters and doctors who gave them vitamins and youth potions. They believed, like most tyrants, that they would live forever. Just to make sure, they also built tunnels meant for refuge from global cataclysm. One of the more quaint and documented opinions of Nicolae Ceauşescu was that an imminent nuclear war was likely. He planned to survive inside the tunnels together with his janissaries. After the radiation cleared, they would emerge to the surface and conquer the world. To this end they would use Romania's petroleum reserves, bought from the Arabs and stored in the empty oil fields of Ploieşti, as well as the fleet of used airplanes amassed at international garage sales, to transport things from one ruin to another. In this way Romania would emerge as the world's greatest postwar power, and Ceauşescu ruler of the scorched earth. The royal couple waited patiently, but in style, for their dream of a new world. The interim period, the "golden era," was only a prelude to the "age of light," which was sure to follow. It's enough to make one gag on all utopian undertakings.

"They had gold toilets and a gold bathtub!" said Maria dreamily for possibly the hundredth time since she had found out. "We never had enough hot water for a bath. We boiled snow in the winter to wash our little ones. . . . We made our own soap."

"To decorate the walls above their gold toilets, the Ceauşescus removed original paintings from the National Gallery and replaced them with fakes," said the pianist gravely. "My nephew worked at the National Gallery and made a protest. They sent him to the canal for five years. . . ."

At the mention of the canal, Romania's most dreaded work camp, they all crossed themselves once more.

"They stole these paintings to take with them in the tunnels," continued the pianist, and closed his eyes wearily. It was very late at night, but no one was able to sleep. An infernal vision was being invoked. In a slow, tired voice the pianist spoke obsessively about these paintings. The Ceauşescus needed these paintings in their underground hell to remind them of the destroyed world. The art they liked was on the pastoral side: green fields, sheep, sunsets, little village huts painted realistically by nineteenth-century academicians. . . . "Look," he said, animated all of a sudden, "they would have taken our national art underground, but aboveground they built dozens of palaces in that grandiose Stalinist-Hitlerite style, chapels really, over the entrances to their tunnel world. To understand his mind, you have to go back to medieval Romanian tyrants who tried to expiate their guilt at killing thousands by patronizing art and doing good works—that is, building fortified churches and monasteries that served the dual purpose of pleasing God and serving as a place of refuge. . . ."

The Timişoara family listened wide-eyed to this monologue. Like most simple Romanians, they were in awe of "educated" people. They prized culture and learning. But in their simple awe, terror, and elation I found them more compelling than the learned pianist pursuing his phantoms on the edge of sleep. So I was grateful when we left the realms of speculation.

"Listen," Dinu said, "Elena went to hell and was frying in this big old caldron. And all this time she's screaming, 'I cannot boil or fry in anything but a golden caldron!' "

"And how about those shoes?" shouted Maria. "She had thousands and thousands, encrusted with jewels, rubies, opals, and diamonds. . . ."

"Like Imelda Marcos of the Philippines," said the all-knowing twelve-year-old.

"I wonder if dictators share one imagination," interjected Mark Vedel when I translated.

"And how about those dirty pictures?" said the brother with a leer.

I thought about Manuel Noriega's pornography collection, reported in the United States just before I left, and wondered whether dictators all have the same taste; perhaps they even trade porno mags now and then. But it isn't that. It's just that the arrogance of power that treats people like things is inevitably attracted to pornography. And the kinds of feet used to trample over the people need be clad in potent gear.

There was something more than simple shock at the decadent riches of tyrants that bothered my friends here, and the drunker we got, the more clearly I saw it. It was almost as if at one time they had believed Ceauşescu when he told them that they all must make sacrifices. They had believed that he, too, sacrificed. To have it revealed that he lived in this way while they suffered was *indecent*. This is where the real obscenity was. Ceauşescu had betrayed a quality Romanian people value very highly: modesty. The Ceauşescus had been dead for four days now, but the hatred their people bore them had not abated.

All their voices were hoarse, and I imagined that it was from being able to talk and incessantly doing so at long last. But no, they told me, it was from shouting so much during their revolution. It's a wonder they had any voice left. "We went to the first demonstration," the older brother explained, "after they tried to take Reverend Tökes. We shouted at the Army, 'Join us, brothers!' and then, when the Securitate started shooting soldiers who didn't want to fire at us, we screamed at them: 'Murderers!' "

"And worse!"

"And worse! And then they started shooting us, and we screamed in fear! We started running, and some mothers picked up their children and put them in front of themselves, thinking that the beasts wouldn't have the heart to murder little babies. . . . But they did. . . ."

Maria covered her children's faces and started to cry. There were tears on everyone's faces. She wiped her eyes and crossed herself, then kissed her children hungrily. "We'll never let them do that again, never. . . ."

"We screamed and we screamed," her husband said. "The next day everybody started screaming in the factories and offices. The whole city was one big scream against the murderer. Nobody worked. In the afternoon we broke open the armory at our factory and got guns. We started shooting back. The Army came to our side!"

The story was already familiar to me, but I was moved to hear it retold, even if the witnesses were dead drunk by now and ready to confess that they had been the leaders of the revolution all along. Bits of their story came out word for word from TV and the newspapers and had already become part of whatever they had seen with their own eyes. It was hard to tell what was theirs, the stories were so intimately interwoven. They had already forgotten that they'd read certain things. . . . The wine bottle, looking very empty, came around for one more sip. The Finnish journalist opened a bottle of vodka.

"I've been shouting since the revolution started," said the brother. "I love vodka. Don't like Russians, though. . . ." He passed the bottle to Maria, who demurely refused. "They shot at us in front of the cathedral. I hope God was watching. . . ."

After a brief silence filled with sighs and vodka, during which I could hear the pounding of my heart and the sound of the rails, metal, against metal in the night, the younger man said softly but audibly, "We are all guilty!"

"Now, how's that . . ." Maria said reproachfully. But it wasn't really an objection. It was just a formal protest not to bother strangers with such intimate thoughts.

"We are all guilty," he repeated more insistently this time.

"We had to do what we did to live," said the husband, "and you're drunk. Din-din. . . ."

"If you call that living!" said the younger man bitterly.

I glanced at the snowy fields outside and thought, *When that snow thaws, there will be a lot of ugly things sprouting from the ground. But they'll have to sprout if things are to change.* . . . Then I fell asleep again, for another hour or so, but not quite as peacefully this time.

When I woke, the sun was a blinding disk risen over the snow barely above the pines on the mountainous horizon. I had a hangover. Romania, I thought, must have a hangover. The emotional roller coaster of the past weeks must have brought people to the edge of exhaustion. They had destroyed their evil chieftain, whom they had publicly praised for decades, and they must have that sinking feeling I now had in my gut—though mine was due to wine and vodka—that nothing was certain anymore. An age had ended, but many parts of it were still inside everyone.

But I was at least partly wrong because when I opened my eyes, there was still a happy part of the world in full swing. Mark was standing there with an Englishman named Duncan, a resident of Budapest, holding a bottle of champagne over my head. "Happy birthday to your country! Happy New Year!" they toasted. It was the crack of dawn. I took a long swig. There were many more people on the train, standing in the hall, talking and laughing. Duncan's champagne made the rounds, followed by a bottle of wine proffered by a young man from Arad, no more than sixteen years old. He, too, had tales of the Revolution. In Arad the Securitate had fought the students for hours before being subdued by the Army. He himself had made Molotov cocktails from wine bottles just like the one we were drinking from. "It is better to fill it with wine and then refill it with wine than to fill it with gasoline and use it only once!" he shouted oracularly. I had to agree.

Just before Bucharest, roving gangs of caroling Gypsy children jumped on the train, singing the traditional New Year carols. They touched everyone with their colorful sticks ending in paper flowers and wished us "Happy New Year" and that we might "be as hard as stone/

as strong as steel/as tough as song," and that "God" should "bless us."
It was a lovely thing to wish one in the bright snowy morning of new
Romania. We showered the tykes with coins.

A few hours later we pulled slowly into Bucharest. The mysterious
city of my youth was covered with ice and snow. Towering over the
cupolas of churches and apartment buildings in the distance was a
monstrous white building sprung from the mad imagination of some
mega-Mussolini. It was Ceauşescu's horrible new palace. "I took some
children there," Dinu said, "and they started crying. The rooms are so
big they're scary."

There were throngs of people milling about the train station as we
pulled in. On the walls there were handwritten posters: "Take care of
the children!" and "Thank you, soldiers!" There were long lines at a
newspaper stand. The train came to a long halt. I was home.

5

Bucharest

There was a sheet of ice on the platform. I slipped when I tried to lift all the bags. There were some porters with handcarts, but they were carefully avoiding the icy sections. Duncan finally succeeded in snaring a daring fellow who drove a little truck that slid crazily on the ice. We loaded the bags and ourselves, and the little truck plunged into the frenzied mobs. People were bundled against the cold in layers of sweaters and sheepskins. Women wore their scarves wrapped around their faces. People were loaded with suitcases, bags, backpacks, woolen bundles, string-tied cardboard boxes, and were clamoring to leave the city. We came to a stop in the middle of a group of agitated adolescents. From there on the crowds were too thick to negotiate. "Who lost you, munchkin?" our driver asked a skinny kid shivering at the edge of a group of slightly older children. The kid said that he and his friends were waiting to go home for New Year's. Their school in the provinces had come on a winter visit to Bucharest, and they had been stranded by the fighting. All passenger trains were late because emergency relief trains with food and medicine had priority. I asked the boy how long his school was going to stay closed. He said, "Not long, unfortunately," and I could see that he was not at all unhappy about the schooling he'd received in the last few days.

"Did you see fighting?" I asked him.

He put his frozen mitts together, making like a machine gun, rat-at-at-tat . . . smiling. Great vacation.

I disembarked with all my bags and tipped my driver a one-dollar bill, which made him ecstatic. I had been told by a veteran Eastern European newsman that the one-dollar bill was the basic unit now. Anything bigger there was no concept for. The old exchange, a pack of Kent cigarettes, still opened doors and got things done, but the single dollar was more potent now. I had a stack of one hundred one-dollar bills and six cartons of Kent 100s. I was set for an army of maître d's and a forest of greasy palms. While Duncan went in search of a taxi, I let myself sink into the roar of the station. The place made a special music, a pure whirlpool composed from the sounds of my native language. There were sudden peaks of MĂ, familiar form of "you," shouts of ASCULTĂ,which is "listen." I did. There was also a low moan under the words, a kind of steady wailing like that of a wounded creature set suddenly free. . . . Or so I fancied. A young man holding a piece of paper interrupted my reverie to ask me, of all people, who looked foreign and lost, where the station manager's office was. I had no idea, but he showed me his piece of paper anyway. It was a testimonial, signed by several residents of an apartment building where he had taken refuge during the fighting. He had been most helpful. The tenants commended him for spending all his waking hours on guard duty, checking everyone who came in the door. He hoped to get a free ticket home for his patriotism. I wished him luck and gave him a pack of Kents. His boundless gratitude was embarrassing. He declared himself ready to serve me for life. He didn't need to go home right away anyway. His wife and children could do without him for as long as I needed him, even if it was his whole life. There were few taxis outside, and many people waiting for them in the sub-zero cold. I considered employing my new-found friend, but Duncan showed up with one of the customs officers in tow. When he saw the officer, my patriotic friend vanished. But the officer was most friendly to us and had a taxi in no time. He bundled us up in it, without checking our bags, and refused the pack of Kents when I proferred it. "Welcome back!" he said. Shook our hands. And there was the V sign again.

After honking desperately at people who didn't move, the cab made a suicidal dash over the sidewalk into an iced-over narrow street. We nearly skidded into a wall and stopped a few inches from the window of a charming little photo shop called Baby Photo that reminded me of my mother's photo shop in Sibiu. Under the ice patterns on the window were stiff formal portraits of people who had prepared for the occasion. An older gent posed solemnly for his grandchildren in his funeral suit.

A young girl with roses on her white hat, at the center of a family of starched-collar bureaucrats, smiled vacantly. We backed away without damaging that serene little grouping forever. When the driver, cursing—he had a three-day beard and a pirate eye patch—finally extricated us from the alley, he stopped for a peasant couple camped on two enormous leather bundles filled with sausages for the market. Between them was an enormous straw-wrapped glass barrel of tzuică. The driver's explanation was terse: "They'll pay me with one of those sausages and a swig. . . . Better than money." Anything was undoubtedly better than Romanian money, which resembled toilet paper but had less value. Timişoara Dinu had told me on the train that the new government had started paying workers with new bills, a sign of respect. But I saw very few of those. Filthy paper bills were kept in circulation until they shredded completely. The sausages went into the trunk, but the bottle stayed, squeezed between the knees of the man, who wore a short embroidered sheepskin and a black sheepskin hat. His wife's well-rounded haunches just about pinned me to the door. I had a hunch that these two rotund figures had done well under the old system and would continue to do better under the next one. In a hungry country the sausage maker is king. Upon hearing that I was from America, they offered me a sausage and a swig. I took the swig and the sausage. The tzuică seared my throat, bringing back the taste of long-ago drunken evenings in some of the worst taverns in Bucharest. When I handed the driver the dollar bill, I also slipped him the sausage. He grinned.

The Inter-Continental Hotel in Bucharest is the modern-day equivalent of Dracula's castle on the Argeş River, a fortress built to resist cannon. It can be seen from almost anywhere, just like Ceauşescu's palace. Its facade was scarred by fresh bullet holes from top to bottom. It looked like a giant with measles. The older buildings on University Square all around it were also pockmarked every few inches as if someone had been firing precision rounds in a kind of mad game. Hundreds of windows were broken; parts of roofs were seared. University Square was a solid sheet of uneven, thick ice, blackened here and there by the grime of cars trying desperately to cross. There was an overpowering smell of wax in the air from the hundreds of candles burning at makeshift shrines under small Christmas trees.

The entrance to the lobby of the Inter-Con was a madhouse of reporters, cameramen, doormen, men in suits, and swarms of Gypsy children with paper flowers on sticks who all but put their quick little hands in your pockets. Their lively faces, caroling and begging, gave a festive air to the whole place. Duncan said good-bye and got back in the taxi. He had friends in Bucharest. I felt as if I were at a crossroads. I was tempted to leave my suitcases and walk away. I imagined renting a room somewhere in Bucharest with a view of Cişmigiu Lake. I had enough American dollars to live modestly for the rest of my life. I could change my name once more and tell nosy neighbors that I was a provincial literature teacher from a remote Transylvania burg who had come to the capital for "culture." I would establish a new life, consisting of regular visits to a small café and long evening walks by the lake. I would dress in an old-fashioned coat and tails from the last century and die a few years hence, a figure of mystery. I'd had this fantasy in many forms before—becoming a gas station attendant in a small town in Utah, for instance—but here it nearly became real. I wasn't sure, though, whether such a change of identity was yet possible in Romania. But the revolution would prove itself only if it succeeded in reestablishing the possibility of anonymity for its citizens, a great gift in a country where sticking one's nose in others' business had been the order of day and night. In spite of the cold, there was an indefinite familiar smell to the street, not the diesel smell of Budapest, but something older: crushed linden flowers and smoke. Under the ice and snow were the idle footsteps of my old walks, the fallen leaves of adolescent autumns, the shadows of complicated Byzantine porticoes. . . . I had the momentary illusion that all I had to do was to start walking, that my footsteps would find the shadow of my old footsteps, and that if I followed my old path, I would somehow cancel time and be nineteen years old again. Suppose that there is a moment in the midst of a revolution when it is possible to transcend time. There is something in the Romanian psyche that keeps searching for that moment. There is a man in a story by Mircea Eliade, the great Romanian religious scholar and novelist, who leaves an enchanted garden only to discover that thirty years have passed. Conversely, leaving the garden of my exile, I might discover that thirty years had *not* passed. Exiles—and Eliade was most consciously an exile—do not believe in chronological time. We hold the places of our youth unchanged in our minds and stay secretly young that way. On the other hand, what if age catches up with us when we return? What if death, a patient creature that never strays far from one's birthplace, waits for us just behind the old pantry door? I felt my hair beginning to turn white, my back begin to bend under the question mark of old age . . . and in Bucharest today the possibility of death was not at all remote.

Alas, I was also a foreigner and soon had proof of it. Porters, doormen, and bellboys, unmindful of my reveries, swarmed all over me. They were a peculiar lot, trained by Ceauşescu's secret police. They shared, no doubt with their colleagues all over the world, the distinction of being utterly corrupt, purveyors of thousands of small services available for a tip. In addition, they were the heirs of a long Oriental tradition of baksheesh, a word often translated as "tip" but implying somehow a deeper level of servility, learned at Turkish courts while ferrying between harem and chancellery. The ones who grabbed my bags first were surrounded quickly by agitated others, who looked as if they, too, were carrying my bags, imaginary bags for which they needed to be tipped. Others, who seemed somehow also to be part of my retinue, stood apparently idle though they communicated with small tremors, winks, and hand signals that they were unreservedly at my service in all the vast undefined realms from money speculation to protection. After my bags and I spun three times through the swiveling glass door (the only working door; the others were locked), I found myself suddenly in the tower of Babel, being shouted at in a dozen languages. "Check my reservation!" I screamed in Romanian. It was a mistake. Speaking Romanian is not the way to get things done in Romanian hotels. The uniformed hoteliers at the concierge desks were imposing authority figures who ruled the world of small fry in the lobby with disdainful gestures. A raised eyebrow suffised to send them scurrying. They did not need to hear Romanian from their guests; they heard enough of it from the multitudes under their heels. In Romanian I had no reservation.

Noah Adams, freshly scrubbed, having no doubt taken a shower and eaten dinner, spotted me standing there, black smoke coming out of my nostrils. He came to my aid with a sly grin on his face. It was all very amusing to him, I'm sure, but here I was, lugging all his electronics, denied in the lobby of my own country, condemned for speaking the language of my birth. And I was starving. After the Hungarian pure butter sandwiches that I hadn't eaten I'd had only wine and vodka in the way of sustenance. I hadn't slept or washed in an aeon. I was very cranky.

After hours—though they may have been Danube minutes—of negotiations, a room was "found," thanks to Noah's authoritative blond midwestern English and three packs of Kents. Noah also assured the bell captain that indeed, even though I spoke the native language, I was, in fact, a member of a powerful news organization capable of sending magnetic thunderbolts of damaging information to the staff's superiors, even if, momentarily, they didn't know who these were. I should have been more grateful but I needed a shower and a bowl of hot borscht. We gained admittance to one of the hotel restaurants via another pack of Kents. We sat down to scan the spattered mimeographed menu. The menu read like the dream book of food I had been longing for since 1965. There was stuffed cabbage with mamaliga (cornmeal mush), smoked ribs, ghiveci eggplant, moussaka, mushroom stew, sour meatball soup. In truth, only two things were available: steak and fries and sour meatball soup. I had them both. The sour meatballs (supă de perişoare) is a wonderful thing, though I wasn't sure where the meat in the meatballs came from, a suspicion that was strongly reinforced by the so-called steak, which was a piece of burned gristle of unknown provenance garnished with thin, greasy straws made from potatoes drowned in rancid oil. "What do you suppose it is?" Noah asked me.

"It has to be between beef, pork, and lamb," I reasoned, "because horses are too valuable and rats are too hard to catch. And people love their dogs and cats. It's a nation of pet lovers."

Noah approved. He had asked me already in Hungary if people there had pets, and when I told him that they loved their pets to distraction, and they'd gone as far as to invent certain breeds like schnauzers, he was most gratified.

Noah, the National Public Radio anchorman whose voice is familiar to millions of Americans, is a quiet man with a somewhat distracted air, caused, I think, by an all-consuming curiosity that leads him around odd corners or into dark arcades, under bridges, etc. In Budapest we would walk along talking, and I would notice, after a time, that Noah had vanished. A diligent search usually uncovered him staring in absolute fascination at some bizarre item in a window or an unusual feature of a building. One afternoon in Hungary we went looking for a hat. Noah had a card with the name of a shop where he'd been told hats were made by ancient furriers who bought furs from hunters. When we did find the shop, after a two-hour cab ride and a thirty-minute walk, Noah became so entranced with the small family of furriers he stayed for hours, trying on hats. He liked the intensely happy and intimate atmosphere of the shop with the telephone ringing every few minutes, tended to by daughter and mother with shrieks of delight, the pipe-smoking father with a toddler on his knee. Since we could communicate only through gestures, there was a great deal of speculation on what kind of animal had died for what hat, so everyone played charades, barked like foxes, howled like wolves, brayed like donkeys. The entire storeroom was dragged out for our inspection. Foxes, beavers, sheep, bears, seals, and minks, sewn into skillful and often grotesque shapes, were pressed down on Noah's patient head, while the entire family of furriers walked around him with mirrors. At long last a Gorbachev-style fur hat with flaps was found to fit, and we left the ancient place. "That was interesting," Noah said, a journalistic understatement. Though no words were exchanged, he had immersed himself somehow in the life of an old imperial trade and learned quite a lot. His distractedness was some kind of gift. Radio fame is pretty anonymous. Noah told me that once he was the guest of honor at a fund raiser on board a ship. He arrived unannounced, and nobody recognized him. After a while he found himself in the pissoir next to a man who asked impatiently as he unzipped, "Have you seen Noah Adams yet?" Noah said no. Noah wore his Gorby hat all through dinner because it was cold in the restaurant. We talked about our plans. My job, as I saw it, was to wander around, poke my nose into places, talk to people, and surprise my old friends with telephone calls out of the blue of time. I had several notebooks and pens, and that would suffice me for the entirety of my poetic wanderings. I am not a newsman, and I wanted Noah to know it, a distinction that became very useful later when we met up with Michael Sullivan and Rich Rarey.

Michael Sullivan, NPR producer, fiendish workaholic and newshound, was presiding over an electronics-crammed room that was a continual news explosion. Deborah Amos, the Prague-based NPR correspondent, was also in Bucharest, as was John Hackenberry, whose reputation for fearlessness and intensity preceded him. All the sorry phones of Romania had been drafted in the service of the news media. Michael had an open line to Washington that he never closed for fear of losing contact for days, as was not unusual. News stories had to be filed both by phone and by satellite. Time on satellites cost a pretty bundle, and the timing had to be precise. Intense competition from other networks, as well as newspapers and magazines, made the whole atmosphere surreally charged. Rich Rarey, the technical whiz, worked with tape decks, earphones, and razor blades at the small hotel table, seemingly oblivious of people swirling about him. Michael Sullivan worked on two stories at once with Rich, was holding a phone conversation with three editors in Washington, laughed at a joke by Hackenberry, and read a scribbled sheet of paper Deborah handed him. It looked an awful lot like work to me. I had started to beat a hasty retreat when Michael said, "Great! Can you have a story for me in two hours?" He then turned to Noah, "Can you get some people to talk about the future? Get Andrei to translate. . . ."

Rich, who could somehow hear through his earphones, said: "Most important, did you bring the champagne?"

Everyone's eyes turned to us; it was an extraordinary sum of attention from people who moved faster than sound. We had, or rather, *I* had. I'd lugged six bottles of Hungarian champagne with me. It was New Year's Eve in Romania in 1989. A new decade was beginning tomorrow. For a moment the room was quiet. Not for long. "Goddamn it!" screamed Sullivan at someone in Washington. "I don't care if it's your goddamn day off! I just stuck a microphone in a dead child's grave, so *please!*"

The lobby was a vast hive of journalists from all over the world. A turbaned reporter from India was gesturing grandly to a tall African. An Arab man handed me a blue mimeographed invitation to a party that evening at the Palestinian Embassy in Bucharest. He was at some pains to staff the party in order to quash the rumors of Palestinians fighting for Securitate. A storm of languages swirled about the lobby, giving off the warmth of attention and interest. . . . Interviews conducted in every corner, flashing lights, rolling television cameras—a guarantee to the young Romanian revolutionaries that they were not alone. Everywhere on the globe, with the possible exception of Albania and China, Romania was being watched, discussed, admired. Even in China the rebellion smashed in Tiananmen Square flared again briefly when graffiti appeared in Beijing: "REMEMBER ROMANIA!" In Moscow, during the largest demonstration since the Bolshevik Revolution, the crowds clamoring for democracy carried banners that also said "REMEMBER ROMANIA!"

French television crews with pyramids of equipment zoomed and spinned. French newspeople were everywhere, in the lobbies, on elevators, on the streets, searching intensely for fragments of the Romanian Revolution. The French had a special interest. France had fallen in love with Romania. In 1989, in the year of the bicentennial of their own revolution, after they had been saturated by ceremonial imagery of *la gloire* and *la patrie*, the Romanian Revolution exploded like a magnificent illustration of all their history. It was the grand finale of all the fireworks shows put on by every *mairie* from Paris to Strasbourg. Romania gave the French the third dimension of their grand commemoration: reality. For that reason also, the French government adopted the Romanian cause, and French aid was quick in forthcoming. Because of their proprietary attitude, the French newspeople didn't enjoy great popularity among their fellow newsfolk. I asked a young French producer in the elevator if she found the French of Romanians satisfactory. She bathed me in an icy stare and said, "They speak our language since birth!" She then turned to her cameraman and said, "We really have to do something about Jean-Marie. . . ." Not really. It is true that many cultivated Romanians speak French well. Before the Communists, the better cafés in Bucharest sported the French newspapers, and most people read them. Romanian literature is Francophile, and Romanians are some of the best French writers. Eugène Ionesco, Tristan Tzara, Benjamin Fondane, Voronca, Isidore Isou, E. M. Cioran, and Paul Celan all are French writers of Romanian origin. But as for "speaking it from birth," that's nonsense. Outside Bucharest the throngs speak no French whatsoever. But the French newspeople may be forgiven their arrogance because their disappointment was much greater when things started to unravel. Much of their busy and seemingly incisive reporting—like our busy and incisive reporting—turned out to be manipulation by master manipulators. And since we were, in our turn, manipulators, the game of mirrors was practically infinite. After the French got out of the elevator on the fifth floor, an Australian newsman who'd heard my rebuff said, "Don't mind it, pal. The French! They always bring silence to elevators, a fact they don't notice because they are always talking." Downstairs a woman from Cable News Network, until now the source of all my television news from Romania, was arguing with one of the desk employees about the weekly phone bill. Eventually she paid: forty thousand dollars. American dollars, I believe. I changed one hundred dollars at the miserable official rate. The street paid ten times as much; but I wanted a receipt, and I meant to do no illegal things. My old reflexes were beginning to reassert themselves.

I attended briefly a National Salvation Front news conference. A Romanian reporter asked the government spokesman, Aurel Dragoș-Munteanu (who had replaced Silviu Brucan), why Romania was selling babies. The newsmen present were being their noisy selves, and Dragoș-

Munteanu called them to task. "Here you are," he said, "always being so tough. . . . But the toughest question comes from one of your Romanian colleagues, and none of you are paying any attention. . . ." That admonition didn't do much good. The reporters went on snapping gum. Munteanu's answer was that "contractual obligations" undertaken by Romania had to be honored. At that time the horror stories of orphanages and the AIDS epidemic had not quite taken hold. Aurel Dragoş-Munteanu was a personable man with a relatively gentle sense of humor, unlike Brucan, whose demonic humor struck most reporters as downright sinister. Whatever might be said about Brucan—and much has—he enjoyed himself enormously in the spotlight. His bald, thick-lipped face with large, brown eyes terrified a young reporter from *The New York Times* who told me that Brucan leaned as close to her as one can without actually touching and said, "You and I have something in common, dear!" He then laughed his disconcerting laugh. She spent most of a sleepless night searching for clues to what the ex-ambassador, press spokesman, and soon-to-be foreign minister meant. At last it dawned on her: They both were Jewish. Silviu Brucan, who knows more than anyone about the recent history of Romania, is not part of the government now. Munteanu, who had been head of television under Ceau-şescu before practicing his party school but mellifluous English on the world press, is now Romania's representative to the United Nations and sits on the UN Security Council. I left the news conference as noise-lessly as I'd come in. There wasn't much to learn here, unless it was the fact that reporters, like third graders, were constantly craning their necks to see what the person next to them was writing.

Michael's orders notwithstanding, I planned to disappear as quickly as possible. I had already filed a story from Budapest, and I was going to take my time with the next one. I was a poet on a mission of return, not a word-counting kamikaze. And Noah ought to get his own translator from among the vast ranks of the Romanian unemployed. I wanted to practice speaking my native tongue again slowly and simply. I wanted to enjoy the sensual pleasure of the sounds, look leisurely for forgotten words and meanings, reshape my mouth to the exigencies of a whole other world view. In short, my Romanian was rusty. I needed time.

My room, overlooking University Square from the sixth floor, was distinguished by two large bullet holes, one in the tin girding of the small balcony and one in the sliding glass door leading to it. There was still a scent of melted metal and explosive around the shattered glass. It was snowing outside, adding a fluffy blanket to the ice. Since Christmas Bucharest had had ten inches of snow, alternating with fierce cold. I looked out through the snowy curtain. Much of the battle of Bucharest had been waged from the roofs of high buildings. Journalists, the majority of whom stayed at the Inter-Continental, had been a particular target. If I'd been lying on this bed a few days ago I would have been in the direct line of fire. Every single building I could see had been damaged by fighting. People had been returning to some of their apartments because several balconies were in the process of being straightened out. Others were a mess of fallen plants before gaping holes of broken glass. It looked as if every balcony at the Inter-Continental had been a firing nest. On the other hand, the hotel had taken enough fire itself to make it seem that every balcony facing it had sheltered someone with a machine gun. It was almost too much, this too neatly symmetrical duel. Two gargoyles with rather resigned Balkan stares surveyed the street from the top of the university buildings. One of them had had its ear nicked by a bullet, but it hadn't changed its visage much. These gargoyles had seen everything. For a moment I almost envied them.

Next to the bed, on a small stand with a painfully "modern" lamp, was the telephone, my tenuous link to the outside world. There was no telephone book because none was ever published during the dictatorship. Everything had been secret, including phone numbers. To dial out, I had to dial 8, then wait for a tone, which rarely came. To dial another room, I had to dial the operator to ask for it. To call the United States, a reservation had to be made six hours ahead of time, the best deal in Bucharest. A private citizen had to reserve three to six days ahead of time. Outside Bucharest waiting periods were even longer, up to three weeks. I called the hotel operator to ask her if she could find a number for my old friend Adrian.

"Adrian M.?" she asked. "I know him. He is a friend of mine. I will call you back with his number," she said. I was surprised. Adrian had been one of my best friends in Sibiu. He was ten years older than I was. I had heard that he worked for Romanian television, but we had not been in touch for the past twenty-five years. I wanted to see him, and I was especially curious about Romanian television, where he worked. I wanted to know what Adrian did there. The operator's matter-of-fact acknowledgment that she knew my friend prodded that little demon at the back of my mind, a dormant creature that was suspicious of everything and bade caution. Hotel telephone operators in Romania were

Securitate operatives. I had a personal desire to see Adrian, but it was a complicated thing. (More anon.)

I called room service and ordered coffee, rolls, and cheese. "And listen," I added, "I will give you an American dollar if you bring me a stack of newspapers." I knew how hard the new newspapers of Romania were to find. A few moments later a tuxedoed waiter came in with a covered tray. On it were coffee, rolls, cheese, and a two-inch stack of newspapers. It was a well-spent dollar.

I settled in with the December 29 edition of *Adevărul* ("The Truth"), the National Salvation Front newspaper. For the first time in my life I was reading a Romanian newspaper that wasn't all lies. It was a strange sensation. *Adevărul* had the same weight and texture as the Communist newspaper that had preceded it, a rag I remembered well. Its front pages used to be covered with worthless economic facts and figures and the speeches of party brass. Only in the back pages could one find anything worthy of reading: sports; poems; brief news from around the world, mostly the Soviet Union. But I was not holding one of those. The large headlines proclaimed an astounding number of new laws passed by the National Salvation Front: the end of one-party rule; a call for free elections in April; the abolition of the death penalty; the separation of the judicial and executive branches of the government; the restructuring of the national economy on the basis of efficiency and accountability; the restructuring of agriculture on the basis of small peasant holdings; the restructuring of the educational system along student demands; the elimination of lies and propaganda and the institution, in their stead, of criteria of justice and competence in all areas of public life; freedom of the press, including newspapers, radio, and television; respect for the rights of minorities; freedom of worship; the restructuring of trade to serve the domestic needs of Romanians; the cessation of agricultural exports and of petroleum products in order to give people food and heat; the restoration of the ecological balance, including measures to develop a nonpolluting industry; the restructuring of foreign policy to promote neighborly European relations with a view to belonging to a united Europe; the changing of the name of the country from the Socialist Republic of Romania to Romania; the permanent removal of the socialist emblem from the tricolor flag; the naming of a commission to begin drafting a new constitution; the removal from power of all the ministers of the old regime, the changing of the name of the militia to the police;

the recall of ambassadors; freedom for all political prisoners; the restoration of the citizenship of Romanians who had fled the country.

I stopped reading at this point, overcome by it all. It was too much to take in. Each one of these laws needed a chapter unto itself. One third of the first page of a twelve-page newspaper contained the principles for the complete transformation of a country of twenty-three million people from a Communist dictatorship into a Western democracy. So many fundamental reforms were certainly not the result of a week's worth of sleepless visionary nights. What I was looking at here must have been the fruit of countless underground meetings deciding the future of Romania after Ceauşescu. Who had done it, and when, in a country where everyone was under constant surveillance? I was not inclined, at that moment, to speculate on the provenance of these laws. The point was that they had been proposed. Of course, my poetic self yearned for something miraculous, the idea, somehow, that all this was the brilliant and concentrated work of intelligent men over the course of one week. If that was true, what excuse did I or anyone else have for not radically changing our entire existence, writing grand epic poems? I was infused with the vibrant energy of the revolution and I thought, for a moment, that I had been swooped over by a beam of light and placed on the very stage of history.

An hour later I was still waiting for the hotel operator to call me back with Adrian's number. I called her. "If he's a friend of yours," I said, "don't you have his number handy?"

"Have patience," she said—a word I heard many times from her in the coming days. "I will call him to ask him if it's all right to give you his telephone number."

"I'm an old friend!" I shouted.

"I know," she said.

Howzdat? "You know who I am?" I said.

"Now, why wouldn't I know?" she asked, bemused.

I could think of many reasons, the chief one being that unless she was indeed a very, *very* good friend of my friend Adrian, I had nowhere revealed my connection to him. We said good-bye for the moment, and I sat there, looking at the cold apparatus. I should have waved my copy of "The Truth" under her nose. See? It says right here that the age of suspicions and lies is over. In black and white . . . I didn't want to seem overly paranoid to myself, but *what*, I asked myself, *can she know?*

That I'm a friend? That I am who I am? Does she know my name? Has she already called him and he is not sure whether he should talk to me or not? After all, only a week ago I had been a voice on Radio Free Europe, a man on the short list of enemies of the state. I could hear them thinking, *Is he a spy? Why has he come back so quickly?* Adrian, after all, had been in the cultural section of Ceauşescu's television, whose job had consisted solely of singing the praises of Ceauşescu. My old friend had always been both mysterious and cautious. And his friend the operator felt sure enough of herself to have fun with me. Making phone connections in this hotel was the single most important link in the chain of police ears that stretched from Bucharest to wherever a voice could go. Ah, paranoia, the familiar taste of which still clung to these walls like ectoplasm. I had definitely returned to a world whose rules I had forgotten.

I went back to my newspaper, which seemed brighter, more real, and more idealistic than the slow-creeping world about me. There was an appeal from the front for the cessation of acts of revenge and the need for national unity in the days ahead. A small article assured those who had not had their vacations in years that they would be paid now. I read a small, poetic piece by Gabriela Adameşteanu wondering where the janissaries of the Securitate could have disappeared, in their new suits and their squeaky shoes. And how could a nation "sick with fear" heal itself in the days ahead after finding its orphanages full of unwanted, abused children, ordered by the dictator to be born against the wishes of their parents? "A whole people," she wrote, "not yet born/ Is condemned to be born." I looked at a photograph of Ceauşescu with a quote by playwright Eugène Ionesco: "Ceauşescu is Satan!" I turned the page. There were two eyewitness accounts of the events in Timişoara, December 16–24. Photos of the first massacre. Bodies loaded onto flatbed trucks. People trampled, shot, and run over by the panicked crowd. A woman crushed under the treads of a tank. A wounded boy wrapped in bandages on a hospital bed. Destroyed, partially burned movie houses, apartment buildings . . . Raging fires . . . Timişoara under cannon and machine-gun fire . . . Revolutionary guards in the windows of government buildings, official residences, museums, and hospitals, holding antiquated weapons taken out of civil defense armories . . . One account described the reaction of a crowd gathered in the town of Piteşti on hearing about the executions of the Ceauşescus. "No one was surprised," wrote the reporter. "One man murmured, 'It isn't enough,' meaning not that the punishment was too gentle, but that there is no appropriate punishment for someone responsible for wasting millions of lives." A cultural manifesto signed by prominent writers and artists called for "an immediate end to the construction of Ceauşescu's palace" and for the "restoration of cultural patrimony," an allusion to Ceauşescu's destruction of peasant life. On the next page there were biographies of martyrs and interviews with wounded fighters in hospitals.

And here, once again, were the tunnels. A brief article, written in spare soldier's language by a certain Major Mihai Floca, described the tunnels under Bucharest being deactivated by his elite commando unit. He wrote of giant refrigerators stuffed with a variety of meats, stores of foods that "most people have forgotten the taste and color of," immense closets filled with quality clothes and shoes, comfortable dormitories, ultramodern workshops equipped with the latest electronic monitoring equipment and computers, caches of weapons, sophisticated bombs, germ warfare shells. The brightly lit "labyrinth" was vast, leading everywhere, under secret buildings, under the television and radio stations, under the Ceauşescus' many palaces and safe houses. "They were prepared to live forever in there," he concluded sternly. What is it about Commies and tunnels? Harrison Salisbury reports in his book on Tiananmen Square that the Chinese troops that burst out of the Great Hall of the people and the historical museums ringing the square had slipped there secretly from tunnels under the Forbidden City. "There is even a branch railroad line with an underground station in Zhongnanhai," writes Salisbury. If one considers that the chief metaphor used in Communist propaganda is the "light of communism" or the "dawn of the new age," the tunnels become even more baffling. On the other hand, it makes perfect sense: A movement born and elaborated underground that came to light through violence and then ruled illegitimately must always make provisions to return to the darkness of its beginnings. The only thing it has to oppose to that fundamental fear is rhetoric, Orwell's twisted words. Light is dark.

After an hour the operator called and gave me Adrian's number. I dialed it.

"Happy New Year, Adrian," I said.

"I can't believe it," he said.

Well, that was all it took. His voice rang with both insincerity and genuine emotion. He *had* been forewarned by his friend, but he was also truly happy to hear me. And I was happy, too.

"We have some friends over for New Year's Eve. Come over!"

I promised.

It proved impossible to find a driver. There was a curfew after dark, and fighting was rumored to go on still in the neighborhood Adrian lived in. I called him back. We wished each other Happy New Year 1990 and made plans to meet at the television station the next day, January 1.

It looked certain now that I would be spending New Year's Eve with my fellow newsmen. That was fine, but I regretted not being with Adrian. I was still on my Western island. There was a wall of glass between me and the snowed-in but still smoking country of revolution outside.

Michael, Rich, and Noah were in the bar, watching television. The Inter-Con bar was a world in itself. The journalistic fauna hung in clusters about small tables, picking bits of news from one another, ever ready to run to the telephone bank on the mezzanine. I suspected that some of them never actually left this bar, becoming the source of unsubstantiated rumors that traveled quickly around the world. I heard here that Ceauşescu's palace seen from the air spells his name. That a Libyian commando who was Arafat's best friend had turned up dead in a Bucharest hospital. That captured members of Securitate in Sibiu were kept in their underwear in an empty swimming pool in the below-zero weather. That North Korea had had a MiG standing by to pick up the Ceauşescus on December 22. Some people had shortwave radios and got their news from BBC, finding out what happened under their noses from reports broadcast from thousands of miles away. The lack of good translators made things difficult for those who didn't question the Romanian tendency to exaggerate or lacked respect for the exceedingly prolific Romanian imagination. "Every Romanian is a poet," says a saw, and these were the days for it. Poetic rumors zoomed like fireflies through the charged air of the Inter-Con bar. One of the few sensible people filing out of the Balkan stew was David Binder from *The New York Times*. A veteran of this part of the world, he was both bemused with and tolerant of his colleagues. He took everything with much needed salt. A reader of Romanian literature, he was more interested in philosophical questions, having learned that the key to a people is their sensibility and national character, not the "facts" that often turned out to be fabrications. The so-called facts changed as often as the National Salvation Front spokesmen who held press conferences every day in the hotel and whose chief qualification seemed to be a good knowledge of English. Binder asked me if I thought that there was a cruel streak in Romanians. He had been reading up on the peasant rebellion of 1917, another remarkable explosion of popular hatred. "Only after excessive suffering," I told him. Essentially Romanians are a gentle, hospitable, and good-natured people. Pushed far, they will use their imaginations to make exemplary gestures. The Securitate men impaled on the wheel Petre told me about were neither more nor less dead for being impaled. But impaled, they were *unforgettable*. That was the point, whether any impalement had taken place or not.

Lounging about the bar in skimpy outfits, ladies of the night did the best they could with a sprinkling of phrases in a dozen languages. I heard an Italian cameraman ask two girls: "Are you two lesbians?"

"We don't have that in Romania yet," one of them answered earnestly.

"Maybe when democracy comes," the other said, just as sincerely.

We had a number of quick brandies against the cold outside. At a quarter to midnight we passed through the revolving doors of the Inter-Con fortress, and like the people in some fairy tale, whose world changes every time they spin around, we found ourselves on the icy streets of Bucharest. It had stopped snowing. Above there were stars, little frozen pinpoints of light. There was a generous but cold half-moon in the sky. And not far, in the center of the square just ahead of us, burned the candles at the martyrs' shrine. My ungloved hand was cold around the neck of the magnum of Hungarian champagne that I had brought with me from the other Europe.

I felt quite affectionate toward our little group with our tiny wires and urgent need to tell the world everything we saw.

6

The Revolution Is Televised: Seize the Means of Projection!

Adrian was not in front of the building, and even if he had been, I couldn't have seen him. Once we got past the tanks ringing the outer perimeter, with their holey flags snapping briskly in the freezing wind, I found myself within one of the densest cluster of humans in my experience. The whole nation, it seemed, had gathered outside the high wire fence surrounding the television station. Most of the unsettled mob was pleading with the soldiers just inside the gate, while the rest had climbed on tanks and were either making speeches or speaking into the ears of the motionless gunners.

"Twelve years at hard labor!" shouted a tubercular man, his three-day beard covering a narrow face, eyes rimmed in triple black circles. "I have no place to go. All of my people are dead and gone, gone and buried. . . ." The soldier who kept him from bodily crashing through the gate was sympathetic and bewildered. His round, apple-cheeked face was right up against the drawn visage of the former political prisoner, like a twelfth-century allegory of innocence and experience.

"They gave him a raw deal," a fat man in suit and tie explained to me. "Wait till I tell the people what they did to me. . . . The bastards

gave all of us a raw deal, years of raw everything except meat. . . ."
When he laughed, I saw that he had two gold teeth.

"What's your business?" I asked him.

"Cows . . . I'm supposed to feed ten thousand cows on fifty acres
of bad seed. You tell me . . . Until now we just let them die of hunger, or stole feed wherever we could find it, or bought it on the black
market. When time came for the report, we lied. That was the deal,
and people starved. . . ." He was the director of a livestock collective
near Bucharest, responsible for supplying the capital with milk.

"I heard," I told him, "that babies went without milk for
years. . . ."

"Yes," he said, "tell me about it."

A doctor in a dirty surgeon's smock rushed to the gate and threw
himself against it. He was immediately allowed in. "Are there wounded
people in the building?" I shouted after him.

"There is an infirmary inside, but I think everyone's been moved
to hospitals. . . . I'm here to speak on our AIDS tragedy. . . ."

Few knew that yet another story would soon shock the world: the
AIDS babies. Tests by Romanian and French virologists revealed that
at least one in four babies in state orphanages had full-blown AIDS.
The likely cause of this catastrophe was contaminated blood that had
somehow found its way to Romania from abroad. A minuscule amount
of this untested blood was used to inject sickly newborns in the belief
that it would boost their immune systems. This turn-of-the-century
medical practice is considered useless by most doctors today, but it still
had currency in Romania. At the onset of the AIDS crisis alarmed Romanian doctors attempted to warn world health organizations but were
forbidden to do so by Ceauşescu himself, who did not believe in AIDS.
A doctor who tried to smuggle out a report was arrested. The dictator
did not want the world to know about the overflowing Romanian orphanages, miserable, understaffed places that were the direct result of
his policies against birth control and the decree to increase the Romanian family to the required five children. Pregnant women were fre-
quently checked at their workplaces to ensure that they were not having
abortions. Women who had them anyway lost their jobs. The abandoned babies were raised by the state in orphanages, and it is widely
believed that the strongest among them were selected for special Securitate schools, where they grew fanatically devoted to the dictator. These
were Ceauşescu's so-called janissaries, named after the Turkish fighters

who were kidnapped from conquered countries, reared in harems, trained as warriors, and sent back to fight their own people. One thing is certain: The draconian birth policies brought about an artificial baby boom in the mid-seventies. Ironically, the young students and workers who fought on the streets to overthrow Ceauşescu were the very children he had ordered into being over the wishes of his people. The AIDS crisis was a direct result of the dictator's policies, but there were more questions than answers. Where did the blood come from? How did babies in orphanages in cities far apart contract AIDS? Was the same blood used and reused? Why was the policy of injecting babies continued against contemporary medical practice? Why did Romania have only one blood-screening machine (in Bucharest), and why were disposable syringes and surgical gloves in such short supply? I wanted to shout these questions at the doctor, but he was quickly gone.

The TV station bore the scars of heavy fighting. There were hastily patched windows; parts of the roof had been blown out; the facade was riddled with bullets. On the other side of the street, past the three tanks arrayed in a semicircle, there were several demolished villas and charred apartment buildings. That is where "they" lived and had some of their offices. "They," in postrevolutionary parlance, was understood immediately to mean "terrorists," just as "He" and "She" meant the Ceauşescus before the revolution. "They" had fired their guns and lobbed grenades from their houses, drawing shell fire until there was nothing left. These houses, among the best in Bucharest—shady porticoes covered with grape arbors and flowers in the summer, tiled roofs with sparkling snow in winter—were said to have come fully stocked, courtesy of the dictator. Styled eclectically after French, Spanish, and Turkish villas, they would have been doomed in any case. The architecture of the future, planned by the regime's architects, had called for moving all of Ceauşescu's loyalists into fortresslike apartment buildings around the unfinished presidential palace. Those apartments, too, came furnished, with full refrigerators, courtesy of the leader. In the end, no doubt, the country would have been made entirely circular, with the leader's family at the center and wider and wider rings around it, in order of loyalty. At the far periphery, the dubious and distrustful would have passed their days in small, unlit pens in the patrolled confines of factory zones. Ceauşescu's industrialization plan, carried out through "systematization," envisioned Romania as a 90 percent industrial country by the end of the century. While seemingly opposite in its goals from the Khmer Rouge restructuring of Cambodia, the Romanian plan would have been carried out with similar ferocity. Instead of driving the population like cattle out of the cities into rice paddies, the Ceauşescus envisioned a hive world clustered around smokestacks, feeding the royal center. The model was the Kremlin of the fifties and the Stalinist architecture of vast building blocks—discredited even in the Soviet Union.

A strong smell of smoke wafted from the burned villas. The tanks, their cannons pointed right into the middle of the street at the crowd of which we were part, made me anxious. I was not convinced of the firm commitment of this Army, which had so many branches, sides, and levels. I had the thought, unavoidable in the presence of so many loaded guns, that some of the soldiers might be Securitate, and some of this Securitate might not have been the Securitate that had joined the people. And these people, for that matter, in the midst of whom I found myself, were they the "right" people? Revolutionaries? All it would take is for one of them to be "not the right people," with a big, fat grenade under his shirt. I must confess that for the next few days this thought continued to cross my mind, especially in the waiting rooms and halls of official buildings, where dozens of armed men leaned casually or tensely on their AK-47's or slept on cots along the walls with their weapons on their chests. It had been reported that inside the television station a "terrorist" came out of an air-conditioning vent and stabbed six people before he was subdued.

In spite of such thoughts, an air of genuine, joyous anticipation possessed the crowd. These people had come here to go on TV to tell their stories. Some of them had waited the whole night in the cold. A woman in her early twenties with black glitter glued to her eyelids and her cheeks jumped up in the air waving a lace glove to attract the eye of one of the soldiers, who strenuously avoided her. "Yoohoo there, Doru, I brought the tape!" Clutched in her other hand was a cassette tape.

"What's on the tape?" I asked her.

"My song," she said, "my love song to my country. . . . It has no words or music yet," she added apologetically. "It's only an idea right now. But"—her eyes shining—"they have musicians and singers inside who can write it and sing it . . . and I'll dance to it. . . ." She tried to catch Doru's eye again. "He's my boyfriend, he promised to put me on TV today . . . maybe tomorrow. . . ."

One by one, the aggrieved, the ecstatic, and the curious were led to a small bulletproof booth on the other side of the fence. There they were searched, gone over with a metal detector, and allowed to use the telephone to speak with a producer. If their cause seemed reasonable—almost all causes were—they were allowed inside to speak before the nation uncensored and unedited.

Our press credentials helped us move to the front of the line right away. "American media," whispered someone close to me. "They always treat foreigners better?"

"Eh, friend, they've got to tell our story to the world," a patient uncle said to him.

The machines by means of which we would tell Romania's story to the world drove the metal detector crazy. We set our tape recorders, cords, wallets, money on the table. Noah's trusted pocketknife had to stay behind. Our tape recorders got a thorough check. We were made to operate them to show that they were indeed tape recorders, not bombs. This gave Rich an opportunity to turn on his equipment and to leave it on. He taped everything. The metal detector looked crude, probably unable to detect plastic explosives, but every object in our possession was examined. It was embarrassing to gaze upon the contents of my American pockets: cigarette packages, gum, crumpled notes, twisted paper clips, tiny mics, chocolate bars, pens, notebooks, tapes, and mini-cassette recorder. Seeing these things lying flat on a metal desk with three guards going through it was a revelation, a kind of crosscut of my life. There are moments, even in revolutions, when the overriding sentiment is embarrassment, not enthusiasm. The only private place is still behind the eyes. The revolutionary guard who escorted us to the television building apologized for the security. Noah assured him that we were very pleased with the security and willing to undergo it. That was true. I remembered the satisfaction I felt at the strict seriousness with which Lufthansa Airlines treated our luggage. Everybody's bags were lined up on the tarmac, and you had to identify your bags. Any bags left over were quickly blown up.

We passed through a series of dingy rooms and hallways. Armed men and women sat on metal chairs at metal desks or leaned against the walls, smoking. Bucharest was a smoky world just now, and the revolution made it twice as smoky. Pulling on unfiltered Mărăşeşti cigarettes, bitter-tasting, the defenders of the station, sleepless for days, emanated an indistinct but lovely aura of delinquent youth, with their tricolor armbands, unshaved faces, and carelessly—but stylishly—slung

Andrei Codrescu

guns over T-shirts with rolled-up sleeves. After two more passport checks we were delivered to a small studio where a middle-aged man received us anxiously. "Your friend Adrian," he said to me, "will be right along. I am coproducer of cultural programming." I could tell that he wasn't quite sure if he was coproducer anymore. He had been in charge of what used to pass for cultural programming on Romanian television. Uncertain of his new status, but with the polished manner of the intellectual bureaucrat, he told us what he no doubt imagined to be the correct new revolutionary policy. "We are finally free to show what we were forbidden to," he declared, passing a sweaty palm over a nearly bald head. Pressed as to what that might be, he listed "foreign movies, documentaries, rock 'n' roll music." He offered to fetch the new programmer in charge of formerly forbidden rock 'n' roll. As for documentaries, he promised to find the new documentary producer. For every new program there seemed to be a new person, leaving him just slightly . . . Well, he could still conduct tours in English . . . wasn't his English just dandy? It was. Learned at the party school, practiced at international conferences. . . .

I remembered well what "cultural programming" was on Romanian television when he and Adrian used to run it. (Until a few days ago, actually!) All through my youth old men clad in mightily used shiny tuxedoes performed orchestral pieces on "folkloric themes" with their backs to the viewers. The orchestra, clad in similar attire, held on for dear life to ancient instruments. I used to imagine them all suddenly lifted from their stools and stands, flying in perfect formation out of the studio into the night. I would follow them in my mind over the rooftops and guide them into the windows of apartments, where startled people would start screaming with horror. Or else I would try to imagine them naked, their sagging bellies sadly flapping under routine arrangements. Other fare included plays and performances of poetry by decommissioned actors from the National Theater. One such television event wrecked one of my mother's more serious relationships and nearly caused me to be killed. My mother was in love with an Army captain, a gentle, tall man who was, on the whole, a tolerable chess partner but whose feet, when he removed his boots, filled the house with an unbearable odor. I would read my sixteen-year-old surrealist poetry to this man, watching his small Army forehead wrinkle in puzzled concentration. Bit by bit, he came to admire my poetry and think of me as an awesome intellect, particularly after some of my more lucid efforts were printed in the back pages of the local newspaper, *Tribuna Sibiului*. My pseudonym then was Andrei Steiu. Unbeknownst to me, his admiration had become so total that he began showing some of his Army comrades my poems in the newspaper and claiming that *he* was Andrei Steiu. One evening an ancient gentleman who presented every Saturday a television program called *Poems from Around the Country* chose one of my poems. He announced that evening on TV that he was going to read the work of a sixteen-year-old from Sibiu, named Andrei Steiu. Next day my mother's captain was called before a special party meeting convened to discuss his lie. He was demoted to a lower kind of captain, and my mother stopped seeing him. When I passed him on the street, he vowed to catch me and administer me a "beating unto death," which I took to mean that poetry is serious business.

The Romanian television of my youth was such an exceedingly boring thing that people never needed sleeping pills. Except, when it wasn't, and then it was unbearably exciting. At the time of President John Kennedy's assassination in Dallas, Romanians made their first satellite linkup. One evening, while we prepared to fall asleep, our little TV went crazy: Big American buildings appeared. Cars appeared. Americans appeared. Guns and policemen appeared. These were scenes coming live to us from the scene in Dallas, Texas. A confused Romanian commentator tried to explain what it was that we were seeing. He could not. We did understand him when he said that President Kennedy had been shot. But we did not believe him. "It's the Russians," said my uncle Rihard, "a goddamn Russian plot." When I pressed him on how the Russians could get close enough to kill the President of the United States, my uncle Rihard snapped, "The Russians didn't kill him! It's a plot to drive us all crazy by *pretending* that they killed him!" Uncle Rihard believed that everything we were seeing had been staged in order to drive us all out of our minds. Not for a moment did he entertain the idea that the President had actually been killed. Most people in the country shared his opinion.

When television was first introduced to Romania in the early sixties, there were no shows. A factory making TV sets had distributed these to all the "cultural centers" in the country. Every village, big or small, had one of these centers. They were for the most part places for people to come and play chess, listen to the radio, drink coffee, and whisper rumors. When the TVs came, these places made room for them on red-clothed tables placed before the respectful audience. The audience was rigorously and hierarchically arranged by position, sex, and age: party functionaries in front; old men behind them; women and children at the back. The party secretary called for silence and turned on the little set. A grating noise pierced the reverential hush, followed by black-and-white test patterns. Everyone watched these for some time, nodding respectful heads at the wonders of modern technology. When enough abstract art had been absorbed, the party secretary carefully turned off the television, and everyone dispersed into the night, breaking off in small, thoughtful groups contemplating the wonders of the world to come.

The world that came, unfortunately, was that of Ceauşescu. The benign boredom of Stalinist TV gave way to the glorification of Ceau-şescu, who required that his praises be sung in every medium. A curi-ous little museum in Bucharest was looted during the revolution, but I hope, for the sake of the future, that it will be reassembled. It contained Ceauşescu images done in paint, charcoal, wood, metal, ceramics, weaving, and video. Only an Elvis shrine would compare with this, the difference being, of course, that representations of Elvis, from black velvet to ice sculpture, were motivated by genuine affection. On tele-vision, Ceauşescu took two hours every evening to sharpen his clichés. Occasionally—the occasions became more numerous as his self-esteem increased—there were ceremonial pageants in which Ceauşescu would have the crown of Michael the Brave and the scepter of Mircea the Old presented to him. These mock coronations were received at first with the unbelieving derision of people who thought that they had now seen everything, but soon they passed into the realm of routine and became the subject of jokes. Peasants in native costume provided the back-ground for these ceremonies, holding grapes, flags, and sheaves of wheat, while singing "folk arrangements" to the holy name, which doesn't rhyme with almost anything in Romanian but was made to, thus giving rise to a number of unnatural words soon gathered into special clothbound dictionaries given as gifts to party members upon promotion.

I had little idea what Adrian's job consisted of during these years of "Ceauşification." But here he was, Adrian himself, grown stylishly older, with silver hair, in a light beige suit with a wide striped tie. On his face was that little grin that endeared him to me in my childhood, a grin that said, "We'll have all kinds of fun if we're careful about it." When I became a young firebrand poet and distanced myself from him, it was partly because of this carefulness, but I still missed his grin.

It *was* good to see him. We embraced. Here we were, grown older and different, a Romanian and a Romanian-American, survivors in an insane century. Ideology was flotsam over the swirling current of ancient sympathy.

After our embrace we fell into a familiar mode.

"I will introduce you and your colleagues to some very important people," Adrian said, frowning, as if he weren't sure whether such a wild man as myself would behave properly in their presence. I found myself oddly doing the same thing. He was aiming to rein in my wild horses, while I tried to rein in my colleagues, the real wild horses. My journalist colleagues were remarkably blunt. They thought nothing of asking someone how much money he made, if he was a party member, if anyone in his family had ever gone to jail. Honest answers to these sorts of questions were not easy to come by in a country that until last week had lived in fear of precisely those facts. A perceptive gulf separated us. Yet many people amazingly *did* answer those questions. It was as if they were trying to throw off a lifetime of caution in a few moments. They told us their names, their addresses, their life stories, the stories of their families, their own versions of their country's history. They even recited lists of American Presidents—proud of the hitherto forbidden knowledge. Deborah Amos called these people cassettes: You push the button, and the discourses of a lifetime rush out, a complete confession. Foreign journalists in those first few days after the revolution had become priests, privy to the unconfessed secrets of everyone. Those who told their stories believed, naively, that every word they spoke was going to be aired in America. They believed that in this way they would be protected from retaliation or revenge.

But Adrian knew better. "Too many people are coming out of anonymity too soon," he said wryly. I reflected briefly on our differing conceptions of anonymity: Mine is to be able to exist eccentrically but unbothered, while his is to be unnoticed while seeming to do his job. I felt an odd split in myself in Adrian's presence. On the one hand, I had the impulse to protect him from my NPR colleagues—and friends! I was embarrassed about having journalists with me, as if I were some sort of personage who traveled with a crew of Boswells ready to take down his every word, while knowing full well that to my old pal I was still Andrei Steiu or Andrei Perlmutter, and that was as it should be. Among friends one remains the same age and in the same place where the friendship began. But that was only part of it. The other part, and by far the most peculiar one, was that the Romanian in me was an infinitely more polite creature than the American in me. The polite, even delicate Romanian elicited information obliquely, through reminiscence, wit, and inference. The American was direct, rude, quick to get to the heart of it. In addition to the historical circumstances that made everyone confess, there was a basic psychocultural difference between Romanians and Americans. The reason—incomprehensible to a Romanian—why it was possible for an American to be so direct was that an American wasn't offended if he was told that it was none of his business. Telling an impertinent questioner off was the right, democratic thing to do. But for a Romanian it was rude not to answer a direct question, so he preferred to lie rather than honestly tell his tormentor to "fuck off." Also, Americans did not judge the information they obtained in the same way that Romanians did. They were rarely shocked by it, and they never considered it a confidence unless expressly told that it was. The American press, of course, has no concept of confidence.

In any case, while thoughts and memories assailed me, my colleagues the bloodhounds were sniffing stories. All about us the young men and women who televised the revolution moved with ferocious energy, carrying cords, manipulating antique equipment, having heated arguments. The place reminded me of a technocommune in California, a nest of video hippies.

Adrian introduced us to a newscaster who'd been on the air twelve out of twenty-four hours every day since the beginning. "I went home once"—she laughed—"in a tank . . . to change my clothes!" She had an open, strong-featured face about which fell a mane of unmanageable red hair. She moved in blue jeans and T-shirt with unselfconscious ease and determined strength. She switched from Romanian to English and back quickly, filling in the missing links with sweeping gestures. "I am *not* a television journalist!" she proclaimed emphatically. "I'm a microbiologist. And all my colleagues"—she pointed to several armbanded young people about the room—"have met on the street in the battle for the station. We occupied Studio Four on December twenty-second and have been here ever since." They were a young architect, an engineer, two students, and another biologist. They constituted the National Salvation Front committee in charge of Studio Four, the active center of the revolution. "None of us knew what to do," she said, "so we decided to start at the beginning . . . like a new world. Show everything, ask everyone . . . how do you say? We are all TV generation. . . ."

I asked her the question that had been on my mind since returning: "How did you know what to do when the revolution started?" It was a question that needed clarifying. Watching the Romanian revolution on CNN, people all over the world were struck by just how *revolutionary* the Romanian revolution was. The scenes they were seeing were reminiscent of the French and Bolshevik revolutions, living tableaux. The people atop tanks with their arms stretched in the victory sign, banners behind them . . . The tricolor armbands, the headbands . . . a beautifully photogenic but nonetheless horribly bloody revolution, summoned, it seemed, from historical skies by France itself . . . But while Miss Liberty, wrapped in her *drapeaux*, with a defiant breast pointing to the future, rose in living color in the minds of the French, it seemed suspicious to others (particularly to the more phlegmatic but still insufficiently skeptical Anglo-American journalists) that there was something almost *too perfect* about the Romanian revolution. It was already known, despite everyone's professions of spontaneity, that planning had gone on. Students had already admitted that they had been teaching themselves techniques of nonviolence for demonstrations: when and how to link arms; when to sit down; when to call for retreat. But these techniques of nonviolence, which worked so well in Prague and elsewhere, did not work in Romania because the "terrorists" opened fire on the crowd. So much for planning by the students. The "other" planning, by Securitate and Army, was still a mystery. If I had known then what I know now, I would have asked my television friends some tougher questions. But I wanted to believe then—as did the entire world—that the Romanian revolution had been a completely spontaneous and brilliant event. I was asking the young reporter to confirm my belief, to tell me how she and her fellow revolutionaries had thought of running to the TV station, without a plan. She didn't disappoint me. She said that this had indeed been the case, that she met the others when joined by the same thought, they entered and occupied the TV building. "The reason," she told me, "why we instantly knew *what* to do is that we all were educated in Marxist history, which is the history of revolutions and popular revolts. We knew from our classes that words have power. . . . We learned how to organize a strike committee . . . how to use every typewriter and piece of paper to make copies to glue on walls. We knew how to make glue out of anything for wall posters. . . . We knew how to organize a food detail, an infirmary, a dormitory, how to stay up all night working, how to talk to workers from factories, and soldiers. *They* educated us." She laughed.

I had no doubt that this was true. At least the knowing-how-to part. I too, was brought up in a Communist school with Marxist history and the know-how of revolution. One of the ironies of all the revolutions in East-Central Europe, whether violent like the Romanian or "velvet" like the Czech, is that they were learned in the very schools meant to shore up the regimes they overthrew. I thanked Miss Liberty, whose evident charm was enough to erase whatever critical sense I might have had. I later heard that she was the lover of the front's second most powerful man, but that could have been a rumor, of which there was no shortage.

A small group of armbanded young revolutionaries was having lunch on the floor; there was a large black bread, smoked bacon, and oranges lying on an embroidered towel. "Join us," one of them said. They made room. I was starving. The oranges, shining like pure gold, were certainly the centerpiece of the modest lunch. They were clearly proud of these oranges, whose absence from Romania had lasted a decade. These were among the first oranges to appear in public outside the privileged tables of the *nomenklatura* since 1980. "Have an orange," one of them urged us, but I knew that these oranges were too good to eat; they had to be contemplated, inhaled, palpated for a while, hugged perhaps, for someone to become fully cognizant of their presence. These oranges had been freed from the caches of the toppled aristocracy; they were former political prisoners. "I will not eat a . . . political prisoner," I said, and amazingly they laughed, understanding the metaphor precisely. I said this in Romanian, and until now, even after Adrian introduced us, I had not spoken to anyone in Romanian, holding back for the right moment. This was the right moment.

You do not belong in a place until you have made a joke in the native tongue. That's the true passport of acceptance. Now they converged on me. "How long have you been away? What are the names of your books? Have some slănină [raw smoked bacon]." One of them gave me a tricolor armband. I put it on proudly, feeling like Arthur Rimbaud on the barricades of the Paris Commune. I was savoring these moments because I knew that the tremendous energy of these days was unique. Even as they were speaking to me, two young technicians were wiring me up. I protested feebly. "I can't . . . I'm embarrassed. My Romanian isn't what it used to be." But it was to no avail. Embarrassment is useless in a revolution. I was drafted to make a statement. They wanted me to speak on television, without notes, unprepared. I was to follow, ironically, a former political prisoner who was speaking softly, in short sentences, his eyes lowered. Before I knew it, I was sitting at the long table with the tricolor behind me and the hand-lettered sign that said, GUEST OF FREE ROMANIAN TELEVISION. "I bring you the greetings and good wishes of American writers . . ." I began. "I am an American writer of Romanian origin. . . . I have waited twenty-five years for this day. . . ." Unbidden, the words flew, in good Romanian, as if, unspoken for all these years, they were only waiting my return to take their rightful place in my vocabulary. I spoke for two, maybe three minutes. I looked to the young woman standing behind the cameraman, and she rolled her hand, meaning "more." But I had said what was in my heart. I tried not to appear too moved and kept myself from bawling like a baby. But it was a close call. I had said the words "democracy," "the Ceauşescu tyranny," "Radio Free Europe," "Romanian language," "revolution." Those were words that for the greater part of my childhood had belonged to the secret language of silence. Not only had I said them aloud now, but I had said them on television before the entire country I once had to leave.

In fact, the entire country *was* watching. Next day I was recognized on the street. A couple leaving Bucharest's only Chinese restaurant at the same time as Rich and I greeted me by name, a real shock since I was sure that I had never seen them before. "We saw you on television." Well, I was touched, of course. I didn't know yet that all over the country, my old friends, high school and college buddies, old neighbors, friends of relatives, and friends of friends, had watched me and were telephoning each other to see who would get to see me in person first.

For the rest of the day, with Adrian darting in and out and my colleagues interviewing people in different parts of the building, I watched the activity in Studio Four. An extraordinary amalgam of images was being cooked for the nation. The televised revolution was being conducted with tremendous energy. On the basis of what I saw before me, I could believe that Romanian television had created the revolution. Some of the members of the National Salvation Front—not Iliescu or Generals Guşa and Vlad—looked the same age as the young revolutionaries who made sure the station stayed on the air. The faces of the members of the government and those of the young guards became confused in the minds of viewers. Many people thought that the revolutionary newsmen were the new government, and vice versa. Adrian professed to be an admirer of the young people, mostly students, who treated him rather disdainfully. He reproached himself, in a rather demonstrative manner, for having believed that young people "had only disco, rock videos, and loud entertainments in their heads." He said, "What a bitter lesson in civics they taught us! What a history lesson, written in blood! How immature we so-called adults seem all of a sudden!" I still knew Adrian well enough to give him a sidelong look. It was as if he were talking for the sake of a third party, listening either from inside his head or in the wall. Or perhaps he was speaking to the American media.

Nonetheless, on the air, twenty-four sleepless hours a day, the young broadcasters had rallied the nation to the defense of the revolution. Their own refusal to go to sleep kept the nation awake during those critical days. Could they all have been "planted" in place? Hard to believe. How much of what I saw was illusion, how much mirrors and smoke, how much was genuine emotion, how much careful planning? Romanians are urgently asking those questions today. They didn't occur to me then. Overcome by the raw energy of everything, I watched in wonder.

A lean peasant dressed in the ethnic costume of the Maramureş region sat under the tricolor, speaking. On his left he had a bottle of plum brandy, and on his right, a pleated bread called cozonac. He was bringing New Year's wishes from his village to the entire country. After traditional greetings involving the bottle and the bread, he thanked God for the good weather during the revolution. "The peasant," he said, "is the salt of the earth. Without us there is no food, but more important, there is no soul." He began describing in vivid colloquialisms the misery of the peasantry under the Communists. It was an articulate, powerful description of a hell that went against the grain for decades. He described forced collectivization, resistance, and suffering. He mentioned his friends and relatives by name and named also their children. He told the story of the "disappeared" from his village, the theft of young men. It was a well-documented chronicle of pain, unfolding in a rhythm akin to folk epics, hypnotic and eerily beautiful. The region of Maramureş is one of Romania's chief traditional storytelling areas. There is a cemetery in a Maramureş village where all the crosses bear the inscriptions of a local artisan. It is called the Happy Cemetery because the obituaries are brief and to the point. "Here lies Ilie Such/He led a life full of cheer/If he hadn't drunk so much/He wouldn't be here." The Maramureş invoked before me on TV was a cemetery, too, but not a happy one. Suddenly the speech changed in tone and became political. "The peasants are this country," the man said, "and we demand land and an immediate end to collective farming." He also demanded a six-hour workday for "our sons, the miners." He concluded by calling home all those who had left the country. "Brothers, come home!" he said, talking directly to me. It was a masterful demonstration of political skill that flew in the face of those disbelieving cynics who think that "Romanians don't know democracy." This was a democratic man speaking, with a sense of a just world that came from farther back than the Enlightenment. It came from the commons of villages run on democratic principles since before the Turkish occupation. Here it was, a preliterate world, on color TV. I have no idea what party this peasant ended up joining, or founding, but here was its articulate spokesman of the moment, risen from seemingly nowhere. Romanian television had issued a call to Romanian citizens to come have their say before the nation, and everyone, it seems, had taken TV up on it.

The peasant from Maramureş was followed by an announcement of new decisions of the front and reports of fighting still going on in Transylvania. The commentator, who, amazingly, was the same man who read the Ceauşescu news before the revolution, shuffled through papers obviously composed seconds before. He stumbled over words, held the papers at an angle, pushed his glasses over his nose. He announced that a number of guests had appeared at the station with various messages and that they would soon speak uncensored. There was a momentary blank screen. Then a number of people took seats at the long table. It was obvious that they had just arrived and had not rehearsed anything. Two of them were revolutionary guards, who described the situation at a factory near Bucharest. They and their comrades had been running things while the old administrators, who were still around, helped show them how things worked. There was a nervous woman from Constanţa, a city on the Black Sea, who said that already, a week after the revolution, the party hacks and secret police were taking back their old jobs. She named them all and lost her nervousness when indignation took over.

The immediacy was stunning. I had never seen television like this.

I thought again of the Chinese tragedy, how, at the May 1 demonstration in Beijing, TV newsmen, forbidden to broadcast the truth, carried
banners that said, DON'T BELIEVE WHAT WE WRITE. WE WRITE LIES. Happily I thought, *this doesn't seem to be the case here.* Ha!

Just as I had that exalted thought, the station began showing an
MTV video taken from who knows where. Near-naked Americans leaped
about in a shower of sparks and fog that was like a mock revolution.
Surely no one in Romania had ever seen such a thing. In the coming
days MTV and rock 'n' roll became a real presence on the starved little
screens of Romania. In fact, hundreds of taboos were broken. Bare breasts
appeared on a sudden afternoon at the very start of anno Domini 1990.

I sat in on Noah's interview with the rock 'n' roll programmer, a
grinning man with wiry curls. "I've been stealing MTV from satellite,"
he said, "anything I can get my hands on. The revolution is disregard-
ing copyright at this moment in favor of blowing the minds of Romanians. . . . We issued a call to our rock 'n' roll groups to come play on
television. . . ." There were apparently quite a few rock groups in Romania. They'd played deeply underground with very old instruments.
"They need instruments." The producer pleaded with us. "They are
fabulous; you must listen to their tapes." We did. I sank inside my
earphones into the sounds of a Romanian rock band, trying to make
out the words. "On the shore of a Black Sea . . . blacker than the dirt
in my heart . . . I'll drown with my friends . . . tear the fabric of life
apart. . . ." Not cheerful, but this was angry rock, written under circumstances blacker even than the words. There were jazz influences
here, too, and I remembered listening to a tape of jazz musicians from
Sibiu almost a year before and being surprised at their depth of knowledge about American jazz and their love for it. In fact, as I listened to
this new rock 'n' roll from Europe's recent darkness, I realized how
much these young people loved American music, movies, and style.
They yearned for it in a pure and instinctive way like children reaching
for candy. I remembered that in 1965 my cousin Romi played some
smuggled tapes of the Beatles and the Rolling Stones in the dingy room
where he lived and lifted weights and that when I heard those sounds,
I wanted immediately to follow them to the source, to the heart of the
heart the beats came from. And did, eventually, after leaving Romania.
These younger young people of Bucharest in 1990 were just like me in
1965, and now they too, could follow the beat to its source if they

wanted to, or even better, they could make it issue loudly right from right where they were.

The young broadcasters passed a bottle of homemade wine around. A slim man in a suit with round wire-rimmed glasses had appeared and was shaking hands all around. He seemed no older than the others and easily accepted a slice of bacon, bread, and a swig of wine from them. When he went into the studio, Adrian told me, "That's the new health minister."

"And he didn't even inspect the food," someone said.

When we left the television station, I felt that I had been inside the nerve center of the revolution and that my own nervous system was now intricately connected to that of my birthplace. Outside, the mobs had grown larger and more agitated. The call of liberty had brought them all out to give voice to every discontent. Television had involved not only everyone in public life but every part of everyone, even those inner things usually safeguarded from public scrutiny. How much stranger than if what I saw was at least partly a spectacularly staged play.

7

Someone's Shooting at Me

Before leaving the United States, I'd contracted with ABC News to do a piece for *Nightline* from Bucharest. When the Romanian events began unfolding, Ted Koppel asked me to comment on the situation, and I was happy to do so because all through December our media had employed Polish, Hungarian, and Czech "experts" to explain the Romanian situation. The Rolodexes of our major news organizations were singularly devoid of Romanians. This state of affairs reached its peak during the first CNN live broadcasts from Romania in early December, which employed a translator who spoke bad Berlitz Romanian. After the confusion cleared—though it took an awfully long time—real Romanian exiles with excellent English were found, and things began to make sense. NPR and MacNeil/Lehrer found Dorin Tudoran, a dissident poet who lives in Washington, and Vladimir Tismăneanu, an articulate scholar of political philosophy. NPR also interviewed my friend Radu Bogdan, a professor of philosophy at Tulane University in New Orleans, who also happens to be the nephew of Silviu Brucan, who, in addition to all his former official positions, is by many accounts the éminence grise of the National Salvation Front. These people were able to lay to rest some truly grotesque stories and to straighten the record in various ways.

Romania has always been a completely baffling place to most Americans, with very few exceptions. I am always asked if Transylvania

113

is a real place when I tell people that I was born there. Until I went back, I was beginning to have my doubts. In addition to having difficulty with Romanian names (many of which end in escu and eanu, meaning "son of," as in "John-son"), people have trouble grasping the fact that Romanian is a Latin language and Romanians are a Latin people. When one looks at the map, one finds a solid Slavic sea (except for the Hungarians) surrounding Romania. Historical and geopolitical realities are hard to grasp in this part of the world, which has seen migrations, wars, collapsing empires, and changing deeds of ownership for more than three thousand years. Added to this basic ignorance was the fact that Ceauşescu still appeared to most people in America as a maverick in the Communist world who had opposed the Soviet invasion of Czechoslovakia and had had his picture taken with three American Presidents. When the Romanian people revolted, no one knew who anybody was. Our media consistently confused television employees with political leaders and made serious mistakes in identifying the protagonists. The need for translation wasn't only from language to language but from world to world. The story of translators during the changes of 1989 has yet to be told. Experts, newsmen, and simple readers of newsmagazines suddenly had so much to learn about Eastern Europe they might be forgiven a certain confusion. There was bumbling, but also moments so touching they were angelic. During Secretary of State James Baker's meeting with the archbishop of Prague in January 1990, his translator, a 1981 Czech refugee, burst into tears. Both Baker and the bishop hastened to console him in their respective languages. There were times when I, too, felt like crying while translating and other times when I made my words meaner and angrier than the original suggested. My own adventures and misadventures in the fields of translation have given me reason to suspect that wars and conflicts may be the result of mistranslation. On the other hand, I am always amazed at how little "expertise" in this field big money can actually buy. Has there been a single vampire movie that has employed a Romanian for the correct Transylvanian accent? Million-dollar budgets never seem to include one hundred dollars for a native speaker to provide the genuine article instead of the gibberish passing for "Transylvanian" in Hollywood. Likewise, our TV news, while not strictly fantastic, is often at a loss when a new geography comes to the fore. A news anchor in New Orleans asked me with great interest if I thought that the cause of the Romanian revolution had been the defection of gymnast Nadia Comăneci. "Sure," I told her, "that, *and* Dracula's defection!"

In any case, having become one of Ted Koppel's "experts," I made a deal to film part of my return for *Nightline*. There was some irony involved. I had left Romania with little more than a change of clothes. I was now returning with a TV crew to give people my books. One of my major fantasies of return, the one called "I'll show you!," was certainly fulfilled. On the other hand, the country was bitter cold, young people had died in scores of cities, hunger was widespread, children were dying of AIDS in hospices. At the TV station they were worshiping oranges. I quickly lost whatever childish motivation was involved. I wanted instead to tell a moving story so that well-fed people in the West would reach in their pockets and help.

The ABC News crew in Romania had been there through the dramatic days of street fighting. They were a hardworking international bunch. Robin Weiner, the producer of my piece, was based in Rome; Bruno was from the ABC Tel Aviv bureau; cameraman Alex and sound person Francesca lived in Vienna. Robin was a self-propelled energy vortex. ABC News had taken over the entire Flora Hotel near the giant Stalinist printing plant—once the Square of the Spark, now the Square of the Press—but was also using a room at the Inter-Continental Hotel. Since I was doubling up with Noah, Robin asked me if I wanted to use the room. Of course. When we got to the ABC room on the twelfth floor, it was evident that someone had been staying there; there were breakfast trays and bottles of mineral water among the ABC cables and cameras. As I later had occasion to observe, this was just one of the milder scams that the deskocracy of the Chief Sleazotel ran. But Robin had an instant and most effective flaring of anger before the manager, who meekly erased the debt for the past week. I then moved into the hastily and thoroughly cleaned room. Even the bullet holes in the window had been shined, so great ran the fear of Robin in the Inter-Con. ABC also gave me a car and a driver, Petre. This was true luxury because Bucharest taxis are a nightmare. In sub-zero weather they are a meganightmare.

The first scene we shot was in a snowed-in park near the Flora on January 2, 1990. I walked first away and then back from the camera, sinking into the deep snow that gave way with a hard crunch under my boots. I walked, deep in thought, or so it seemed to me, pondering my return. Here I was, twenty-five years later, each heavy footstep a month of my life, the snow, a metaphor for time, giving way under my heavy tread—but then Alex said, "That was too fast. Let's do it again!" Once more, thoughtful, meditative face fastened on firmly, I walked across the frozen wastes of time toward the merciless eye of the camera. No, that wasn't it either. Neither time nor thought could provide Alex with the shot he needed. Several frozen walks later, a cement grin gripping my scowling visage, I walked toward him murderously slow, intending to attack.

"That's it!" said Bruno, who was also looking through the viewer.

"You did it!" said Alex. Proud and frozen, I allowed Francesca to run her light Viennese fingers under my sweater again to remove the microphone. Four hours had passed, but I had walked *right*. For the next two days we shot every little scene called for in my one-page script. I'd had no idea when I wrote it what painstaking attention my words would get. On the radio an equal script of this size takes one minute to read and two minutes to hear. With the half hour it takes to write, that's only thirty-three minutes. But a paper minute on television can take any number of days. Three, in my case.

I had written about my fantasy of return. I spoke of how I had dreamed that one day, extremely rich and famous, I would glide up the summer boulevards of Bucharest in an oversize limo driven by an angelically blinding hermaphrodite. The adoring mobs at the outdoor cafés leave their steaming sausages and serenading Gypsies to stream toward me with their wine goblets raised high. One of those thus greeting me is none other than my horrible stepfather, who made my childhood miserable. When he comes close enough to receive my blessing, I deck him. It's a hard uppercut to the jaw, and he falls in an uncomprehending lump. We continue up the boulevard then, toward the Capşa Café, where all my literary heroes, past and present, rise from their espressos to cheer. That was a simple (and common) enough fantasy when I conceived of it, but putting it on the evening news presented something of a challenge. Robin worried that the vast viewing audience might not exactly get it if I was speaking about summer while such winter surrounded us. The point was that while I mused out loud about my absurd fantasy, the camera would pan over burned buildings, tanks, and people dressed in black. I would then switch abruptly to the present and tell the viewers that the bleak present they saw was better than any fantasy because it was the real landscape of a free country, and there was nothing better than freedom.

"Perhaps we should find your stepfather," suggested Alex. I insisted that my stepfather had to stay imaginary because I had no wish whatsoever to see him again and that if I did, I would not have the heart to deck him since he was by now, if he was at all, an eighty-year-old man. "Expense is no problem," insisted Robin, suspecting that perhaps a kind of thriftiness was holding me back. I wondered once more at the vast resources available to make a phrase come to life. "They told me in New York," Robin confessed, "to give you whatever you want. I never heard them say that before. . . . Especially *Nightline*." I then knew that my angel in New York was really Ted Koppel in Washington. I once heard someone say that: "I don't know how Koppel got on TV. He's incredibly smart!" TV news doesn't have the greatest reputation for depth, but I must confess to a certain admiration for the seriousness and professionalism of this ABC crew. Beyond the literalness of interpretation that was a quality of news, they were fanatical about accuracy. If the café in question was Capşa, no other café would do. A line in the script having to do with crossing the border caused the lot of them to drive to the Bulgarian border in order to film an authentic crossing and an authentic flag.

The most touching scene—one that I did not mind doing over and over—was a walk I took through the destroyed library building of the University of Bucharest. The books of all those literary lights gathered at Capşa once-upon-a-time were all here. So were the invaluable works of others—three hundred thousand books gone up in flames. There was something else here, too—namely, a very young me, writing poems at those long readers' tables, sneaking sidelong glances at the unbearably intelligent and beautifully unapproachable face of the young woman studying philosophy two seats away. No one can burn her face from my memory. The books will be replaced. As I climbed up the winding staircase going into the bare winter sky, past collapsed floors, I remembered the luminous faces of my old friends, our enthusiasms and hunger. It was snowing. Ten days after the fighting, heavy snowfalls, and frigid temperatures, the books were still smoldering. I walked over the smoking remains of the books and manuscripts of Romania's greatest writers. I picked up a few charred pages. These were the sacred pieces of the Romanian revolution, more holy in their way than the pieces of the Berlin wall, which had come happily down in peace. The books murdered here carried a greater weight and a headier promise. On the half page I was holding was a folk story poem I recognized from my childhood. It was about Ion Handsome-Lad who sacrifices himself for his father, the aging king. Speaking of his once-powerful horses, he says: "One died/ One vanished/ One aged." About the sad king, it is said: "One eye laughed/While the other cried." That was—precisely—how I felt. Elated by the victory, wrenched by its losses. Verily there is little that is arbitrary. The other page I took from the ground was an old German poem in Gothic script, burned roundly about the edges, to form an oval with blackened sides like a mad mirror. It was a page from an early edition of *Faust*. I raised the collar of my coat and looked out through what used to be a grand window but was now only an archway open to the sky. Volunteers with spades and brooms below were beginning the slow and painful work of clearing the debris. It snowed over them, giving brilliance to the black-and-white world where they moved. The soldiers on guard on top of their tanks in front of the former CCP building seemed frozen also in time. It seemed to me as I looked out the window of my bygone youth that everything had come to a standstill in a single frame. Time had stopped. I can't swear that a tear didn't streak hot and salty down my cheek. It broke my reverie and brought me back to the present.

When I went back down, stepping carefully over large missing chunks of the grand staircase, I saw a woman crying, held by her husband on one side and by her teenage son on the other. Her other son, Paul, had been killed at that spot in front of the library. She wept and lamented in an ancient way: "Oh, Paul, why didn't you listen to your mother? You died here! Where are you, Paul? Where are you, son?" People stood around crying and offered her apples and bread, which her husband took and put in a sack at his feet.

A few feet away a woman said to a fresh-faced young soldier who stood next to a tank with a flower tied to the barrel of his AK-47: "Can I give you these two apples? I washed them myself." He wanted to take them but was clearly under orders not to. There had been reports of poisoned food and poisoned water. The apples the woman offered the soldier were, at the moment, precious commodities.

Our NPR crew, an infinitely more modest operation than ABC News, ran on a shoestring budget. On the other hand, we produced a staggering amount of stories, no doubt because of the tyrannical rule of the formidable Mr. Sullivan. There lived in him, hidden beneath a deceptively handsome exterior, an unyielding professional despot. One of the stories Noah was following was about the destruction of villages under Ceauşescu's "systematization" program and the removal of the villagers to block buildings on the outskirts of Bucharest. It was said in Bucharest that the greatest criminals of Ceauşescu's rule had been architects and gynecologists, the former for destroying the outer life of the nation, the latter for killing its inner life.

We arrived at a yet nameless and half-built suburb of Bucharest in two taxis driven by maniacs. The driver of the one Michael and I rode in pushed his Dacia blindingly fast over the snow and ice, making all kinds of unexpected moves, going around trucks at full speed, once crossing some rails seconds before a train passed. . . . It was all I could do to stay in my seat. I told him to cut it out, but he only laughed and said that it was OK because he'd "test-driven cars for Dacia" and knew "exactly how much the bitches could take." That was not reassuring, particularly since the other driver, who must have also test-driven Dacias, began to drag-race our driver. As the roads got worse, we flew over potholes, unfinished pavements, mountains of snow-covered industrial junk. "It would be perfectly ironic," said Michael, "if we ended here, the last heroes of the revolution." He was pretty well shaken by the ride.

We stopped in what looked like a huge construction site, a forest of half-finished buildings exposing pipes, brick, half roofs. Lying about were snowed-in piles of construction materials. Here and there the frozen smoke of a wood stove hung in the lead sky. The whole neighborhood came out to talk to us. They were peasants who had recently become workers. Their wives and mothers still wore country kerchiefs and blouses. But the younger children, especially the girls, looked city modern with makeup and lipstick. An older man made a long speech against communism when Noah asked him if he'd had to leave his village to come here. But when the speech was over, he confessed that he'd lived in the city all his life. A thin man with a deeply scarred face, wearing a hard hat and the clothes of a construction worker, offered to take us to his apartment, where his relatives—former villagers all—lived. We tramped up the cinder-block stairs without a banister. It was a damp cement building, still unfinished in places. We crowded into the tiny living room of his apartment, we with our tape recorders, and as many neighbors as could followed us in. It was a clean and modest room with icons on the freshly painted walls and one or two reproductions of flower paintings by Grigorescu. There was a peasant embroidery on the couch and a hand-stitched tablecloth with roses on it. Before they would let Noah ask any questions, the laborer insisted that we have a glass of tzuică to toast liberty. When this was done, his wife, a shy young girl who looked no more than eighteen, brought some flat homemade bread on a wooden tray. We each took some and then had to have another tzuică to toast America. Every time Noah began to ask questions, they insisted on the rituals of hospitality. That was fine with everyone, especially our drivers, who made two toasts for every one of theirs.

At last their story emerged. They all had been moved from the village of Dămieni, not far from where we were. In Dămieni they'd had a big wooden house with a porch carved by their "great-grandfather." They went to the church on the hill every Sunday. The collective farm where they worked had one hundred cows and eight hundred pigs. They made brandy. There were six of them in the two-room apartment: the man and his wife, their two children, and his parents. The wife said that for her, personally, "it is better living here in an apartment, but now, since the revolution, there hasn't been any heat or hot water." "Was there any *before* the revolution?"

"Sure," she said.

Her mother-in-law disagreed. "It's not better here. . . . It was better in the village . . . in Dămieni!" A heated argument ensued between the two women. The younger one liked the city; the older one thought it was a curse. "In Dămieni," the old woman said, "you could hear a chicken, see a pig, run with a dog, lay your head on a lamb, kiss a calf, milk a cow, and sleep with fluffy little chicks in a hayloft. Never," she said to the younger woman, "will your children hear a rooster, roll in the dust with a pig, butt heads with a soft little lamb, ride a horse, kiss a calf, milk a cow early in the morning, and chase fluffy little chicks around. Never!" Her vehemence silenced everyone until one of the children, a four-year-old girl, came and buried her head in Grandma's lap.

"I want to see the village of Dămieni," said Michael.

"But there is nothing there!" said the laborer after a pause.

"Still, we would like to see it!" Michael insisted.

"Nothing there but snow and the ruin of an old culture house we all paid from our savings to build."

"Not a chicken, not a pig, not a dog, not a living soul . . ." mumbled the old woman.

"Can you show us?"

"It's far," the man said. "It's fifty kilometers from here, near the airport!"

Michael's mind was made up. We would go to the site of the disappeared village of Dămieni.

"Why?" I asked him. "There is nothing but silence there."

"That's the point," he said.

I didn't see any point. Silence is silence. We were making *radio*, for chrissakes! Isn't one silence as good as the next? Couldn't he just open his microphone over any snowy patch? I could hardly see the point of driving another fifty kilometers with the now well-oiled maniacs who'd brought us here. What's more, I knew that Michael had been quite distressed by the ride.

Michael's stubbornness was dramatic. He was unbending. We piled once more into the demonic little vehicles, which raced this time over open country that looked like snow as far as the eye could see. The man of the house came with us, to show us where Dămieni was. Now and then our flying machine would spin 360 degrees over a patch of ice, and every time the driver would laugh hysterically and explain that he knew what these "Dacias can take!"

At long last we came upon another field of snow, distinguished only by a sharp mound sticking out of it like the wing of a crashed airplane. It was the side of an old building. "That was the culture center," the man said. "We sure paid for it. . . ."

Michael shushed everybody. He and Rich proceeded to tape the silence. A small breeze started up, and there was the sound of an airplane overhead. Then more silence. The man from Dămieni interrupted then and, pointing to the sky, said: "I worked at the airport. I know why they destroyed Dămieni." He told us that Ceaușescu could see Dămieni from his private runway and that one day, ashamed that his foreign guests could also see the modest buildings, he ordered the village razed. There was more silence now, a different kind of silence after I had translated what the man said. I hated to admit it, but Michael had been right. There is silence and silence. I cannot very well explain it, but the particular silence of the village of Dămieni that was no more is very different from the silence of a place where people still live. I don't know if radio listeners can actually *hear* the difference; but there is one, and it's significant. There was something else as well: If we had not gone in search of the silence with the former villager, we would not have heard the true story of the end of his village.

"That's also the point," Michael growled. "If you do the right thing, you get a story like that. That's extra. Lagniappe, as you people say in Louisiana."

I had to give it to him. Anybody who's willing to die just to get the right kind of silence deserves a doff of the hat. And a kick in the ass. Journalists are quite insane if you ask me. I observed a whole table of war correspondents at the Inter-Con restaurant, talking about the good old days in Vietnam, Cyprus, and Beirut. Most of them were getting ready to pull out of Romania because the shooting had stopped. They were bored now. They were going to leave the political and economic reporting to less hardy types, eggheads.

Early the next day, on January 3, we went to interview the chief architect of Bucharest. He was one of the men responsible for implementing Ceauşescu's policy of *sistematizare*, including the destruction of Dămieni. That this man was still in place was amazing in itself, but that he was still in charge was even more amazing. A guard in front of the building asked us where we were going. We told him. "The devil," he said, "is going to fry that man in a piss pot. He's under arrest up there."

As it turned out, he wasn't really under arrest but was really in charge. Or partly under arrest and partly in charge. No one knew for sure. The ministry building—the chief architect has ministerial rank—was a pretty turn-of-the century Victorian house. The two soldiers guarding the inner entrance barely glanced at our passports. There was little sense here of the emergency gripping the media or the front buildings. And yet it was here, more than anywhere else, that the evil of Ceauşescu's dream was made manifest. Dozens of historical monuments, churches, and architectural treasures had been demolished to make room for Ceauşescu's self-glorifying monuments. Gone was the beautiful Văcăreşti Monastery, where I had once looked at icons, with its twin Byzantine towers, shady porticoes, and long galleries. Gone also were many old mysteries of my student years where I'd hidden to write poetry and dream. An old city is a sort of wilderness. Destroying it is the same as destroying a forest, an ecological crime. Ceauşescu's forest of apartment blocks, which stands over the ghosts of my youth, is regarded by many as the most ambitious construction project in Europe.

But the presidential palace, built over the three layers of secret tunnels, is the regime's most grimly symbolic building. Its floor space is more than 400,000 square feet and thirteen stories. There are great chandeliers over the immense marble staircase. The central area for receptions is as big as a football field, 240 feet long and 90 feet wide, with tower ceilings covered in gold leaf or pink gypsum. The five-ton chandelier over the main staircase consumes more electricity than two Romanian villages. At the time when average people's apartments were required to use sixty-watt bulbs, the palace devoured eighty-five thousand watts. The marble columns are hand-carved. It is three times the size of Versailles and bigger than the Pentagon. Fifty thousand people lost their homes, so that the site for it could be cleared when construction began in 1984. Its cost has run to more than a billion dollars, and whole industries were set up to feed the palace's demands for marble and lumber. Construction accidents claimed twenty lives. And yet . . . the palace is only two thirds finished! The reason is that the Ceauşescus inspected the building every week and ordered rooms, staircases, and decorations already built to be destroyed and started again. Like insane minotaurs at the center of an ever-growing maze, the couple tried to put traps and walls between them and their fate. The roof had to be built and rebuilt several times and was never finished.

Their story was reminiscent of the legend of Master Manole, the builder of Dracula's Castle on the Argeş. That edifice, the ruins of which can still be seen in forbidding starkness over the Argeş River, could not be made to stand no matter how hard its builders worked. Every time their work seemed finished, the building collapsed. One night Master Builder Manole had a dream that the only way to finish the building was to build someone alive into the wall. The three builders decided that the first of their wives to come with lunch next day would be sacrificed to the castle. The two older men told their wives to stay home, but young Manole didn't. His beautiful young wife came and was immured in the castle wall. To this day, say local legends, you can hear her crying and lamenting on certain nights, not understanding how her husband could have been so cruel to her. One can say that symbolically the Romanian nation was likewise nearly sacrificed on Master Builder Ceauşescu's orders.

The average citizen of the capital lived in a blacked-out city under warlike conditions. But the bombs that destroyed their neighborhoods came not from an enemy outside but from one who lived in their midst.

It was a war of destruction in the name of unlimited construction. Dissident writer Octavian Paler describes it this way in his secret diary:

> In the daytime, when the wind blows from the south, the sky is yellow. The dust that floats like a persistent fog over Bucharest has an origin known to everyone. It comes from the rubble of demolished buildings. It is the dust of a dead city. For several years, since bulldozers have become a threat like the invasions of the Mongols in the past, the sky has become obscured. It is practically impossible to defend yourself from this new form of history that is invading your privacy. You can close your windows all day. In vain. The dust slips through cracks and covers everything, the furniture, the books, your typewriter. On the streets there is no defense. The first car that passes stirs up a cloud of dust that prevents all your efforts not to resemble the wild curs that wander in packs through the rubble of demolished neighborhoods. This omnipresent dust is symbolic. It is part of the past of the city, carried by the wind and blown over the present. It rises, as if from a cemetery, from the walls that have become one with the earth.

We were greeted at the entrance of the modest ministry building by an unshaven young man with a tricolor armband. "I am the Salvation Front representative in charge of the ministry," he explained. He pointed apologetically to two boys sleeping on cots in his small office. "My men . . . they've been on duty since December twenty-third." The next room, however, was immense, dominated by a long polished walnut table. A lit chandelier hung over it, though there was probably sufficient wintry light coming in from the leaded cathedral windows. Three polished bureaucrats in well-tailored suits rose to greet us: the chief architect of Bucharest, the dean of the architecture school at the University of Bucharest, and the ministry archivist.

We took seats at the table in the grand salon and were offered coffee, espresso, in delicate porcelain cups. This is de rigueur in the better offices in Bucharest. The young man from the front said without much hesitation: "Ceauşescu's *sistematizare* policy was criminal. The destruction of Romanian villages and historic buildings were acts of cultural genocide. All new building must immediately be stopped." He then excused himself and left us with the specialists.

Noah asked the chief architect if he had been in charge during Romania's accelerated building program. He freely admitted it. "What is going to happen now to Ceauşescu's building program?" asked Noah.

"We will have to finish what we started," the chief said without emphasis.

"But . . ." said Noah, "didn't your new boss from the Salvation Front say just now that *sistematizare* was a criminal program? . . . How can you maintain that this program must be continued in spite of what has happened? Isn't there a decree stopping all construction?"

"The law is vague. There will be time to reconsider everything. I defer to my colleague Dr. Professor Academician. . . ."

The professor pursed a pair of purple lips under tan horn-rimmed glasses. He took up a pointer to a map of Bucharest on the wall. "This," he said, "is Bucharest in the seventeenth century. This"—he pointed to another map—"is Bucharest in the early twentieth century . . . and this . . . is Bucharest now. The city has been exploding in population and size without respite for three centuries. Such growth cannot be tolerated without central planning. There are objective conditions in the development of a city. . . ."

I had a moment of nauseating wonder. "Objective conditions!" Those two quintessential Marxist words had been repeated ritually throughout my young life and throughout the life of Romania for forty-five years in order to justify any number of crimes. "Objective conditions" led to the silencing of political opposition; "objective conditions" were in place when opponents were murdered; "objective conditions" were there for cheating people of their own labor, stealing their wealth, privacy, and well-being, censoring writings and art. The "objective conditions" had prevailed long enough. I had been hoping that neither they nor the notorious "indications" from above held any more currency in this new country. Yet here was this unperturbed Communist bureaucrat speaking not only as if nothing had happened but as if all were objectively destined to go on as before. I almost lost my translator's cool. I wanted to hurl the delicate espresso cup in his porky face.

"Your positions are diametrically opposed to those of the front," insisted Noah. "Aren't you afraid that you will lose your jobs?"

"I never wanted this job in the first place." The chief architect laughed with an air of amused and worldly superiority. He was—how should I say it?—*suffused* with power. He exuded authority like a feline.

"Don't get me wrong," said the professor. "I am not against peasants, and I would be the last one to destroy their villages. . . . My father was director of the Museum of the Peasant—"

At this point my hackles, whatever those are, stood. "Hitler," I said, "collected artifacts for an eventual Museum of the Jew, to be built after all the Jews were dead!"

"That's impertinent!" said the hitherto silent archivist.

"I will phrase my contempt more elegantly next time," I said.

Whatever else might be said about these unrepentant minions of the old regime, they were supremely confident that as soon as the kids upstairs got tired and went home, things would return to normal. I hoped that they were wrong, that the kids upstairs weren't just playing revolution. They had died on the streets protesting against these men. They could not allow them to steal their revolution. But I could see that it was going to be a long struggle. The polished dinosaurs before us were expert politicians. The young were long on morals but deficient in politics.

Our interview ended on a note of palpable hostility. Our group was generationally and temperamentally sympathetic to the young revolutionaries. On the way out Michael asked to speak privately to the front leader who had met us. He told him that the men upstairs were the enemies of their policies. The young man nodded and gave a short, knowing laugh. "We are keeping them around," he said, "so they won't go home to get their friends and begin to *organize* against us. . . . They are safer in their old holes. . . ."

I wonder.

8

Adrian: Writers Improvise the Revolution

My driver, Petre, was familiar with Adrian's neighborhood by the lake. "A nest of vipers," he bluntly characterized it. Petre was a swarthy young man with a bandito mustache and a wicked grin. He had been active since the first hour of the revolution. He had organized a taxi strike in order to stop party members from attending Ceauşescu's rally on December 21. For that he'd been fired on the spot. He was rehired next day when it became obvious that the rally was actually going to be the end of Ceauşescu. He used his taxi to ferry demonstrators to the front lines. When the Army tanks began moving on the demonstrators, he and his fellow drivers abandoned their taxis to form a barricade. He had been working with ABC News since the first day. He was now proud, he said, to work for me. He refused my offer of a tip and would not take cigarettes. "I am doing it for my country," he said. I believed him. He drove a Dacia with an ABC News sticker on the right of the window. He, too, drove fast and carelessly over the snow. "Every Romanian driver thinks he's Mario Andretti," Robin told me.

It was already dark, past the six o'clock curfew. "Your friend Adrian," he said, "he lives in a place where a lot of Securitate used to live. He must be a big man." I was not thrilled by either his observation or by his astuteness. A "big man" in yesterday's Romania was not a particularly good thing now. "He works for television," I told him.

That pacified Petre, and he proceeded to tell me his part in the battle for the television station. It was a good story, and I almost didn't notice that we were in an underground passage under the street. I did see some small barred windows in the wall to my right. And then I heard the shots: pac . . . pac . . . pac . . . pac . . . four or five in a row, from a small automatic weapon. Petre stepped on the gas, and we flew out of there. We hadn't been hit.

"It's the first time in two days," Petre said. "It must the ABC sticker!"

On the way back we went *over* the street, and Petre covered the ABC sticker with a towel. It had been some day: I had been shot in every sense of the word, first by Romanian television, then by ABC, and now by a gunman. It's the curse of a poet in a revolution, to experience all the meanings of words.

Adrian's wife, Betty, waited for us at the frozen intersection of her block of buildings under a sign that said, THE TENANTS OF BLOCKS 5–56 SUPPORT THE NATIONAL SALVATION FRONT! She had filled out a little, but she hadn't changed much. Same dark eyes with a wink in them, a proud carriage. She greeted me warmly. I've known Betty since we were mere children. In fact, she had been present at one of the crucial and more symbolic occurences in my young life. I started writing poetry at thirteen. By sixteen I felt myself to be of that special race of men who are really horses with wings. I carried my poetry notebook everywhere, from café to café, slapping it wearily on marble tabletops. I was Rimbaud, Baudelaire, Eminescu, and Tristan Tzara all rolled in one. But I had not yet typed my poems. It was all very well to be a handwritten genius in Sibiu, a small provincial town at the far edges of the former Austro-Hungarian Empire, but I would never transcend my circumstances until I had *typed*. My friend Adrian, who was also a poet, and ten years older than I, had a typewriter. He also had a leather jacket and a mysterious job, which reminded me of my mysterious father. His typewriter was a potent object. All the typewriters in Romania were registered with the police. That way unauthorized material could be traced back to the source. I had been hinting in my oblique and disdainful way that the time had perhaps come for Adrian to let me type my poems on the old Underwood. It wasn't a personal thing, you see, but the fate of Romanian literature rested on it. One day Adrian saw the wisdom of my desire and left me alone with his typewriter. I intended to type all the poems in my overflowing notebook. But just as I had flexed my fingers, there was a knock at the door. I opened it, and there was Betty, twenty-two years old, with a brown cardboard suitcase. She had, it seems, met Adrian on a train, and he'd told her to come visit when she found herself in the big city. There she was, with a kerchief on her hair and big dark eyes. I bade her to make herself at home, and I resumed my important work. But I couldn't concentrate somehow. Every time I succeeded in typing a word I would steal a glance at the young girl lying on the bed with her arms under her head, watching me. Her breasts rose and fell in time to her breathing but not in time to my typing, though at first I did try to match them. In the struggle between my waning desire to type and my growing desire to touch her breasts, my future personality was being formed. It appeared that I was not yet ready to make the transition from the dreamy intimacy of handwriting to the metallic responsibility of public domain. It also appeared that I was not yet courageous enough to leap on Betty's breasts. On the other hand, I might have summoned the courage had Adrian not come home. He found me with my handwritten poems strewn on the floor all around me and his future wife asleep on the bed. The typewriter lay untouched, as did Betty.

Further attempts at typing that year were fruitless as well because every time I began to touch the keys I would strain my ear for a knock on the door. It was not until I left Romania that I could sit at a typewriter and just type, as if it were a normal thing to do. By then things had changed. I liked the staccato din of modern American life. I liked the typewriterlike hum of New York and its rushing humans, who looked to me like the madly dancing keys of a shiny, vast keyboard. America moved at the speed of its keyboards. I began composing directly on the typewriter. Knocks on the door, when they came, did not break my concentration. *Au contraire*, I used the excitement to spur me to greater heights of typing. Whenever I thought of my sad Romania, I thought of registered typewriters, forbidden copiers, a place where writing was deemed more dangerous than bombs, a place of sadness, silence, handwriting, and the shyness of boy geniuses.

But I was back now, in a revolution that shattered all that silence and that would soon need all the technological know-how of my new country to bring it into the twentieth century, and here was Betty, grown stouter, but still familiar. She led me by the arm past rows and rows of vestibules and building blocks. It was a middle-class neighborhood. There were small parks between buildings and a big lake at the outer edge.

Adrian's ancient mom remembered me. She lived with them, as did their twenty-six-year-old daughter, who'd been a baby when I left. She was now a computer engineer working in one of Bucharest's top institutes. We sat about the living room, drinking toasts to our reunion. A big TV dominated the room. I very much wanted to know everything about their lives in the years just past, especially those intimate details possible only among friends, but where to start? Adrian showed me a number of poetry books that he'd published in those years and told me about several unpublished manuscripts, particularly his "Dacian" novel, which had fallen prey to censorship. I gave him one of my poetry books. We then fell silent. Adrian had always been rather taciturn, but there was something else. I had somehow breached a code of etiquette by first meeting him outside his house at the TV station. I had forgotten the Romanian sensitivity to manners, a fact that my media colleagues disregarded completely. Consequently, they were not surprisingly thought of as boorish Americans, but I was expected to act differently. Schnapps, toast, and greetings before reminiscences, reminiscences before politics, politics before business. There was an ironclad order to these things. Until now my use of Romanian had been adequate to the task of translating for NPR. I had not had time, in the heat of interviews, to be self-conscious about words. But here, among old friends, it was a different matter. I felt that I was expressing myself woodenly, that I groped helplessly for words, that I couldn't say what was on my mind. At times I translated sentences I formed first in English. And Adrian was not forthcoming. I felt the intense curiosity of the women of the family, so I addressed my remarks to them, three generations of them. Just at the point when the warmth of the schnapps, Betty's vivaciousness, daughter's curiosity, and grandma's toothless grin were beginning to make me feel at home, Adrian said, "My cousin is coming over. He's a big radical. He thinks we should have capitalism immediately. He wants to talk to you." That was too bad. The last thing I needed after days of political talk was a man with a mission.

I was right. Adrian's cousin was intense and overbearing. He made me load a cassette into my minicorder, and for the next ninety minutes he bored me and everyone else with his exploits during the revolution—which included accompanying large numbers of terrified women to their apartments and calming them down—prefaced by his own history of Romania, his opinions about the Great Ronald Reagan, and other vast and impersonal matters. I managed to exchange a number of soulful looks with Betty during the radical cousin's soliloquy, but it was too little and too much. Several times either Betty, her daughter, or grand-mama protested the long-winded speech, but in vain. Even Adrian, embarrassed at long last, tried to put an end to the plume of words rising irrelevantly into the Bucharest evening. He, too, was unsuccessful. It was in this way—through the portentous speech of his cousin—that Adrian avenged himself on me for bringing the press with me earlier. It was tit for tat: my outsider against your outsiders. In that circle, with people between us, we somehow failed to meet.

It was fairly late when I said my good-byes. Betty gave me a little plastic box with two costumed Romanian peasants in it. I signed my book for them. The two dolls in the plastic box looked dressed for one of Ceauşescu's rallies, and I wondered if they weren't the standard gift offered to foreigners at the TV station in the earlier days. Or perhaps they were representations of us and the stiff way in which we had met, guarded, in costume. In any case the baffled cousin, who never finished his story—it undoubtedly had no end—was puzzled when, in parting, I told him that he ought to type his story on an old Underwood. Betty understood. Even Adrian seemed to.

All the way back I couldn't stop thinking about my friend Adrian, the TV bureaucrat. He reminded me of the three architects I'd met that morning. All of them were well-off men of the old regime. They probably knew each other under social circumstances. All of them undoubtedly knew or were known to the telephone operator at the Inter-Continental. What will become of this old, interconnected intelligentsia?

Adrian had been a friend, but I had never admired his writing. In Romania certain poets have near-divine status. In the general corruption of the Ceauşescu years, only writers, especially poets, had kept their integrity. In some ways Romanian literature was one of world's most sophisticated. It carried, in addition to the charge of its language, a mission of humanity, an intrinsic dissidence. Curiously enough, the writers I had admired twenty-five years before were still admired today. Even Adrian, in all his sophistication, deferred most humbly to people like literary critics Eugen Simion and Nicolae Manolescu.

Lying on my bed at the Inter-Con, I tried to grasp an image of the future of Romania. I couldn't. There were people with power, know-how, and connections who watched the storm from a protected place above the clouds. Very far below them thrashed the hungry and angry masses, demanding a better life. Between these two remote layers students, poets, and young revolutionary workers were busying themselves tearing down the old signs, posting new beautiful visions of democracy on the bare walls of sinister dormitory buildings. I was afraid for them.

Early next morning—I hadn't slept more than one hour, and I was beginning to resemble the haunted, unshaved radicals of Bucharest—I went to the Writers' Union on Calea Victoriei to speak to Mircea Dinescu.

The Writers' Union was a luxurious French-style building with a fin-de-siècle interior. A wrought brass and iron staircase twisted elegantly into the upper rotunda, where tall, upholstered brass doors led to official chambers. The doorman wore a uniform as elaborate as his door.

I remembered him! Twenty-six years ago, when I was a very young and hungry poet, I conceived the mad notion of presenting myself to the union with my handful of published poems and my head full of millions of yet unwritten ones, in order to get free food at the union restaurant. This gent put an immediate end to my impertinence with a firm shake of his luxuriant eyebrows.

Well, I was back now, and I was an American, and I was asking to see the president of the Writers' Union, Mircea Dinescu. I wiped my snow-covered boots on the Oriental grate. Behind my ancient nemesis there were three young soldiers with machine guns. One of them was noisily slipping bullets into his chamber. "Well, I'm back now," I said, "and I want to see the boss!" The old man let me in, but I can almost swear that the old generalissimo smelled a rat. Not the rat I am, but the rat I was.

As I climbed up the metal staircase, I wondered how many bosses the old fox had seen come and go.

Dinescu, the man who told the nation that its tyrant had fled, is a short, energetic man with a spare crew cut. He looks like Napoleon. Immediately after the revolution he was named provisional head of the Writers' Union. His last book, *Death Reads the Newspaper*, had been published outside Romania during the dictatorship. Branded a dissident, he spent the two years before the revolution under house arrest.

In Dinescu's office chaos reigned. Several people argued in various corners of the salon. Ana Blandiana was also there, and I was delighted to see her. I had met her when I was no older than seventeen, while she'd been twenty or twenty-one and seemed to me an elder and wiser—and incredibly beautiful—creature from another world. Her first book of poems, *First Person Plural,* had been a revelation of the first order to my generation of poets, the first generation to breach the lead skies of Stalinism in the mid-sixties. A Transylvanian like me—born in Timişoara in 1942—she embodied the idealism of the revolution. She was still beautiful. And warm. We greeted each other effusively. Someone handed me a delicate cup of espresso. The ornate surroundings weren't quite in keeping with the revolutionary atmosphere, a fact that I noted gently to Dinescu's visible distress.

"Fine," he said. "You think we should live in a cave?"

"We are making you a member of the Writers' Union," said Blandiana, "and tell Dorin Tudoran"—a prominent Romanian dissident now living in the United States—"to come back, too!"

"That's right." Dinescu, phone cradled under his chin, nodded.

While I sipped my coffee, Ana told me about the soldiers who carried her triumphantly to the radio station, a story I already knew, though hearing it from her made it intensely alive. "One kid even knew a poem of mine, the one beginning 'I wish I were a herder of snowflakes.' " I knew the poem, too:

> I wish I were a herder of snowflakes
> I'd like to have large snow flocks in my care
> Which I shall have to drive across long skies
> And bring them whiter, purer, back from there.

Dinescu was screaming on the phone at some uncomprehending authority that yes, indeed, the union was going to become fully independent, pay its own way, publish its own books and an independent self-sufficient newspaper. It was obviously not clear to the official on the other end of the phone how this was going to be accomplished or even where one would begin, but eventually he gave up. Neither was this clear to Dinescu because after he slammed down the phone, he smiled a wide gap-toothed smile and explained that he would very much like to know what an independent newspaper needed. I set about making a list with his Mont Blanc pen, a gold-nibbed writing machine that felt wonderful: computers, typesetters, layout tables, disks, paper, software, programmers. "Here you are, working for the revolution"—Dinescu grinned—"and that's my pen." Sure enough, I'd almost put it in my shirt pocket.

The various discussions in the room revolved around the new independent status of the union, a hitherto unknown situation that had to be conjured ex nihilo. When two rather ink-stained elderly editors with holey sweaters came into the room—straight it seemed from a Victorian clerking house—Blandiana indignantly asked them how in the world a man who was one of Ceauşescu's best flunkies had been named that very day head of Romania's news agency, Agerpress. "I can't believe it!" she exploded. "This guy used to sit at Ceauşescu's right at every official function!"

"He was protocol, not Securitate," said one of the meek ink spots.

A general discussion followed in which the reappearance of old party hacks in important jobs was discussed, bemoaned, and cursed. I related my experience of meeting the three evil stooges of architecture. Everywhere, it seemed, the apparatus was beginning to function again. Born-again dissidents (Romanians called them *de-azi de dimineaţă*, meaning "born this morning") popped up like mushrooms after rain. They beat their chests in public and on television, claiming that locked there, invisible to all but to God, themselves, and their immediate families, had been many anti-Ceauşescu sentiments.

Dinescu's office was the revolution in miniature. The unexpected had to be addressed at every turn, and it sprang up everywhere. On the telephone, over the next thirty minutes, Dinescu and Blandiana argued with various invisible functionaries over the meaning of democracy, the need for paper, the question of whether old Communist journals ought to be kept alive by the state, the convening of a writers' congress, the question of a Stalinist editor organizing a street demonstration to protest the loss of his journal, and a few other, less monumental things, like baby-sitting and a kilo of oranges. A mountain of telexes containing invitations to round tables and speeches abroad were piled on Dinescu's desk. "We cannot leave to go anywhere now!" he exclaimed. "If we absent ourselves for even an hour, they will steal our revolution!"

There it was again, the fear of some horrible trick that would make all the spilled blood meaningless. I had been hearing this more insistently since the morning. The unresolved questions ignored in the heat of battle were asserting themselves. What had happened to the thousands of Securitate men allegedly arrested by the Army? Where were they? When would the trials begin? The conversation turned invariably back to the events of December. It was hard to believe that only thirteen days had passed since the dictator had been deposed. But certain nagging questions were already asserting themselves. There was a suspicion—more or less articulate—that two events had taken place in December: the revolution and a palace coup. The revolution had been spontaneous, but the coup had been planned. Front President Iliescu, Prime Minister Roman, All-Purpose Brucan, Vice-President Mazilu, General Stanculescu, and many others had appeared too suddenly at the helm of the people's revolt. They all had been conveniently present at crucial moments—at the CP headquarters on December 21, on television that same evening. The entire leadership constellation was connected to the Communist party in complex and mysterious ways. But if these people had indeed been plotting against Ceauşescu, what prevented them from telling everyone about it? What were they still hiding? There was no question in the minds of anyone present that Ceauşescu had been overthrown by a popular revolution. Only honor would accrue to those who'd had the foresight to prepare for it. "Perhaps," ventured Blandiana, "the popular revolution took the plotters by surprise . . . though it served their ends well. The palace coup may now be using the revolution to install another Communist junta in place." It was a bold assertion. There was momentary silence. This was the first time that I had heard such a cogent supposition, one that threw a very different light on the multiplying mysteries of recent events. Speculation multiplied as well in the coming days, and soon every Romanian had his pet theory.

Literary critic Nicolae Manolescu had one of the bleakest: "We thought we were in a revolution . . . but were in fact caught in the crossfire between two Securitate gangs." I refused to believe him. The thought that this beautiful revolution with all its martyrs had been stolen made me too angry. "I may be wrong," Manolescu conceded, "but one thing is certain. Romania is quickly becoming a plotless detective novel."

"But that is not what I returned to read!" I shouted. "Romania right now is a poem, not a novel!" Manolescu looked at me slyly. Well, he was a literary critic, a writer of prose. I am a poet. There is never an end to either speculation or genre rivalry. For the moment, no matter what the truth, the young revolutionary guards now occupying media offices, factories, and ministries had no choice but to stay awake. Their young adrenal revolt had to outlast the patience of bureaucrats and the real or imaginary depths of twisted alliances and betrayals. I knew, of course, that this was a mighty tall order in the Balkans, a place not known for the persistence of its idealisms. After every revolution (and not just in the Balkans) the bureaucrats had come out, sharpened their pencils, begun their grind again. "The chains of tormented mankind," said Kafka, "are made out of red tape."

The job of my fellow writers here was to improvise their revolution as brilliantly as possible, so that there was no turning back. I could hear their hearts beating loud under the strain of euphoric sleeplessness and worry. A note from downstairs announced a man with a manuscript of poems from prison.

"Oh, I'm tired of politics," said Blandiana. "I want to talk poetry!" But clearly she was enjoying all this. This *was* poetry, a big revolutionary poem improvised on the go, a sensual, passionate, and inspired poem like one of Ana's own.

It was another matter for thousands of others, an army of official scribes whose nauseating bows and scrapes to Ceauşescu had oozed unread on the front pages of newspapers. Some of them had quickly changed their rhymes to praise the revolution instead of the dictator, but they had been (so far) met with disbelief and derision. Their larger-than-life dean, the court poet Adrian Păunescu, had been nearly lynched by a furious mob who remembered his bootlicking verses. He tried to climb over the gate of the U.S. Embassy to escape, but he was too fat. At the last minute a Romanian police patrol took him into custody and saved his life. I had met Păunescu in 1965 before I left. Not yet a court poet, he used his gift for grandiloquence and bombast to impress the girls at an outdoor tavern where we were drinking. "Here is to *vino* and *veritas!*" I recall him shouting. Even then I had my doubts that there was much *veritas* under the *vino*. But he had once been a generous and careless being, giving off the raw energy of poesy and youth, and I was sorry to see how far and how low his natural power had taken him. It is most distressing because it seemed—at least at the beginning of 1965— that the habit of writing empty phrases in praise of tractors and Communist bosses was a thing of the past that had died with Stalin. How wrong I was! "He is the honey in the words," went one panegyric to Ceauşescu, written soon after his ascension. "A visionary sweet-kissing of the homeland's earth," trilled a somewhat bizarre other. Păunescu began leading huge nationalist rallies in chants of "Ceauşescu! Romania!, Romania! Ceauşescu!," whipping the crowd into a frenzy with his bombastic verses.

The curious relation between poets and tyrants is a subject worth exploring. In many cases court poets like Păunescu legitimized tyrants by covering brute reality with sentimental clichés. At the same time some of the strongest dissidents in Eastern and Central Europe were poets who are now part of new revolutionary governments. The difference was not simply talent, because some of the spineless lyricists were not devoid of it. There was a more fundamental difference, a basic sense of right and wrong. As a young poet in 1965 I was certainly headed for trouble, or at the very least for the Romanian Army, because I not only was unwilling to write paeans to the leader but had already penned some fiery manifestos calling for instant liberties. Ceauşescu's requirement to have poetry written for him, and later for his wife, should have been a signal to the outside world that the little man who would soon impersonate—with great success—an international statesman had already, in the mid-sixties, begun the process of becoming king. Poets are seismographs, but who listens to them? The majority of Romanian poets either stayed out of politics in disgust or became dissidents and exiles. One of them, Marin Sorescu, was watched by Securitate and received death threats simply because one of his books had been found at a center for transcendental meditation, an illegal practice in Romania.

Other punishments for unauthorized thoughts were more hideous. Many writers suspected of dissidence received summons from Securitate to meet with a certain colonel. When they arrived at the secret police headquarters, they were shown into a bare waiting room. After a few hours someone would come to tell them that the colonel was unavailable and that the appointment would be rescheduled. Many people chalked these incidents off to psychological intimidation. However, six months or a year later many of those invited to the Securitate headquarters became sick with cancer. They were diagnosed with large, unusual tumors. Cancer is a private and shattering thing. Few of these people made any connection between their visits to Securitate and their devastating illnesses. In 1988 Mihai Ion Pacepa, the head of the Romanian secret police, defected to the West. He revealed the existence of a program to kill opponents of the regime with lethal doses of radiation. The room where the writers had been waiting for the invisible colonel was equipped with a cobalt device that radiated them. The evil flower of such an idea could have only originated in the deep murk of a Byzantine tyrant's mind. Ceaușescu's vision transcended time. The revolution had now upset all the poets' little islands, whether surrounded by the barbed wire of censorship and fear or dedicated to dictator worship, and the future was uncertain. Nor did the dead rest easy. The talk of reconciliation was still part of a quickly evaporating euphoria.

"The people want blood," said Dinescu thoughtfully, referring to that day's demonstration for the reinstatement of the death penalty, abolished by the front after the execution of the Ceaușescu. "We should forgive!" he said emphatically.

"We should," said Blandiana ironically, "but how do we make *them* forgive?" The author of *First Person Plural* was a master of pronouns.

"I'm afraid we may slip into anarchy," one of the editors said. He was one half of the inky pair.

But anarchy and creativity are often indistinguishable, and this was one revolution that needed all the creativity it could muster to succeed against inertia, paranoia, and plots hatched in palaces and tunnels.

After I had said my good-byes, I put my hand in my pocket and found there an appeal I had received the day before from three sweet-faced young people. "We, the Romanian yoga community, are asking all the yoga groups in the world for help. . . . We have been arrested, beaten, persecuted. . . ." I sailed past the doorman and flashed him the V sign. He didn't respond. This isn't anarchy, old man. It's the coming out of people kept for so long in the dark we are surprised that they exist at all. You would doubtlessly stop these yogis at the door, but Dinescu and Blandiana would, I believe, receive them upstairs. It's not only possible to run a country with poets but necessary.

On the way back to the Inter-Con Petre stopped the car in the middle of the street. "Listen," he said with evident emotion. "I am forty years old, and I have never heard this sound!" I listened. The church bells of Bucharest were ringing loudly and clearly for the first time in four decades. As we lurched back through the snow, I thought of those four silent decades. No bells, no loud voices, no loss of control, no rage. For all those years Romania'd been a nation of whisperers, people buried deep under a snowlike blanket of fear.

Back in New Orleans, on February 6, I gave the yogis' appeal to Allen Ginsberg, who promised to help. Allen told me that he had just received an invitation from President Havel to return to Czechoslovakia.

In 1968 the students had elected Allen Ginsberg King of May, a great ceremonial honor that entitled him to all-night foolishness. One hundred thousand students paraded their belaureled poet-king through the ancient streets of Prague, singing and carrying on. When the "king" returned to his hotel in the morning after the revelry, he was met by two secret policemen, who put him on a plane for London and confiscated his private diary. In May he received his stolen diary back from the hands of the country's president. The powers that be should never underestimate poets. On the other hand, one must watch closely those who hate both youth and book learning. The student-worker-soldier alliances formed in the spontaneous heat of the revolution may unravel when the age-old tactics of manipulation and intimidation, mixed with working-class resentments against privilege and wit, reappear. A sign at one of the first pro-Salvation Front demonstrations by so-called miners on January 16 read ENOUGH THINKING, LET'S GET WORKING! That's a frightening enough thought to make me *never* sleep again.

9

Where the
Heart Is

I was ready for a stiff drink and a hot bath when I returned to the Inter-Con, but my lord and master Sullivan was waiting for me. "We have to get your story on the satellite tonight. . . . You have an hour to write it." I thanked him profusely in language I rarely use and set down to write it. I put through a telephone call to America, hoping that it would come before I passed out. I was beginning to have a grudging respect for the exhausting profession of journalism, which, in its way, was very much like the revolution. One could not afford sleep while events were unfolding. I was no more than a page into my story when the phone rang. It was not America. A newspaperman named Octav Buruiana was in the lobby, wanting to interview me for *Libertatea* ("Liberty"), one of Romania's new papers. "Fifteen minutes!" I told him.

Buruiana was an intense young man with the dark-rimmed eyes of the revolution. He showed me his press card with his photograph. "Old habits," he said. "You never knew if anyone was who they said they were. . . ."

"I'm a trusting soul," I told him.

He asked me several questions, and I answered as briefly and honestly as I could. At one point I shocked him. He asked me how quickly Romania could have American-style democracy, and I told him that American democracy had taken a long time, that it had plenty of flaws,

141

and that I was here precisely to sound a number of cautionary notes since as an American I knew well what those flaws are. "There is no point in quitting the worship of Lenin for the adoration of Vanna White," I told him. I then had to explain who Vanna White was, and that alone took longer than ten minutes. At the end of the interview Buruiana revealed another purpose to his visit. The newspaper he worked for was still in the hands of the Communists. He had succeeded on the first day of the revolution in printing certain articles that had been rejected by his editors. He had gone directly to the printers, who had threatened to go on strike if his articles were not published. Since then he had been increasingly isolated within the paper. He now wanted to start a truly independent newspaper. He asked my advice.

"Do it," I told him.

The old press law, which institutionalized censorship, had been abolished, and there was as yet no new press law. Buruiana believed that this was the ideal time to publish a nonaffiliated newspaper that would attempt to make it entirely in the marketplace. His ideal was an American-style newspaper with opposing editorial opinions and as much news as fitted. I gave him all my Romanian money, some two hundred dollars exchanged at street rates. It was a mere pittance, but it cost less than that to print the first issue! When he left, I wondered if I had done the right thing. After all, I really *didn't* know him. What if he was a scam artist? I had been warned that such were already operating. Thinking back on his intelligent intensity, I dismissed the idea. In a revolution you must trust strangers. One's old friends are a more complex matter. On February 28, 1990, I had registered mail at the LSU campus office in Baton Rouge. The package contained the four first issues of *Observatorul* ("Observer"), a weekly independent newspaper. There was a note from Mr. Buruiana, the editor, thanking me for my modest help. "Let the world know," he said, "that this daily is in no one's pay." It is a vigorous, polemical, smart, well-written twelve-page paper. On the back page of the first issue was my interview, headlined LET THE YOUNG HAVE THEIR SAY!

When my call to the States came through, I was only still half done with my piece, and satellite time was fast approaching. "How are things at home?" I asked Alice.

"We are watching everything about Romania!" she said. "We are all in the revolution!"

I talked to my son.

"I got an A on my report!" Tristan said.

That was good. And it gave me a good reason to keep my eyes and my heart open. It was eight hours earlier and spring in New Orleans, but everything was connected. After our conversation I wrote furiously. I dashed up the stairs and got the story to Michael seconds before the satellite left the skies of Romania for another part of the globe. That spinning little object was more powerful than all the bureaucrats in the world.

Next morning, I was ready to leave Bucharest. The past three days had been remarkable. Even those things that under normal circumstances are banal and uninteresting, like watching television or having lunch, had been made sharply significant by the times. Time itself was stretched to accommodate the rapid unfolding of a thousand events. As in a fairy tale where the hero grows ten years in a day, a minute was a day, a day was a year. Three years had thus passed in three days, but my heart was still yearning for the real return, to the town of my birth, Sibiu, in the Transylvanian mountains. My childhood was there, and the friends of my childhood. I wanted also to see my uncle Rihard and my aunt Elena, my only living relatives still in my homeland. I'd heard that they had been moved from their house to an apartment building in the town of Alba Iulia near Sibiu. An address with several long, scribbled numbers had reached me via one of our old neighbors, who now lives in Canada. They had no telephone, and they were very old. I had written to them, but there had been no answer. I didn't know if they were still living.

We heard contradictory reports about the state of the road and the situation in the Sibiu region. One man had it that the fighting was still raging in Sibiu, which had been the headquarters of Nicu Ceauşescu, the princeling. The roads were dangerous; attacks by armed gangs were a certainty. But somebody else said that he had heard on the radio that peace had been restored. The Army was in full control, and there was only scattered shooting. We also heard that a dam had been dynamited and the highway was closed. Rumors swirled about us like snow, and it kept snowing.

For five hundred dollars Dumitru would take us to Transylvania in his eight-seat van. "I can't think of anybody else crazy enough to go now," he said. He had a crooked grin on his Gypsy face that showed his gold tooth to good advantage. He smoked hand-rolled cigarettes on the other side of his mouth. One of his eyes was semipermanently closed in cynical prescience of all that was transitory. Dumitru looked capable of driving off a cliff just to see somebody's expression. He was good enough for me.

We left the Inter-Con fortress very early on the morning of January 4 and took the nearly deserted icy highway out of Bucharest, in the direction of Piteşti. Gusts of snow whooshed past the van windows. We moved through and over snow past Ceauşescu's frozen palaces, bathed in the eerie milk of dawn. By the Botanical Garden, Dumitru pointed to the ice-encased branches of the exotic trees and said: "He was ready to get that for himself, too." Had he gotten the garden, he would have razed it, no doubt, and grown cement towers on it. In front of the Political Sciences Academy there were two patched flags, the first I had seen. I felt my heart tighten. Dumitru pointed them out to me: "That's wrong, he said, "We ought to keep the goddamn hole in that flag till hell's frozen over and ready to cross . . . like this road. . . ." I agreed wholeheartedly. Dumitru was keeping an eye on events. I wished also that he'd keep his eyes on the road. Like all our other Romanian drivers, he drove as if ice were what all roads were normally made out of. We were soon sailing along at speeds that exceeded the numbers on his dial. The road was full of potholes and uneven patches of ice. We lurched from hole to hole and weaved and spun like a small drunk airplane in a crosswind.

As we reached the outskirts of the city, we saw immense lines for milk, bread, and newspapers. People stood in the numbing cold, talking, moving their hands, pounding the ground to keep warm. They were dressed in long gray coats with lambskin hats pulled over their ears. Some wore several sweaters, and the women looked like onions with a half dozen skirts wrapped around them, as well as elaborate layers of kerchiefs around their heads. I remembered being a child in those lines, endlessly fascinated by the ceaseless chatter of the adults, gathering news tidbits for my mother, little bits of salacious gossip for my friends, even rare words I didn't understand, which I put in a little notebook I had, called "Strange Words I Heard in Line." These were the working people of Bucharest, of Romania. They had stood in line for forty-five years patiently waiting for the barest necessities. A revolution was going on, but the lines were still long—the same as the week before, the year before, the previous decade. . . . Are there, I wonder, people on this earth, whole countries, whole continents perhaps, doomed forever to the lines of misery, anticipation, and scarcity? As the world I know in America grows more satiated, more colorful, more overstimu-lated, these lines get longer, more desperate, the people in them more drab . . . and there is less at the counter when, after aeons of standing, they arrive, hands outstretched, the sweaty money they hold worthless after all that time. . . . Still, there is a difference between these lines and those of my childhood. No one is listening, waiting to report peo-ple's discontents. . . . At least I hope so. Every word people speak now would have been considered treason only moments ago. And what of those people whose jobs had been to listen and to report? Do they feel shame, or embarrassment, or fear? They certainly haven't disappeared; they are doubtlessly still in the line, listening. (After all, they, too, have families they have to feed.) Full of unusable information, would they eventually disintegrate? Publicly confess? Get religion? I had the fleeting vision of a revolution that works on the honor system: Bad people arrest themselves.

Throughout my childhood I believed that one had to lower one's voice whenever speaking seriously. A normal tone of voice, possible to overhear, was reserved exclusively for trivia. One would use several tones in the course of a conversation, even within a single sentence. For in-stance, my mother would send me to stand in line for bread. As she handed me the ration book, she would say in a normal voice, "Get two loaves and five rolls," and then, lowering her voice, "if there are enough coupons," and then, lowering her voice even more, "and find out what people are saying." This last phrase was well understood. We stood in breadlines not just for bread but also for the news. The breadline was our newspaper since the actual newspapers printed nothing but lies. Rumors, innuendos, and mishearing made the rounds faster than print anyway.

Soon we were outside the city. The highway was frozen solid and slippery. The first billboards on the road listed the output of neighboring factories: threshing machines, plows, seeders, tractors. They were grimy, in contrast with the immense snowfields beyond them. Here was the proud iconography of my childhood. The only things conspicuously missing were the oversize portraits of Lenin, Stalin, Marx, Gheorghiu-Dej, and Ceauşescu that stood grimly in the grime above the lists of machines. When I was a kid, I used to think that those gents made all those machines, and I couldn't figure out how five old people could make all that by themselves. Later they told me that I was going to help them when I grew up. I was a young pioneer. I often looked up at the immense brass statue of Lenin in front of the printing house and felt my insignificance. In January an enthusiastic crew worked for three days to pull Lenin off his pedestal. The crew originally hoped to bring him down in an hour. But like other bulky monuments of the ceremonial Communist past, he was more stubborn than originally thought. Three trucks carted him away to be stored for either an auction, a new lease on symbolism or—my favorite—the "dustbin of history." All through my school years things the Communists didn't like were always thrown into the "dustbin of history." Everything interesting and everybody fun was there: Henry Ford, Winston Churchill, Leon Trotsky. Now Lenin joined them.

A tall billboard leaned backward in a field, its slogans covered with snow. It was perfectly white like a cinema screen. It was waiting for something truthful and powerful to be projected on it, the story perhaps of these days. Even the snow was doing its bit for the revolution. "Look at that," said Rich, "a Transylvania drive-in!"

We began to see the first pointy haystacks that are characteristic of rural Romania. I have never seen haystacks like these anywhere in the world, and I watch for them. There are countless popular sayings involving haystacks. "Timişoara," someone told me, "was the spark over a very dry haystack." With snow on them they looked like the peasants' lambskin hats. They are baled by hand by young people who work singing until way past dusk on long summer days. When the stars come out, they fall exhausted on the hay, and many romances begin that way. By winter the romancers have married, and the hungry cows eat the snowy hay. In the days of the Turkish occupation highwaymen used to hide in the haystacks from the Turkish patrols, which would stab the haystacks at random to see if anyone was there. Angry fathers whose daughters hadn't come home for supper would likewise pitchfork their stacks. Many a curious scar, called the love fork, adorned the young men of rural Romania. I had always loved the touchingly tender way the Romanian haystacks dot the fields, a kind of writing legible only to crows.

The sub-Carpathian hills were beginning just ahead of us. On the side of the road a woman was walking with a bundle of snowy sticks on her back. Gathering sticks for fire in the snow is the job of old women who like to walk alone in the deep woods, mumbling to themselves. They show up in fairy tales as witches. A man walked out of the forest just ahead of her. He took off his hat and bowed. For hundreds of years

Romanian peasants have walked like this between villages. There is a whole protocol to such meetings on the road. After the men take off their hats and bow, the women curtsy. They exchange a rigorous set of greetings and good wishes, and then it's on to the news of their villages. When enough news has been exchanged, they go their different ways and can't wait until they can pass on the news of the road. Thanks to the newless Communist newspapers, the village telegraph still works in the same personal fashion.

The countryside now gave way without warning to the industrial hells of Piteşti. Huge oil refineries were spewing obviously unregulated black clouds into the air. Children with sooty faces played on mounds of dirt-streaked snow. No amount of washing would suffice to get that grainy soot off. This was one of Ceauşescu's grandiose megaindustrial complexes out of which he poured rivers of molten steel into the flesh of the country. This is where he would have liked to move the populations of the clean little Carpathian villages. Piteşti was a living illustration of the ecological tragedy of Eastern Europe. One of the first political groups organized after the revolution was the Romanian Ecological Movement. After Chernobyl everyone had become aware of the fragility of the environment. I am told that there are still herds of sheep in the regions bordering the Ukraine that sport X's inked on shaved circles of skin. Those sheep are radioactive. Even their wool has to be treated before it is sold. They graze listlessly on hillsides with their X-ed sides, creatures of the industrial nightmare.

On January 2 I met two young men in the Inter-Con lobby who were handing foreign journalists the mimeographed manifesto of the Romanian Ecological party. The next morning they were back with a revised program. They had first formed the Romanian Ecological party, but after a stormy night of discussion they had decided to constitute themselves into a *movement*. It was a wise thing. As a movement they could drive home the point that environmental concerns transcend politics, that air and water are not partisan issues. An extraordinary story of devastation had been unfolding since December. The town of Copşa-Mică was called by *Time* magazine—with a bit of hyperbolic journalese—the blackest town in the world. The slogan of the Romanian Ecological Movement is "A clean being in a clean country in a clean world!" Insofar as these words take the environment for their target, they are good. But there is also an echo of nationalism in them. It disturbed me at the time. It disturbs me much more today when I find that an unholy alliance is taking place in many Romanian cities between ecologists and nationalists of the far right who see in the word "clean" a license for race hatred. Piteşti—and not only Piteşti—needs the Romanian Ecological Movement in its most active, physical sense. REM should concentrate in closing down polluting hells, which are, in any case, completely inefficient, a job that is more than sufficient. As we drove past the rows of soot-covered trees and grotesquely shaped mounds of dirty snow, I remembered similar horrors in West Virginia and, closer to home, Baton Rouge. The huge smokestacks and storage tanks looked very much the same. And come to think of it, the "blackest town in the world" may be no blacker than the downwind river communities near the EXXON refinery in my home state. We also need the Romanian Ecological Movement in Baton Rouge.

"Looks just like home," I said to Michael.

"You *are* home," he said.

I felt suspended—for a moment—in midair. Where was home?

We stopped for lunch at a country inn at Valea Ursului ("valley of the bear"). This was deeply forested hill country. We had been steadily climbing for the better part of two hours. The inn was a low stone building with a wooden porch at the end of a narrow path. A little bell chimed when I opened the steamed glass door. A number of country folk wrapped in long sheepskins with their hats on were watching television. They nodded politely when we walked in, but we were not great objects of curiosity. Their eyes were riveted to the little TV set mounted on the wall between a pair of deer horns.

We ordered porc coup (ciorbă de carne), a delicious sour soup with carrots and cabbage, grilled ham and fries, and mineral water. We were still talking among ourselves, unaware that the room had become very silent. Everyone was glued to television. When I finally looked at the little TV set, I noticed that it was showing, once again, the mass graves in Timişoara. There was a close-up of a mother with her baby to her bosom. They looked peacefully asleep, but they both were dead, shot with a single bullet. There were tears on the craggy faces of the peasants in the room, and some of them crossed themselves. Our conversation, too, came to a standstill as we watched. They were showing photographs of the dead and pronouncing their names, followed by the word *Deces* ("dead"). Simple young faces of boys and girls with country names. Ion. Petre. Trandafir. Ioana. Rodica. Kiva. Dead. Dead. Dead. Dead. The peasants' faces looked carved in stone. These were their names and the names of their children. At long last, a time in which I didn't even dare lift the soup spoon to my lips, the litany was over, and a happier image appeared: Nadia Comăneci at the 1976 Olympics, making her superb debut.

She was only a bitty girl here, years away from tragedy and scandal, an innocent of genius on the world stage. Since the revolution her triumphs were shown on television over and over, a symbol of grace and triumph. Her defection shortly before the revolution was being hailed as an act of defiance to the Ceaușescu regime, like another Olympic performance, her greatest perhaps, involving as it did, darkness and a mined border. She had been a pampered child of the elite, linked romantically to the princeling, living in luxury, but the winner of twenty-one Olympic gold medals risked all that for a night leap into the unknown. The Romanians, who had become increasingly desperate to escape in the past decade, applauded her. Nadia's defection was also hailed in the West, but things went awry there. There'd been a whole generation of young girls named Nadia in America after 1976 in honor of the breathtaking sprite on TV. The little Nadias' mothers did not look kindly on the new Nadia of 1989. At first her escape was seen by the American media as a heroic act, which it certainly was. Immediately afterward, however, it was revealed that she had contacted no one she knew in America, not even her old coach, Géza Cárolyi, the so-called Rasputin of gymnastics whose famous mustache had graced the background of numerous Olympians. Furthermore, she flaunted her relationship with the handsome Constantin, her escape partner, who was reported to be, by turns, a "French friend," then "a Romanian émigré," then her "manager." But worst of all, he turned out to be married, with children. His wife, who lived under penurious circumstances in a small apartment in Florida with their five offspring, first heard about her husband's doings from the news media gathered about her door in great, agitated clusters. When Nadia was asked if she knew that Constantin was married, she answered, "So what?" and stuck out her tongue. The picture of Nadia sticking out her tongue played to great effect on the front pages of every newspaper in the United States, giving rise to billions of comments, millions of which had to do, no doubt, with the fact that the slim girl of yore had become a rather hefty Frau. It was a story made for the tabloids. The aggrieved but shocked wife went on radio and TV—managing to pay her back rent in the process—and Nadia's stock plummeted. In a single week one of the world's most desirable commercial

mercial properties, for whom advertisers would have thrown themselves off cliffs, became a compromised piece of merchandise good for nothing but a *National Enquirer*-type movie of the week. It was an amazing story of riches to rags, the story of a dramatic fall from an exalted pedestal into a cesspool of yellow journalism, something possible only in America, where whatever happens happens fast.

That, at least, was the American view. But I, along with many others, saw the story differently. Not only was Nadia a hero for escaping, but she was also a hero for coming over to the land of freedom, opportunities, and free speech and doing exactly what a free person would do. That is to say, doing whatever she felt like doing, without having coaches, advertisers, moralists, and managers tell her the score. She had had enough of that in Romania. She had fled her gilded cage for precisely all the reasons best idealized by our propaganda. And if she acted stupidly, it was her decision to do so. When the pretty anchor in New Orleans, whom I'd watched for years strain to read her teleprompter through blue contact lenses, asked me in all innocence, "Do you think that the revolution in Romania happened because of Nadia?" I answered flippantly. But in retrospect, it was quite a breathtaking question that may have been one of the most perceptively prophetic—though still stupid—questions ever asked. The revolution did come to Romania not because of Nadia but for the same reason that Nadia defected. No one could take it anymore.

Sitting in a simple inn in Transylvania, before a bowl of peasant soup, I could feel an abyss of perception open between me and the folks at the other tables. They watched Nadia with the religious emotion of worshipers before an icon. If they had known the entire story of her life and of her escape, they would have found a way to transform it into myth and legend and still save the undeniably magical little girl before them from calumny and baseness. But their legends and myths would have soon crumbled before the concerted power of the tabloids. There were no tabloids in Transylvania yet, thank God. But it wouldn't be long. These people were living in the last few privileged moments of the premodern age, seconds before the liberty they had welcomed so warmly would destroy them with its ultrarealism. I couldn't finish my soup.

We passed small villages dominated by the spires of wooden churches. Now and then we saw roadside shrines, big stone crosses with little huts to pray in. They marked places where travelers died, where battles were fought, where miracles occurred. The country we were driving through had seen thousands of years of wars, conquests, refugees, invasions, migrations. The simple faith embodied in the roadside shrines kept the people going through all of it. As the motor of Dumitru's van droned on through what might have looked like beautiful but desolate country to my traveling companions, I began to hear a muted sound, a familiar rhythm not unlike the sound of my computer keys as I am typing. It came closer, then receded, something both comforting and ancient. . . . I looked back and saw, coming around a bend on the road, a wide peasant cart drawn by two sturdy horses. The cart was loaded full of hay, and two peasants in long sheepskin coats sat over it, holding their whips like batons over the clippity-clop of hooves on hard snow. They were almost too unbearably picturesque, like fake peasants performing in a pseudofolk tableau. They lifted their fur caps as they passed. Ceaușescu's propaganda had made so much of the "peasant" that his reality was hard to fathom. One of the subtler crimes of nationalist propaganda is to make even the genuine unreal, to turn the world to postcard and caricature. One of the artistic tasks of the future will be to extract the peasant from the pseudopeasant, folk music from "folkloric ensembles," folk art from "popular socialist art." While I busied myself with these reflections, Dumitru stopped the car so Rich could take their pictures. Both men, a father and son, averted their faces. I was embarrassed for them. What "folklorization" hadn't accomplished, our tourist cameras surely will. The last "real" peasant will soon be living like Ishi, the "last of his tribe," in a museum.

We were in the high mountains now. The ragged crags of the Carpathians stretched before us. Enormous valleys descended between peaks, covered with virgin snow. "These are some of the most beautiful snowscapes I have ever seen," said Noah. I knew them well. I had sailed their paths on skis in my youth. Here began Transylvania, my magical land. Under the snow were the rocks I came from, the rocks that made me, no doubt, the strong and silent type I am. People of the mountains are taciturn, unlike the chatterboxes of the plains. We speak little and slowly and only when we must. There is an ancient rivalry, riddled with jokes and insults, between the people of the mountains and those from the capital. We think of them as glib and sneaky; they think of us as slow and easy to trick. I knew now another reason why I couldn't wait to leave Bucharest for the Carpathians. Here began my true soul.

We passed now through old Romanian, Hungarian, and German

villages with poetic names: Little-One-Asleep-in-the-Forest, Rose-with-Many-Thorns, Bitter Crosswind, Maiden of the Bear. The wooden houses perched on steep hillsides had the carved eaves and columns that inspired Brâncuşi's sculptures. We saw his "Endless Column" many times, supporting simple porches. Every house had a water well in the yard. On the lip of each well was a tin cup for the passerby to quench his thirst. Dracula, whose kingdom extended to these parts, once had a gold drinking cup set on such a well in the middle of a village. So fearsome was his reputation that no one stole it. This story is still told hereabouts. The villages gave an impression of wholesomeness, cleanliness, and plenty. But the plenty was illusory. Still, the village people lived better than the city folk. They had chickens and pigs and the wide mountains. Children were sledding on the steep village streets. There were sheep on the snow following each other the way Commies used to follow the party line.

As we climbed to higher altitudes, there were thick pine forests. The pines were intricately laden with bright snow. Mist scintillated about them. The ice-encased electrical wires shimmered and sang. I remembered now that it was winter throughout most of my childhood. I saw myself half frozen waiting for the school bus; looking dreamily out the frosted window at the mountains while the history teacher droned on about Stephen the Great and Vlad the Impaler; walking on snowed-in mountain paths all alone, listening to the silence. I was a winter child back in my winter mountains.

The Carpathians, a link between the Alps and the Himalayas, have a presence of their own. They are grand, occasionally foreboding and mysterious, but also lyrical and sweet, with delightfully hidden valleys and small idyllic plateaus where opium poppies turn everything red in the summer and the weary hiker can fall asleep to dream of Xanadu. The spice routes from the Orient passed through here. Ceauşescu, his wife, and their son, Nicu, liked to hunt in these mountains. On September 24, 1989, they slaughtered forty-six black mountain goats under optimal conditions arranged by their staff, including aerial spotting. Earlier that month Nicu killed two big bears that had been lured for thirty days to the same spot with food. Nicu shot them when they came for their supper. Shortly before the family itself became the object of a nationwide hunt, the dictator ordered the destruction of a beautiful valley for a heliport to be used in later hunting expeditions. It was never built.

Ahead of us was the proud medieval city of Făgăraş, and beyond that, at the foot of one of Transylvania's highest peaks, was my home-town, Sibiu. High above the road stood ruins of old Austro-Hungarian customhouses, medieval fortresses, and monasteries. This was the road Bram Stoker's Jonathan Harker followed in search of Dracula.

But there were other, more disquieting signs on the road. A burned truck listed to the side of a ravine. It had camouflage markings. A little farther an abandoned olive green bus blocked part of the road. It looked ominously silent, and I slid deep into my seat, expecting an ambush. But there was no one there. We passed also several roadblocks manned by villagers with tricolor armbands and antique hunting rifles. They waved us through after a look at our passports. High above us in a small stone booth on a dam over a raging mountain river stood a sentry with a telescopic rifle. These mountains, which have harbored bandits since the Middle Ages, will no doubt see a new generation of outlaws. High above Sibiu, at Păltinis, was one of Nicu Ceaușescu's training camps for Libyians and Palestinians. In Sibiu fighting had gone on longer than in any other part of the country. I worried for my aunt and uncle, for my high school friends and for their children, but also for the beautiful old buildings in the center square where I had spent my dreamy child-hood. I wanted everything to be exactly the way I remembered it.

10

Sibiu

I feared that my first glimpse of Sibiu would be like my first glimpse of Bucharest, a nightmare of cranes surrounding cement bunkers. It did appear that way at first. We entered the city from its worst side, through rows of new buildings. It became immediately apparent that we were not only in the new part of town but at the scene of recent fighting. Smoke still hovered over certain buildings, little black puffs in an impossibly blue, cold winter sky. As we neared the smoke, we saw burned armored carriers lying to the side of the road, small tanks parked on the sidewalks with their machine guns pointing in all directions, and several large tanks. There was an elaborate roadblock just before the Sibiu Inter-Continental Hotel. When we were waved through, we saw that this Inter-Con had seen more serious fire than its Bucharest counterpart. Several floors were blown away, and the windows were broken on almost every floor. The facade was riddled with bullet holes, and chipped plaster floated in a cloud of dust over the street. Overturned and partially burned automobiles were being towed by military trucks. The buildings on the other side of the Inter-Con had been the center of the fighting. The former militia and Securitate building was a smoking ruin. The Army headquarters across the street had a number of big wounds, but it appeared to have survived pretty well. Tanks with their cannons pointed at the burned skeleton of the militia building stood behind a partially torn high wire fence. I didn't remember this part of town, which looked, for all practical purposes, like every other Ceauşescu proleburb. But as we drove toward the Împăratul Romanilor ("Emperor of the Ro-

155

manians") Hotel in the town center, the streets began to narrow, and my old city started to emerge like a sweet nut from an ugly shell. First, the crooked streets began to rise, and then churches, squares, and plazas appeared. The light was quickly dying, though it was only about 4:00 P.M. The sun sets early behind the mountains in the winter. As we drove past some buildings I was starting to recognize, I wanted to jump out of the car, run through the streets like a kid, and shout incomprehensible but delightful things the way children do when the world is (happily) too much for them.

That is exactly what I did. Rich trailed with his microphone, Michael and Noah walked close by, blowing into their gloved hands, which were nonetheless freezing fast, and Dumitru followed with the van slowly, a difficult proposition because children came from seemingly nowhere and surrounded him. Some climbed on the back bumper just the way I used to when the trolley started going uphill. The bitter cold was familiar in some undescribable way. I remembered the way it felt when I waited for the bus in the morning before school

"Hey," I said to Rich, talking mostly to myself—a hilarious spectacle to our ragamuffin audience, no doubt—"this is the street I used to follow down to the Cibin River with my scruffy friends, until Ilona, our maid, who looked after me while my mother and her husband were away, brought me in, ripped my clothes off, submerged me in a tin tub of scalding hot water, and vigorously scrubbed off the grime. I used to sit in her lap after one of these washings, wrapped in a large towel, and sink deeply into the blissful heat emanating from her. My mother fired her because her soldier boyfriend spent time at the house, and together they ate all the food in the refrigerator. My mother thought that I was starving to death. I was a skinny kid, but I stuffed myself with tidbits pilfered from the market by the river. . . ."

The kids all around us were a noisy, scruffy, and skinny bunch. The older people stared politely but walked by. Mothers pulled little babies and groceries on sleds through the middle of the street. I stopped in front of the building where my father's photo shop used to be. It was a fabric store now. Back then there were pictures of people who posed for a long time in their best clothes. In the fall my father displayed the class portraits of the high school graduates he photographed. I used to walk into the shop and startle the customers with my cap gun. "You really have to stop that," my father once told me mildly in what was his single and harshest display of paternal authority.

I was born on December 20, 1946, on Elisabethstrasse in the lower city of Sibiu, known to the Germans as Hermannstadt and to the Hungarians as Nagyszeben. I was also born the year communism came to Romania on the turrets of Russian tanks and the year my father acquired the photo shop. "Timing is destiny," my uncle Rihard used to say imperiously while holding a cup of tea in one hand and his lion-knobbed cane in the other. He knew wherefrom he spoke: At the height of his military career in the pre-war Romanian Army he was made to resign his commission because he married my aunt Elena, a Jewess. After the Soviet occupation he was sentenced to fifteen years of hard labor on the Danube-Black Sea canal project. He survived in time for the ascension of Ceauşescu, which made everyone's life worse but made his a sheer hell. His timing had been all wrong. Mine was a little better. My father, to whom my uncle never spoke, was a Communist. He was also a rake, an adventurer, a gambler, and not much of a photographer, according to my mother, who divorced him when I was but six months old. What exactly his nonphotography job consisted of I never knew, but he had a big black car and wore a leather jacket, frightening objects in those days. I don't know what kind of Communist my father was, but to Uncle Rihard they all were scoundrels. "The Romanian Communist party in 1946," my uncle proclaimed, "was a thousand Russian spies."

On the main street was the Russian bookstore, Kniga Russkaya, where nobody ever went. I did, after Ilona left, and I became a sullen and snitty brat who frowned upon things and strolled with hands behind back, young head bowed under the oppression of maternal tyranny. Grand plots and magnificent speeches hatched inside me as I gazed with feigned interest upon the shelves of red-bound complete works by Marx, Engels, Lenin, Stalin, and Gheorghiu-Dej. I don't think Ceauşescu's book-writing career had begun in those days. Eventually he rivaled Stalin in volume and volumes.

Nicolae Ceauşescu seemed a very different creature when he first ascended to power in the mid-sixties. In contrast with the stale bureaucracy of Gheorghiu-Dej—whose protégé and unprotesting puppet he'd been—he had a fresh style, which gave some hope that the changes being felt throughout Eastern Europe would also come to Romania. That hope came to a sudden violent end in the Prague Spring of 1968, although Ceauşescu was the only Communist leader to protest the Soviet invasion. He also made friendly gestures toward China, the sworn enemy of the USSR. At the height of the Sino-Soviet dispute, I remember reading, to my astonishment, an issue of the Communist party newspaper *Scînteia*, in which the opposing statements of the Soviet and the Chinese Communist parties were printed side by side without editorial comment. It was the moment, it seemed to me, when Romania staked out for itself a position between the great powers that was both wise and historically correct. Throughout their history Romanians ensured their survival by paying tribute to both East and West although, for the most part, their hearts were in the West.

Just past the Russian bookstore was my favorite newsstand. There was a long line of people waiting to buy the papers. This was most assuredly a new phenomenon. The only place during my entire childhood where there was no line was the newsstand. The papers were more predictable than anything else in our world. We read them to help us sleep. The revolution had accomplished a miracle here. And given birth to another line, ironically. This newsstand was a place dear to me. An ancient little man who used to squat in there before a kerosene stove sold me *Luceafărul*, the literary newspaper in which my first poems appeared. I remember standing there, my heart beating fast, tearing open that first public appearance of my poems, inhaling deeply the fresh ink. My poems, young and full of bravado, were full of rebellious gestures and ominous portents of dissent. It seemed possible, during those heady days, to publish true, heartfelt poems. Now that Romania had stood up to the Russians, I reasoned, my poems would also, somehow, sail past the dark caves of the censors into the rosy light.

It was, to be sure, pure daydreaming, but certain things seemed to bear me out. The Ceauşescu of the sixties was a young, ambitious, anti-Russian nationalist, skillful at raising the emotional stakes of Romanians, who, after two decades of increasing poverty and ironfisted rule, had little left but a kind of quixotic pride, an exaggerated and unrealistic nationalism. I knew, even then, that nationalisms in our little corner of Europe had an exaggerated and absurd way of making themselves felt. My next-door neighbor, Peter, was Saxon German. My best friend in elementary school, Alex Schlesinger, was a Hungarian and Yiddish-speaking Jew. Another kid I'd been playing with since kindergarten spoke Romanian and German. I spoke German with my mother, Hungarian with my grandmother and Ilona, Romanian in school, and all three languages on the street. Whenever we had a fight, which happened often because we liked to scrap and wrestle, we first called each other the usual insults, having to do with intelligence and appearance, and then we proceeded to the next—and to us "natural"—stage, which was national. A "stinking kraut" would be followed by a "filthy kike," by a "dirty hun," and a "lice-riddled Gypsy." The richness of our ethnic-insult vocabulary was wide and deep. It reflected, all too easily, the more elaborate prejudices of our parents, which, in their rabid form, had already resulted in countless tribal bloodbaths.

Romania had not even been a nation until the end of the nine-teenth century, when the Turkish Empire disintegrated. My home, Transylvania, was a disputed territory between Hungary and Romania. Originally it had been the original homeland of all Romanians, but it became part of Romania only after World War I, when another me-gaempire, the Austro-Hungarian, bit the dust. Later Hitler gave Tran-sylvania to the Hungarians because they were better Nazis, and Stalin gave it back to the Romanians to console them for the huge land grab of Bessarabia in Moldavia, an ancient Romanian land that became a Soviet republic. Romanian nationalism, forged at the velocity of callous big power Ping-Pong, was, above all, a certain indignation at the facts. History had been cruel to this small people situated at the ill-omened crossroads of Europe. Their survival depended on the forging of an un-questionable identity, even if it meant building it from scraps and straw. The strong ethnic enclaves of Hungarians and Germans within the Ro-manian majority also made strong distinctions in defense of their iden-tities. All of them experienced, with discomforting regularity, a kind of impotent rage that translated often into xenophobia, anti-Semitism, and a tight-lipped determination to go it alone. Ceauşescu was a master in exploiting this character flaw; he became a hero for pressing old Ro-manian claims for Bessarabia against the Russians, while pursuing a ruthless policy of cultural genocide against minorities in Transylvania and the Banat. As the people began to starve, and signs of revolt began to challenge his regime, the level of nationalistic rhetoric was tuned ever higher, right up to the eternally useful high pitches of anti-Semi-tism, while poets were hired to sing at the court. Happily for me I missed both the heights and the abysmal lows of the Ceauşescu years. In 1965, just after he came to power, my mother and I were able to leave the country. I now know that we were bought by the Israeli gov-ernment at ten thousand dollars a head. The business of selling people, one of the lesser-known activities of the Ceauşescus, began at the very beginning of his reign.

The squares, plazas, churches, passageways, cobblestone streets, gas lamps, and the streetcars all supported my adolescent thoughts and feelings with their mystic melancholy. Sibiu is a place made for the ambitious sorrow of youth, with its churches, reputation for the occult, venerable age, air of superiority and culture. "There are only two cities in the world," the great Romanian-French writer Cioran said, "Paris and Sibiu." When I fell in love, first with Aurelia, then with Marinella, there was a medieval intensity about it as if we were Abelard and Héloïse, Tristan and Isolde, Keats and la Belle Dame sans Merci. In the incunabula collection of the Astra Society there was a religious text dated 1345 that had been bound with the only known page from the manuscript of Tristan and Isolde. It had been glued to the boards of the inner cover. I used to gaze at the unknown monk's handwriting on dark winter afternoons with a sense of foreboding.

As we now glided almost noiselessly over the snow toward the front of the "Emperor," under the feeble winter light of the Victorian streetlamps once advertised as "the first gas lamps in Europe," I realized that Sibiu, my hometown, was the exact opposite of the Communist party. Founded by Saxon Germans in the eleventh century, it was old, beautiful, and mystical. A powerful commercial center in the Middle Ages, it was famous for its printers' guild and its sieges. My elementary school, an ancient fortress that had been an Ursuline convent before the war, had several mossy cannonballs embedded in its walls, mementos of a Turkish assault. Sibiu had been home to Dracula (Vlad the Impaler); to Baron von Bruckenthal, an inventive and cruel man who had been the lover of the Austrian empress Maria Theresa and an art lover; and to Nicu Ceauşescu. Dracula had been exiled to Sibiu and found hospitality among the burghers. He repaid them by sacking their town and impaling half its citizens on stakes. Buckenthal loved the city, but he, too, liked to see a good execution. Aggrieved by the insolence of Horia, the leader of a peasant rebellion, he invented the rack as a special punishment for him. He improved the iron maiden, a German torture instrument, and was known to enjoy whippings, castrations, and elaborate hangings. The Bruckenthal Museum, where I spent much of my childhood, displayed all the baron's implements, along with his truly splendid collection of Flemish paintings, gifts from his lover the empress, who robbed half the Vienna Gallery for him. Nicu Ceauşescu must be considered the low end of this distinguished line, although his torture chambers were second to none. His Securitate compound contained thirty underground cells, where a variety of devices were used. Most common were wooden and rubber nightsticks, sandbags, heavy rubber hammers, "nails," robot cells, and the Mobra motorcycle. The "nails" were thick hooks screwed into the wall with a chain attached. The prisoner, handcuffed with his hands behind his back, had the chain put through the handcuffs. He (I'm using "he" generically; there were many women prisoners) was then lifted up until his entire weight rested on his toes. After thirty minutes he collapsed and fell on his knees with his hands behind his back after having broken the ligaments of his upper limbs. The Mobra motorcycle was a heavy T-shaped iron device. It was affixed to the body of the prisoner, whose hands were handcuffed to the far ends of the T. He was then allowed to walk free. After thirty minutes he would begin to suffer unbearable pain all along the upper body where the neurovascular system is, including the spinal cord. When the pain became truly unbearable, he crumpled. The robot cell was a modern variant of the iron maiden, a small enclosure with a random mechanical hammer inside hitting the body unpredictably at intervals ranging from five to thirty seconds. This device was eventually discontinued because too many prisoners died before they could talk.

I knew none of this when I was a kid. After she lost the photo shop mother became a printer. She learned her craft from men who still worked on Gutenberg-era presses, producing some of the most beautifully designed books in the world. She was also Jewish, and beautiful, and she named me Andrei, a Russian name, just to make sure that the Soviet soldiers would not kill us. They didn't, but they may have killed my father, who disappeared under mysterious circumstances sometime in the early 1950's. I did not know him very well, but people lowered their voices when they spoke of him, something they did quite often, and about many things. The photographs of formal people from the fifties gathered dust in the window of his padlocked shop for about a year. Then they removed them, and the window was empty. I used to stand there looking at the dead flies on the discolored black felt where the photographs were and remember the lively noise of my cap gun. Pac. Pac . . . pac . . . pac . . .

Throughout my childhood we suffered a number of indignities that bothered my mother much more than me. We had to share a small apartment with a large family of peasants who kept enormous garlic bulbs on the windowsill and hung their hand-washed knickers, skirts, and trousers to dry right over our locked icebox. We had important things in that icebox, like a whole salami obtained by my well-connected uncle from a pig farmer in the Transylvanian Alps. This salami we guarded with our lives, and we were ready, at the slightest noise, to rise in the middle of the night and fight for it. For lunch at school, I would take a bacon-grease and paprika sandwich with a raw onion. It was delicious. My friend Vidrighin, whose father was a rich peasant, sometimes brought blood sausage or headcheese to school, and he would cut a thick slice with his sharp knife and give me some. In exchange I taught him German and Hungarian. It seemed to snow all through those years of my childhood, covering everything with a thick white blanket that muffled our quiet world even more. Other parents, the parents of my classmates, also disappeared under mysterious circumstances, but once again we heard only the incomprehensible whispers of adults whose voices were hoarse from performing in those unnatural registers and whose tired faces betrayed the fact that they'd been up all night listening to Radio Free Europe. Older people, whose memories predated World War II, remembered Romania as a rich, lush, colorful country. Its markets had groaned with richly textured, generously plump breads, fruit, and cheeses. The outdoor cafés had been full of people enjoying hot Turkish coffee, ice cream, new cider, spicy sausages, Gypsy violins, and loud, unabashed conversation. Sibiu had grand Habsburg restaurants, particularly the "Emperor of the Romanians" Hotel, where, over plates of paprikás, schnitzel, layered strudel, and innumerable glasses of wine, my father had misspent his youth.

By the time I came around, the happy picture of a land of plenty had pretty much vanished, though pockets of stubborn prosperity continued, because the mountain region surrounding us was home to grizzled shepherds who had refused to collectivize and their peasant markets still flourished. My friend Vidrighin and I made it a practice to go about the market by the Cibin River, tasting fruit and cheeses until we were full, and then we didn't have to go home for dinner. We preferred roaming the crooked streets of Sibiu until well after dusk, when the ghosts came out. An illusion of peace attended my childhood. In the Stalinist fifties, under the dictator Gheorghiu-Dej, dissent was unheard of, news of the outside world was practically nonexistent, and the Soviets, our big brothers, were the chief importers of culture. Kindhearted, generously mustachioed Stalin watched over us from posters on which he was surrounded by happy children just like us, only plumper. I went to the cinema to see big Soviet epics about World War II, and we played "Russians" and "Germans" instead of "cowboys" and "Indians," only nobody wanted to be Russians. At school we all were pioneers, who wore red kerchiefs around our necks, kerchiefs that the more lively ones chewed down to the red knot, while the nerds kept theirs ironed and stiff. At school rallies we had to stand up and salute "in the name of Marx, Engels, Lenin, and Gheorghiu-Dej," and that's the kind of tongue twister that got us started on our way toward a big vocabulary.

We learned history from an old teacher who was so afraid of making a mistake he kept his eyes on the new Marxist textbook translated from the Russian and did not lift them at all, not even when we fired spitballs at his chalky person and bald head. Romania, according to him, was a mostly Slavic territory, which everyone knew was a lie. Romania, with an o, was a Latin-speaking country inhabited by the descendants of Roman soldiers who married Dacian women in the trans-Danube Valley. Assimilated Roman soldiers stayed even after the Roman Empire had withdrawn, and they inhabited the lands of "happy Dacia" for some two thousand years of bloody history rarely interrupted by happiness. We knew that much, but the Russians, in order to justify their claim to Bessarabia, home of the ancient Romanian kings, began spelling Romania with a u, which was a convoluted grammatical argument for the primacy of Slav claims. This teacher's name was Comrade Câmpeanu; but we found out that his real name was Cîrnaț ("sausage"), and we tortured him without respite every day of the week by drawing sausages on the blackboard or writing them on paper airplanes. He tried to teach us Marxist history, for which he was temperamentally and philosophically unsuited because it was the history of revolutions and popular revolts, a view of things neither I nor my friends had any quarrel with. We were fans of revolution or at least mischief, which, in the boring fifties, was about the only way to keep oneself imaginatively entertained. I fantasized breaking the thousands of shuttered windows with their throngs of timid people hiding in the dark with their radios, blowing up the statues of the party fathers, besmirching the beribboned posters of the nine fat men of the Central Committee who glowered above the central square. In reality I managed some petty vandalism, with the help of a cousin who was a school dropout and a thief, but it was small stuff. Once I kicked a public telephone when it refused to return my coin, and it exploded, spewing showers of silver. I spent the day at the police station hinting darkly that my father was a high-ranking party member who'd have their hides if they dared arrest me. They let me go, but it was because my mother, who was beautiful and charming, came.

Being a Jew was another and richer source of alienation for me, because anti-Semitism was alive and well in Romania. I was not admitted to the lycée the first time I applied because a quota system was in effect, favoring, in order, children of workers and peasants, of engineers and professionals, of former functionaries, of former landowners and rich merchants, of former royalists and Nazis, and then, if there was room, of Jews. In addition to this, I wore glasses and was very skinny at a time when there was a fierce distinction between book lovers and muscle builders. A truly existential moment occurred when I walked up the wrong way on a certain street filled with fans of the local soccer club that had just lost the big game. I owe my survival to the kind Fräulein who opened her medieval door when I buzzed a doorbell at random and who whisked me inside moments before the mob got me. And she made me eat a large slice of strudel. There was another moment, when I was much younger and wasn't exactly sure what a Jew was because nobody had explained it to me yet. Two boys from another street were pissing crosswise on the corner when I passed. "Hey," one of them said, "know what happens when two guys piss like this?" I didn't. "A Jew dies," he told me.

The old synagogue in Sibiu was a dilapidated shell inhabited by shadows. The day I turned thirteen, a gaunt old man grabbed me and dragged me in there to be the tenth man at a service that rarely reached the required number. The once-numerous Jews of Sibiu had been decimated by war and later emigrated to Israel and to America. There were only three of us left in my school. I did not associate with them. I studied the fading glow of the gold Jewish letters above the windows and felt moved, in spite of myself, when I touched the frayed brocade that clothed the Torah. The early wintry dark had plunged the place into a mysterious gloom made fantastic by the candles burning in the menorah. Confused as I was about who I was supposed to be in the first place, this experience deepened the mystery. Two contradictory impulses fought within me: to run out of there, change my name, and become something certain and easy to understand or to continue traveling the dreamy paths of my shadow world until I found out who I *really* was. As it turned out, I followed both paths, the first one first, the second one later.

When I started writing poetry, the local Writers' Workshop suggested that I change my Jewish name, Perlmutter, if I intended to publish. I did, to Andrei Steiu, the last name meaning "rock" or "crag." I published a number of poems under this name until I realized that the *u* at the end of Steiu looked like an *n* when handwritten, so that everyone thought that my name was Stein. So much for giving up my identity. It wasn't until I found Codrescu, which means "keeper of the woods," that I realized perfect separation from my old self, but by that time I had left Romania and I had no need of it. When, furthermore, I found out that Codrescu sounded almost like Codreanu, Romania's greatest anti-Semite, I had even more reason to be rid of it. I decided instead to redeem it by making Codrescu more famous than Codreanu, thus reducing the historical slime bucket to a mere footnote in *my* biography.

My life is rife with syllabic terrors.

In the summer we climbed the Carpathian Mountains until we found patches of snow and ice caves. We lay in meadows of flowers and watched the clouds. The natural beauty of Transylvania, which began just outside the crenellated city walls, was the great healer of my shaky childhood. There was a golden glow of ancient afternoons that warmed both the pavement stones of my town and the rocks of the nearby mountains. At night the "first gas lamps in Europe" lit the street where the electric tram ran past pastry and coffee shops. The Corso was where we strolled back and forth to look at girls. They looked back, and we went to the movies. Even in its shabby coat of Stalinism, Romania still had charm. Our adolescence invested it, no doubt, but something was, in spite of everything, objectively *there*.

Situated at the very center of the ancient spice routes of the Orient, Romania was the golden apple that made everyone's mouth water, and consequently, everyone, the Goths, Visigoths, Huns, Slavs, Austrians, and Soviets, tried to swallow it whole. Amazingly enough, it survived the battering rams of a ceaselessly hostile history for hundreds of years until the regime of Nicolae Ceauşescu began accomplishing in a few years what the combined horrors of numberless invaders were unable to. The once brightly lit streets went dark, their cafés deserted. The markets emptied. The long lines of people holding ration coupons became longer, while the barest necessities became even scarcer. Bread became a luxury. People whispered even lower because fear of the ubiquitous security police became greater. The once-lively peasant villages of the Carpathians became heaps of rubble. "Little Paris," as Bucharest was once called, became "Ceauşwitz."

The Russian bookstore was now the Mihai Eminescu bookstore. We went in. Mobs of people shivering in their warmest clothes were leafing through books on electronics, poetry, and children's topics "There were no children's books when I was growing up," I told Noah, "only fairy tales." There was a long line at the cash register, so we went back out. It was dark, but people strolled with great energy. They were not afraid of Securitate. I knew that there had been shooting from the "eyes" of Sibiu, which is what the roof windows in the pointed shingled Gothic houses were called. They do indeed look like eyes, these roof windows, sleepless, semiclosed eyes that watch over the town. The roofs communicate with each other. Young people were crowding in front of the Peace Cinema. They were showing an animated Czech picture and a Chinese opera. This is where I'd taken my first date to a movie. I held her watchband the whole time because I was too shy to touch her skin. Her watchband was sweaty. Finally, we arrived at the main square near the hotel. The statute of the educator and revolutionary Gheorghe Lazăr, who gave his name to my high school, was surrounded by lit candles in memory of the dead. People were kneeling in the snow, praying. Others just crossed themselves and passed quickly. Five or six kids were playing soccer only a few yards from the shrine as if nothing unusual were going on. "How many people died in Sibiu?" I asked one of them.

They all surrounded us. "Hundreds!" they shouted. They fell over one another, pointing to the roof windows. That's where they were shooting from. Pac . . . pac . . . pac . . . They offered to show us the burned militia building, but we declined.

"Did you have friends who died?" They were a little quiet then, but they shoved one of the shy kids up front. "My friend Reza," he said softly. "He came here at night. . . ." I handed them all some gum, and they were off playing soccer again. Life goes on.

We passed in front of my high school, Lyceum Gh. Lazăr, the locus of four years' worth of on-site torture, now closed for the holidays and on account of revolution. I thought I saw Comrade Sausage grin behind a window. We also walked inside the café across from the school where my poet friends and I played hooky, our uniform coat collars raised in defiance, drinking black espresso. . . . The shop was steamy, and there were quite a few rich pastries in the display case. But there was no coffee; there hadn't been any in a long time. A spoon of Nescafé had been better than money for several years. The revolutionary government changed that next day. Coffee arrived on the shelves.

All the same, I had several pounds of dark roast Louisiana coffee with me to give my friends, as I was going to do, first thing next morning. My exhausted friends finally prevailed on me to drag my frozen person back to the "Emperor of the Romans," where I drew a lovely room under the sloping roof. The window looked onto another sloping imperial roof with an Austrian eagle frozen to it. Behind that roof there were others, hundreds of them, sailing through the ages to welcome me. A sharp curved blade of moon hung unsheathed in the sky.

11

The Mysteries of Sibiu

Early in the morning, while it was still dark, I took a quick shower, dressed, and went down to the hotel restaurant, hoping to be the first one there. It was just opening up. The waitress brought me a cup of tea. "Did you hear about last night?" she said.

I hadn't.

"They caught a terrorist on the third floor. He had grenades, two bombs, and about a thousand bullets. . . . The militia came running through here around four this morning. He gave up without a fight, thank God. . . ."

The third floor was where I had been sleeping blissfully, immersed in the peace of my memories. "What room?" I asked her.

"Second one from the elevator, on the right."

In other words, the room next to mine. I gave a respectful moment's pause to the kindness of sleep. The waitress, whose name was Mara, was a pretty girl with shoulder-length black hair. We conversed during breakfast. She brought me a soft-boiled egg in an eggcup, a cup of yogurt, a sliced apple, and a glass of mineral water. Mara was a student in her third year at the Textile Institute, and like all Romanians, she dreamed of going abroad. On December 21 she had gone with the students to the square to protest. She had screamed, "Down with the dictator!" and "Give us back our dead!" and "Timișoara!" along with thousands of her contemporaries. They had befriended the soldiers who guarded the entrance to the Communist party headquarters. "I kissed one of them," she confessed. "He wasn't going to shoot me." She blushed. Later that afternoon, when the workers came from the factories, the crowd started shouting "The Army is with us!" By evening the euphoria had increased so greatly that people were singing and dancing. Children with candles lit in memory of the dead in Timişoara were lifted up on shoulders. Most people decided to stay all night. But just after midnight, on December 22, when it looked as if the revolution had been peacefully won, "they" started shooting. They emptied the magazines of their machine guns directly into the stunned crowd. A friend of hers from work, Mara told me, ripped open his shirt and walked up to one of the buildings the fire was coming from, and shouted: "Shoot at me, brother! Shoot me!" They did. Mara was starting to cry, so I asked her to sit down and have some tea with me. She couldn't. Other people were coming down for breakfast. But she whispered to me, just before going to serve them: "Can I change your dollars?"

The black market in dollars was relentless around all the hotels. Everyone, no matter what his or her status or business, eventually ended up asking that question. The revolutionary government had instituted the freedom to leave the country, but hard currency was unavailable. The ridiculous official exchange rate was set at nine lei per dollar. The street market paid a hundred lei per dollar. The salary of a well-paid professional, an engineer or a doctor, was four thousand lei a month, which was quite a bit of money, but there was nothing to buy. Everything worked instead on the basis of a natural economy where goods were traded directly: shoes for cheese, cloth for bacon. Doctors were paid by peasants in chickens. It was the same all over Eastern Europe, a situation that did not augur well for transition to a modern monetary system, but it was worse in Romania. Deborah Amos, NPR's Eastern European correspondent, had told me that the rule of thumb for the black-market exchange versus official rates was five to one. In Romania it was twice that.

Some of the people coming in for breakfast were Noah, Michael, and Rich. They crowded their sleepy selves around the table and began planning the day. Michael wanted to verify whether the rumor about Securitate agents being held in their underwear in a swimming pool in the sub-zero weather was true. Noah wanted to interview the Army chief who had defeated the local Securitate units. Also on their lists were interviews relating to Nicu Ceauşescu and the rumor that the water in Sibiu had been poisoned. A Belgian toxicologist had testified to that effect. On this last question I could set their minds at ease, Belgian toxicologist or no. Last night, probably only a few minutes before the capture of the terrorist next door, I had gotten up, seized by thirst. Before going to bed, I had consumed a goodly amount of Stolichnaya with a Soviet journalist who'd been in Sibiu for a week. He had also been in Timișoara and told me a number of interesting things, including the fact that on December 10—five days before the protest in front of Reverend Tökes's house—there were nearly a dozen TASS correspondents there. When I asked him why, my friend winked. His wink troubled me. "What were nearly a dozen TASS correspondents doing in a remote Transylvanian town, many days before anything started to happen?" I insisted. He winked again. I have since pondered those mysterious winks at some length. This is how I read them at the time: The imminent downfall of Ceausescu was known beforehand in Moscow. The events in Timișoara had been planned, foreseen, or guessed. TASS correspondents were sent there both to record the beginning of the end and to prove to the world that TASS, a much-maligned news organization, could stun the world with a scoop. Today I have a more sinister opinion. Anyway, after all the vodka I fell into a deep sleep and rose only to search for water. I stuck my head under the faucet and drank deeply. Only several gallons later did I remember that the water in Sibiu was supposed to be poisoned. Noah had cautiously brought a dozen bottles of mineral water with him from Bucharest. But, I told my dear friends, nothing happened, and several lessons may be deduced from this: A rumor mill was at work in the overstimulated populace; Romanian poison was shabby like everything else produced by socialist factories; Belgian toxicologists don't know poison from beer; my body was immune to damage in the place of my birth. Furthermore, I explained to my journalistic confreres, our plans for the day did not coincide. I didn't mind hearing what the Army general had to say. But I was definitely more interested in seeing my old uncle Rihard and aunt Elena, and my high school chum Vidrighin, who was my partner in crime during the peak years 1963 to 1965.

We drove through desolate apartment block buildings in search of Engels Parkway, Block V, Row 12-A, Lane 6, Apartment 12, the place to which my relatives had been moved. When I was a kid, Alba Iulia had been a sleepy old town. My aunt and uncle had a pretty little house with a grape arbor over the front. There was a tiled patio with a little table where my aunt Elena always put lemonade and cookies. I used to be afraid of my uncle Rihard, a tall, terse, military man with a devastating handshake that hurt for an hour afterward. He did not suffer the chatter of children very well, and my cousins and I were very quiet around him. We once heard that he'd had a valet who pulled his boots on in the morning. We got that valet mixed up with a bit from a Russian novel where an officer whips his valet with a cat-o'-nine-tails. We were afraid that in the absence of the valet, my uncle Rihard would use his whip on us. Yet we liked him very much. I used to listen to him without moving a muscle. He would talk about the horrors of the prison camp, the terrible indignities inflicted on the officers of the old Army, and he raved against the Communists, to the distress of my aunt, who tried to shush him. "Please, Colonel," she would say, laying a light hand on his shoulder. "Somebody will hear you."

"I don't give a damn who hears me!" he shouted, putting his hand over hers.

Their relationship fascinated me. Here they were, old, very old people—and not just to me but to my mother as well—and they acted full of affection for each other. Theirs was a romantic and sad story from the beginning. His resignation from the Army for the love of my aunt had made him a legendary figure in the 1940's. That was during the Fascist dictatorship, and harsh as resigning must have been, he still got to keep his pension and his valet. People also addressed him as Colonel Rihard, and he saluted them crisply. He could have rejoined the Army under the Communists if he'd paid allegiance to the new masters. But hopelessly honest and outspoken, Uncle Rihard got into trouble instead. For the frank expression of his opinion he spent the best years of his manhood in the damp undergrounds of the canal. He emerged, surprisingly, with his health almost unaffected (he had a lung problem and could not suffer smoke but was otherwise intact) and began a long campaign to have his military pension restored. He succeeded in having a fraction of it given back to him. I have no idea how my uncle and aunt had been able to hold on to the little clean house with the arbor. They made everything with their own hands, including soap, and there had been two beehives in the back. There was always good honey on black bread with our tea when we came to visit. They had no children of their own. I wrote to them, as did my mother and cousins, after leaving Romania, and we even sent them money. They always acknowledged the money and our letters with curt notes. They never forgave us for leaving. In spite of everything, Uncle Rihard was a patriot.

It was not easy finding the cement cube where they lived. Dumitru asked several people until one of them finally directed us there. Others had run ahead of us and had roused my uncle with the news that a carful of Americans was looking for him. He was waiting there, at the top of the stairs, an erect old man, thin as a stick, unshaved, with deep, sunken eyes, wrapped in two coats and a big long scarf. I walked up the stairs to him. He looked me deeply in the eyes for no longer than half a second and then said my name: "Andrei." He shook my hand, a still-firm grip that I felt for a long time. He then hugged me, and his eyes filled with tears. We walked through the door of his tiny apartment directly into a small kitchen. Seated on a stool before a tiny stove with a pot of warm milk was a very old woman with little hair. Bundled also in two coats and two head scarves, she was warming her hands over the milk. My uncle Rihard brought me gently before her, and we waited for her to look at me. "She's been sick," whispered my uncle. When she finally looked at me, it was without recognition. "Do you remember Andrei, your nephew?" my uncle asked her. She shook her head. No, she did not remember me. She did not remember much. We went into the next room, the freezing cold bedroom where, on the walls and on a night table, were many framed photographs of my family, of me and my cousins when we were kids, a beautiful picture of my mother at eighteen. "Do you know how old I am?" my uncle Rihard asked me. I didn't. "Eighty-nine years old," he said. "And your aunt Elena. She is also eighty-nine years old." I told him that I was a writer, that I worked for radio, and that I was pretty much an American now. Once more his eyes filled with tears. "Why did you leave us?" he said, but pulled himself quickly together. "Tell Americans"—he enunciated as firmly as he could—"about what the Communists did to the Army. Tell them about what they did to the officers of the Romanian Army! Tell them how they tried to kill us and steal our pensions!" I put my hand on his shoulder as I'd seen my aunt do in the bygone days of three decades ago. He calmed down.

"What about the revolution?" I said. "They will give you back your rights."

He nodded, exhausted. The revolution had come too late for him, too late certainly for my aunt, who, mercifully perhaps, remembered very little. I pressed all the money I had on me into his hand. He took it with a kind of wounded helplessness that broke my heart. I could barely imagine what they had suffered, what they were suffering. They lived, at their age, in an unheated apartment, slowly dying of hunger. Decades of this misery had passed, each year worse than the one before. For all that, the colonel's old pride was still there, his handshake still firm. Visibly moved, Michael, Noah, Rich, and even Dumitru took up a collection in the car and got together another few thousand lei for the old folks. I went back up the stairs and pressed it into the old man's hand, who just stood there, tears streaking down his face, unsure if any of it was real. My last glimpse of him was of a thin man with a messy pile of banknotes in his hand, looking bewilderedly after a car from another world that had visited him briefly. He did not seem to know what the money was for or why having come back, I was leaving—again.

In front of the militia building where the "terrorists" were being held, women clamored to get in with bundles of food. They were the wives and daughters of the arrested men. "My husband," a woman said, "he's just a carpenter. He didn't do anything wrong. . . . Why are they keeping him there?" Surprisingly, after some pushing and negotiating, either the bundles of food were taken to the prisoners, or the women themselves were allowed to go in and see them.

We were another matter, however. We needed permission from the garrison commandant, and he hadn't given it yet. "Have patience," a young lieutenant said. "Comrade—I mean, Mr. Commandant will be here soon." It was a charming slip. "Mr." must not have come easy to a soldier trained for years to say and salute "Comrade." In any case, it did not look as if the prisoners were being brutalized if their families were allowed to see them. While waiting for the superior officer to permit us inside, we circled the garrison, which had seen quite a bit of fighting. However, it was the buildings across the street, which had housed the militia, that had taken the brunt of the fire from the garrison. Also destroyed were Nicu Ceauşescu's villa and the houses of his subordinates. The curious thing was that no fire had been returned by either Nicu or his minions.

A kid of about ten gave us a graphic tour of the surroundings and told us all about the battle, which he had witnessed from his window. "The Army blew up a kindergarten," he said, "Just like that . . . boom

. . . boom . . . pac . . . pac . . ." He was very good at sound effects, which Rich promptly recorded with his big black mike. I gave him a pack of gum, which he nonchalantly slipped into his pocket, the natural reward of the storyteller. In the end we did not receive permission to see the prisoners.

It was only noon, and the NPR crew still had time to file stories via satellite if they returned to Bucharest right away. It was a six-hour ride. In Sibiu telephone communications with the West had to be reserved many days in advance. I told them to go ahead. I wanted to see my friend Ion. I also wanted to be alone to wander around with just my thoughts. I would take the midnight train to Bucharest and get there the next day.

I returned to the hotel and called my friend Ion, who was properly amazed. "It's the revolution," he said, with a bombastic lilt I remembered well. "It's brought us everything we ever wanted." He hastened to the hotel in his car. My chum Ion had become a portly man of some dimensions. But sparkling underneath the gravity was plenty of delight. He strolled in and hugged me demonstratively, pointing out to the desk clerks that I was a rich and famous poet. He was on very friendly terms with the girls behind the desk, who all had the same brisk and ironic manner, learned, I thought, at the secret police academy. Ion was familiar also with the lobby fauna of money changers and hustlers who surrounded our embrace like blood-thirsty gnats. *Not again*, I told myself. *Here is the second friend of my youth with connections in the lobby of grand hotels.*

Ion was a journalist, working for *Tribuna*, formerly the Communist paper. He drove me to his house in his Dacia, pointing out the ravages of the last days' fighting. He lived in a middle-class neighborhood of separate houses with their own gardens. While backing his car into the garage, he pointed out to me the house next door. "This poor guy's afraid of coming home . . . they fired all night at his house. . . ."

"Securitate?" I asked.

Ion winced. "So they say." In fact, the whole neighborhood sported scars. "They aimed a lot at us!" Ion sighed.

I made the acquaintance of his wife, Elena, a history professor who, like Ion, had been born in the village of Rășinari above Sibiu. Their three pretty blond daughters were introduced. Miraculously, plates full of ham, cheese, salami, and a steaming soup appeared, as well as the ubiquitous bottle of plum brandy and the jug of homemade wine. "To your return!" toasted Ion. I drank to that and to the revolution.

"Sure," Elena said, "to the revolution, but can anyone tell me what to do about my thesis?" She had a point there. Elena had just finished her doctoral thesis on the Revolution of 1848. It was beautifully bound. It had been scheduled for defense on January 12, 1990. Unfortunately the manuscript was riddled through and through with quotations from the great "scientists" just deceased—namely, Elena Ceauşescu. "It would be easier picking the garlic out of a Sibiu salami than taking Him and Her out!" exclaimed Elena in despair. Everyone had been required to quote the Ceauşescus in everything he or she did, a merely formal task in the case of a paper on, let's say, rock formations. Terrible problem with history.

"You'll just have to write another book," said Ion, trying to change the subject.

"Sure," said Elena, "and call everybody mister!" A domestic fight appeared to be in the making.

"Writing any poetry?" I asked Ion. We had some more brandy.

"Now and then," he admitted. "But I have all your books!" he said enthusiastically, pointing to a shelf where all the books I'd sent him over the years stood proudly dusted.

"He sure does!" said Elena. "They've been proudly displayed at the bottom of our darkest closet for years!" I laughed. I liked her. Among the throngs of instant converts to the revolution I had yet to meet many people with a reasonable sense of humor. Clearly no one had changed completely from one day to another. We had many more brandies. Ion wanted to know how I'd become an American after leaving Romania, a nineteen-year-old steeped in romantic confusion. How to tell him?

I could barely remember. But at nineteen years of age I had all the qualifications I needed: chutzpah and joie de vivre. I first went to Detroit, I told Ion, in March 1966, on a gray winter day that matched the weather in my soul. I spoke no English, I knew no one, and I had only a shabby black vinyl jacket that didn't keep off the cold wind slicing through me as I watched, in utter amazement, the river of cars flowing on the John Lodge Expressway. There were more cars there than I had ever seen, big cars full of people who didn't know me and probably cared nothing about who I was. . . . I had no car, no country, no language, and no warm clothes. To top it all off, I became suddenly short. An average-size man in my country, I suddenly lost two to four inches among the much taller Americans, who became positively gigantic when they uncoiled out of their automobiles. . . . The revolution of December 1989 in Romania was far away in the future, and most Americans didn't even know where Romania was. The few college students I met at the Wayne State University cafeteria knew, however, that it was a Communist country. So was North Vietnam and Cuba, places that loomed immense in the geography of 1966. Communism was the solid bloc of darkness they had been told was menacing their homes and cars. It had the shape of a mushroom cloud without any specific latitude and longitude; it just hovered there, over their heads, ready to snatch them off to fight a jungle war. I felt for them. I had left Romania in part so I wouldn't have to be in its Army. I hated armies more than bad poetry. In fact, armies were bad poetry to me, and the propaganda of governments that sent their young men to die for their ossified ideas or fat wallets was utterly repugnant to me, polluted language that poetry was out to erase. My young friends did know the eminent legendary Romanian Dracula, in his incarnation as Bram Stoker's and Bela Lugosi's vampire. He gave the young people of my generation a certain sexual and nocturnal thrill that wasn't a bad thing to be associated with. Under the amusing bravado of the imaginary Transylvania of movies and comic books there was, however, a real place that I sometimes tried to describe. There is an untranslatable Romanian word that expresses with great precision the kind of unbearable longing and nostalgia that grips one's heart when thinking of home. That word is *dor*. I have felt it many times. Nostalgia for the medieval squares of Sibiu steeped in golden light, longing for the outdoor cafés of Bucharest, drinking new wine, all of us young, intoxicated with poetry and song. I missed the smells of flowering linden trees, the blue reflections of deep mountain snow in the evenings, the old peasant villages that Ceaușescu's insanity almost wiped off the face of the earth. I missed the real fairy tales I was raised on. The story of the waters of life and death, youth without age, the tale of the sheep Mioritza that recites the cosmic poetry of the sky, the story of the poplars that grew pears . . .

As I made my drunken rambling speech to Ion, he started to cry. He, too, was nostalgic for our youth. It was as far away from him as it was from me. What I had come back to find couldn't possibly exist. It was actually funny. We started laughing like two bad boys. I told him another story that held a whole other moral. One day on the street in

New York, in the early seventies, I ran into my chum Alex Schlesinger, one of the three Jews in our elementary school. Ion remembered him well. Alex and I spent the day walking and talking just the way we used to on the crooked streets near the square by the Cibin River. In the evening we took a crowded subway train to Greenwich Village. We were standing there, hanging from the straps, speaking deliberately and loudly in the most vigorous colloquial obscenities we could think of. Tickled pink by the idea that no one could understand the scatological island we made among the weary passengers, we did not notice for the longest time a well-dressed older gentleman leaning on an ornate walking stick who stared fixedly at us. At the end of one of our bouts of jive, he said clearly, in a most well-enunciated classical Romanian: "You should be ashamed of yourselves!" We were. But see, I said passionately, what Alex and I were doing was not simple punkiness. We were celebrating our freedom from being overheard. The fact that we *were* overheard, ironic as it was, testifies to the fact that there are ears everywhere, not just in the walls, and that these ears, as we all know, pick up whatever they can. The existence of these ears was the reason, in the first place, why I left Romania. One of the gifts of the Romanian language that translated to unexpected good purpose into American English was its keen sense of the absurd. Americans, for the most part, take themselves entirely too seriously. They rarely see the absurdity of the television shows that they watch, or the hilarious silliness of shopping malls, or the dizzying frivolity of the unending fashions invented and discarded by the market. But the absurd, in its political, social, and cultural modes, has been a fact of life in Romania since the night that a self-important Turkish pasha spent in a Romanian hovel. The howling of a baby kept him up all night. In the morning, the pasha conceded that his self-importance came to naught before the hungry screams of a baby and that a baby, no matter what his origin, is bigger than a pasha anytime. Literate Americans I met were familiar with the plays of Eugène Ionesco, the thinking man's Dracula. Ionesco is the father of the theater of the absurd, a literary genre that is the equivalent of vampirism because it sucks conventional meanings out of things until they are rendered ridiculous and sad. . . .

In any case, between nostalgia and language I made a life as well . . . I met my wife, Alice, in Detroit. I spoke to her mostly in sign language until I learned her brand of midwestern English, which is what I still speak. My two sons, Lucian and Tristan, both were born in

America but were named after Lucian Blaga and Tristan Tzara, Romanian poets. The twenty-five years that stretched between the Romanian child and the American adult were filled with the gritty substance of a dramatic time. So much happened! But the bridge was never broken. Even in the midst of my most American experiences, there remained the incontrovertible fact of my accent, which influenced even the simplest communication. After I became known as a critic of the Ceauşescu regime on both Radio Free Europe and National Public Radio, I acquired a plump enough dossier to land me in one of the dictator's darkest dreams. One time, in a San Francisco café, I met with the vice president of the Romanian Writers' Union, someone both Ion and I knew, who spoke to me in a stream of platitudes, while his young keeper, an athletic blond with a Nazi crew cut, sat silently by us. When the Nazi went to the bathroom, the agitated writer whispered a warning to me: "Don't return to Romania as long as you live! You won't live long if you do!" When the Nazi came back, looking suspiciously at his charge's mouth, as if he could sense that some treasonable thing had escaped it, the river of platitudes started flowing again. I was sure, though not resigned to the fact, that I would never see the land of my birth again.

After I confessed all this, there was a long silence. I felt keenly the weight of the years between us. After a few silent shots of brandy Ion asked me, looking quizzically at me, "Why did you really come back?"

Well, there it was, the question.

"To tell you the truth, Ion," I said, "I came back because of my craving for Transylvanian goat cheese. Nowhere on earth during my years of wandering have I found the depth, pungency, and *character* of Romanian goat cheese. Romanian goat cheese is God Pan's personal stash, his beaded wisdom!"

My buddy Ion, who used to carry his ten-inch curved blade to school to frighten soft city boys, loved his family cheese to distraction. It was a soft coat of arms to him, passed on by his father, a rich shepherd who owned thousands of uncollectivized sheep and goats never touched by the Communists, whose representatives were found in mysterious ravines with ten-inch shivs sticking out from between their shoulder blades.

I'd said the right thing. I could see a large, cloth-wrapped cheese taking shape behind his forehead. "Ion, you're just the way I remember you!" We were becoming sloppily drunk and sentimental to Elena's disgust. She was a sober person. Some hours later, when I looked at the

Vidrighin family cuckoo clock, I realized with a start that I had to leave if I wanted to catch the train back to Bucharest.

When I stood up to leave, Ion began practicing the Romanian art of aggressive hospitality. That's when your host offers you everything in the house and you must fight not to take it. The object, for the guest, is to leave the house with as few things as possible, while the host considers his victory great if he can succeed in standing naked on the frozen earth while waving good-bye to you, dressed in his clothes, bent to the ground with his possessions. My skill at this art—honed for years in prolonged bouts with my mother—eventually left me in possession of only three things: a square cube of goat cheese weighing eighteen kilograms, about the size and shape of a small house; a six-foot Sibiu salami hard enough to waste two Securitate agents with; and a bottle of 150-proof plum brandy, a whiff of which is known to have felled sturdy Soviet truck drivers.

Ion drove me with great panache to the train station, where he tried to force a few hundred lei into my pockets. I escaped this last gift successfully. On the train to Bucharest I feigned sleep, but Ion's cheese wouldn't let me; it filled every cranny with its goaty boast. It had a kind of war shout smell. My fellow traveler removed himself to the corridor. I followed him there, and we had a brief conversation. He was a factory director on his way to Bucharest to meet the new minister of labor.

"We all worked for Securitate," he said. "I had a pen name, and I reported on my workers every week in a letter I dropped in a special box. We have to come clean. . . . There is no other way. . . ." He flicked his ashes out the window.

In deference to him I put the cheese outside the door. That caused the people smoking there to move down several windows.

We arrived at the crowded train station in the morning. I had no trouble cutting a swath through the crowd, which moved respectfully out of the way. When I arrived at the Inter-Continental Hotel, I was beginning to weary of the power of my cheese. Once in my room, I pondered ways to dispose of it without having it suspect me. Yes, I was afraid of it. While I was talking on the phone with Michael, telling him that I'd returned, I noticed that the room was beginning to take on a panicked color, a kind of *living beige*. Michael told me that the Soviet foreign minister, Mr. Eduard Shevardnadze, was in the hotel and soldiers were posted everywhere. I gripped the package firmly and put it outside on the balcony, where it was very cold. There was a soldier with a telescopic rifle on the balcony below me. But instead of scanning the area with eagle eyes, the sharpshooter looked helplessly up. He seemed to be smelling something above his head, which disoriented him. The other sharpshooters, perched on various ledges about the hotel, began to lose their concentration as well. At one point every single one of them forgot his rifle and looked helplessly at my balcony. It would have been an ideally opportune moment for an assassin. Pray to God, I told myself, that terrorists do not get hold of Vidrighin's goat cheese. Convinced by now that during the long years of my exile I had lost the fortitude necessary to live with such profoundly mythical cheese and convinced that traveling with it would make my life sheer hell, I resolved to give it away. Two of the bellboys I first approached exchanged knowing looks and refused, but later that afternoon I gave the cheese to Dumitru, who felt strong enough to accept it. My last glimpse of Carpathia's god-cheese was in the trunk of Dumitru's Dacia van, being snapped shut. I swear I heard it *wailing*.

The last thing that Ion and I had discussed before he gave me the cheese was our twenty-fifth high school reunion, six months hence. I told him that I would return in July for the reunion. By that time, I hoped, a happier country would have emerged from the bloody ruins of the Ceauşescu years.

12

Interim:
Worlds Collide

I returned to the United States on January 7, 1990. Nothing seemed quite real to me for a few days. I felt the extraordinary material fullness of America. I had come from a country that was empty of things, and I now experienced a kind of surfeit as if objects crowded me from all sides. I spent time at the corner drugstore, gazing at the rows of medicine bottles, thinking that they were soldiers in a war taking place thousands of miles away in Romania who had landed by mistake in New Orleans, where they were not needed. I looked at illustrated magazines without reading them, feeling the vibrancy of the colors and the fine quality of the paper. I stood in front of the deli counter at the A&P, seeing the cornucopia through the hungry eyes of a Romanian. Everything I touched was covered by a film or by gauze. I now understood why my mother kept her furniture covered with plastic for four years after she had come to the States. It wasn't real to her, but she wanted to protect the illusion, just in case. Here was, believe it or not (once more!), that wonderful mythical America, where the streets are paved with gold, and dogs, as my grandmother used to say, walk around with pretzels on their tails. I also couldn't quite believe how *quiet* things were here, and I live in New Orleans, which is not half as quiet as, let's say, Salt Lake City, Utah. In short, I missed the revolution, particularly its energy, sincerity, and enthusiasm. I think revolution is good for you. I missed Romanian television, where newscasters with downcast eyes shuffled handwritten papers, followed by peasants and Gypsies who'd walked eight hundred miles to talk unrehearsed about their troubles. I couldn't concentrate on *Wheel of Fortune* somehow. *America's Funniest Home Videos, Jeopardy*, and the *New Dating Game* were exactly where I'd left them, their hosts smiling their perpetual smiles.

On the other hand, it was certainly good to walk a whole block and not see a single AK-47. It was miraculous, too, to hear people holding blithely forth on the most extraordinarily banal subjects as if their lives depended on it and not glance either behind them or to their sides.

Also good but strange was the sensation of walking into Macy's and finding a hat that actually fitted. In Bucharest, before leaving, we went in search of something to buy with our mounds of leftover lei and found only a hat store. We spent enormous sums there, and consequently, we filled our suitcases with all sorts of proletarian felt hats in differing shades of gray that all were too small for normal heads. The salesman explained the minuscule size of these hats as some kind of measuring mistake made at the factory at the beginning of the last five-year plan. Since no one dared point it out for fear of being seen as critical of the plan, these hats were produced in a steady stream for five years, and now there were enough of them to behat an entire race of lilliputians. Doubtlessly, too, the bureaucrats who had allowed these hats to be produced had heads that would quickly retract inside fat necks. In any case, as I explained to all the recipients of my curious gifts, our heads are bigger here, but that is not to say that there is more stuff *in* them. I explained that the heads of Romanians at this time were filled with visions of a beautiful Jeffersonian democracy born wingedly full-grown out of their dreams and desires. Every Romanian wanted to be an American. Promised free elections in April by the National Salvation Front, Romanians hastened to form scores of new political parties. The front decreed that 250 people were sufficient to form a political party. For the next three months the telephones of Bucharest rang without surcease as every household tried to organize and hold a vision of the future. Considering the political inexperience of people who hadn't had a say in their own governing for more than a half a century, the results were surreal, touching, and not without moments of brilliance. By February twenty-nine parties had already registered. Many of their platforms were indistinguishable, occasions for the free practice of rhetoric. The only apparently substantial groups were organized by two former exiles,

Ion Rațiu, who returned to Romania after forty years in Western Europe, and Radu Câmpeanu, a businessman. Rațiu's party, the National Peasant party, and Câmpeanu's National Liberal party were pale replicas of Romania's prewar "historical parties," which had faded from the memory of most Romanians, who were, for the most part, born after 1947. The dispersion of the people into political grouplets was a successful tactic of the front, which at first declared that it would dissolve before the elections but then, suddenly, announced that it would constitute itself into a political party.

It was not the first decision taken and then rescinded by the front. Among the earliest front decrees had been the one outlawing the death penalty. It had been decreed after the execution of the Ceaușescus for ostensibly humanitarian reasons, but it was intended, in effect, to protect those who were soon going to be put on trial for "genocide" for their parts in the violence of December. Thousands of outraged demonstrators surrounded the NSF headquarters in early January demanding justice, the ouster of Communists from the provisional government, and the reinstatement of the death penalty. They chanted, "Death should be answered with death!," "Down with communism!," and "Kill the Communists!" The televised eight-hour confrontation ended when Ion Iliescu climbed on top of a tank, promised a nationwide referendum on the death penalty, and outlawed the Communist party. Standing beside him on the tank were prime Minister Petre Roman and Vice-Presidents Dumitru Mazilu and Gelu Voiculescu-Voican, Ceaușescu's executioner. The crowd believed that it had won and began shouting, "Victory! We are the people!" The front leaders also announced that the trials of Securitate agents in Timișoara would begin right away. Also promised was United Nations supervision of Romania's first free elections since 1947. Not all the demonstrators were convinced. Iliescu, Roman, and Mazilu all were Communists who had held important party positions in the past. In a few weeks Mazilu was forced to resign when it was revealed that he had been a Securitate colonel under Ceaușescu. Since then he has been revealing details of a long-standing conspiracy to overthrow Ceaușescu that has been greatly embarrassing to the front.

When I spoke to Mazilu on the telephone in November 1990—he was in Los Angeles on a speaking tour—he denied having ever been a Securitate officer. "I was a professor at the Ministry of Interior—Securitate school. . . . That's all." He complained about his treatment at the hands of the government and accused Securitate of still running the

Andrei Codrescu

country. He claimed to have also written the revolutionary platform on the days following the news from Timişoara. On December 21st his wife hid this document behind the refrigerator while armed civilians took him away in a jeep to shoot him. After driving around without finding a place quiet enough to do him in—the demonstrators were massing on the streets—they let him go. He went to the Communist Party Headquarters where he read his proclamation minutes before Iliescu, Roman, and the rest arrived. This was the platform later adopted by the front with two important points missing: immediate privatization of land and factories, and the withdrawal of Romania from the Warsaw Pact. "These points," Mazilu said, "were removed by Iliescu and Brucan . . ." The voice over the phone oozed sincerity at every point of this unbelievable tale of Superman Mazilu. My friend the poet Denisa Comănescu, who was visiting from Bucharest, happened to be present during this phone call. She tried hard not to shout in dismay while Mazilu recited the story of his heroic innocence. "How newly born he sounds!" she said afterward, shaking her head. Anyone who knew the realities of Romanian life under Ceauşescu would have the same dismayed reaction. How could anyone teaching at the Securitate school not be a Securitate officer?

A few days after the demonstration Iliescu announced that the decision to outlaw the Communist party had been "hasty." The Romanian Central Committee was made legal again, though no one publicly claimed membership, and its fate was left to the January 28 referendum, which was also going to decide the fate of the death penalty. Not long after, the front announced its decision to become a political party. In the face of protests from the barely organized opposition that lacked even typewriters to spread its message, the elections were postponed to May 20. Silviu Brucan—whose sinister laugh became one of the sound signatures of post-December Romania after the airing of Ted Koppel's unsettling documentary on ABC—breezily announced that "if the front did not participate, a political vacuum would be created. The newly created political parties could not fill that vacuum." In effect, Brucan and the front were doing what old Communists knew how to do best: dismissing people as politically immature and incapable of conducting their own affairs. Romanian democracy was off to a rocky start. The protests that inevitably followed, including a strongly worded statement by the U.S. State Department, gave the ruling front yet another occasion to change its mind. The National Salvation Front, announced

Brucan, would split in two: a provisional National Council that would administer the country until the election and a political party. The National Council would share power as well as television time with opposition parties. Romanian television had, it seemed, come completely under NSF control. But according to many observers, Romanian TV—in spite of what I witnessed with my own eyes—had been controlled all along, even at the height of the fighting in December.

The disturbing political developments in Romania were being shadowed by simultaneous revelations of great human tragedies. Tests by Romanian and French virologists had revealed that an even greater number of Romanian babies than previously thought were infected with AIDS. The exact percentage was not known, but preliminary data indicated already that Romania had joined the top three countries ravaged by the epidemic.

I must confess that after my return from Romania I followed the developments there with a rather uncritical eye. I wanted, more than anything, to help. Several organizations had sprung up with the purpose of providing much needed food and medicines. After stories of Romanian orphans and the AIDS epidemic began appearing in the American media, many relief organizations turned their attention to the human tragedy occurring in Romania. Adoption agencies began sending people there for babies. Desperate childless couples headed for Romania without an inkling of how to do business there. Many hotels filled with people determined to adopt at all cost. It was discovered that before the revolution the Ceauşescu government had been selling babies. (In addition to Jews and Germans!) Shortly after this revelation the National Salvation Front declared a moratorium on adoption. Babies could now leave Romania only with President Iliescu's express consent. This did not deter the applicants.

I was interested in helping Romania's fledgling opposition parties and the struggling free press. I formed a nonprofit corporation called rather grandly Romanian Information Technology Effort (RITE), and I began talking obsessively to dozens of people about the possibility of sending computers, copiers, video camcorders, fax machines, tape recorders, and typewriters to Romania. I was being plenty foolish. Software for computers did not exist in Romanian, and translating it was a mammoth job. Copiers needed paper and maintenance. Fax machines presupposed open phone lines. (The culture minister, Andrei Pleşu, said that he had six nonworking faxes in his offices, all donations.) Only tape recorders and manual typewriters did the job, and I wasn't able to get any of those. Romania was still struggling along in the prehistory of communications while we had passed—almost unnoticed, it seems— into its posthistory. Still, I met enthusiastic people willing to do all they could. A man in Philadelphia, an American who spoke good school-acquired Romanian, said that he would go to Romania for a year to teach computer use if someone paid for his stay there. I was unable to find anyone to provide a stipend. In fact, several of my better efforts were stymied for lack of easy access to contacts in Romania, where the bureaucracy operated very much as it always had, with Balkanic disdain, inaction, and mountains of papers and stamps. At the same time the much ballyhooed "fall of communism" did not produce immediate aid from the United States. I now believe that the United States was, in fact, wise to wait before committing help to a neo-Communist dictatorship—a military dictatorship at that.

As my idealistic efforts gathered self-propelled steam, the bad news from Romania grew at an alarming rate. On January 28, twenty thousand people, a majority of them young students and workers, the same people who brought down Ceauşescu, demonstrated against the front's decision to field its own candidates in the May 20 elections. People carried placards depicting the sickle and hammer and the swastika with an equal sign between them. The crowd chanted, "Down with Iliescu!," "Down with communism!," "Resign!" The government appealed to its supporters on television. Trucks full of well-organized factory workers were driven into the square. Patriotic songs were broadcast through the huge loudspeakers that were still in place around the central buildings and had been used for propaganda slogans during the Ceauşescu years. (The speakers had been used to broadcast simulated machine-gun fire during the fighting on December 22 in order to sow panic in the population.) Iliescu's workers attacked the demonstrators and tried to clear them from the front of the palace. Iliescu made a speech that was drowned out by the jeering of the angry crowd. His defenders chanted his name and hurled insults at the demonstrators. One of those insults, soon to recur was: "You are immigrants! You are not Romanians!" An ugly kind of nationalism began rearing its head here. Later that day the loyalist workers went on a rampage throughout the city. They smashed opposition party headquarters and beat up anyone who happened to look different, especially bearded students and people wearing blue jeans.

On February 18, 1990, a different breed of antigovernment demonstrators appeared. Unlike the resolutely nonviolent students and intellectuals, these men wielded iron rods. They smashed their way into the provisional government headquarters, shouting the opposition slogans. Hundreds of troops, backed by ten armored carriers, pushed them back. The iron rods and style of these protesters were more in keeping with the tactics of Iliescu's workers, and many opposition leaders denounced the action as the work of agents provocateurs from Securitate.

In the weeks preceding the election, demonstrations against the front became widespread. In Timişoara, the "cradle of the revolution," a group of intellectuals issued the Proclamation of Timişoara, the most important democratic document to issue from Romania thus far. Point eight of the declaration called for the banning of all officials of the Ceauşescu regime from seeking political office.

The demonstrators, now gathering regularly in University Square in Bucharest and elsewhere in the country, demanded also an independent television station. On April 22, 1990, a large demonstration marched on the television station, calling for Iliescu's resignation. In a sudden predawn raid riot police attacked and beat the demonstrators who had spent the night in University Square. Thousands of demonstrators, now including many better-organized student associations, protested the brutality of the police in the next days. Several protesters began a hunger strike. Iliescu denounced the demonstrators as *golani* ("bums"). It was a shocking word. *Golani* was how Ceauşescu had described the demonstrators in Timişoara in November. Using almost identical language, Iliescu also called the demonstrators Fascists, right-wingers, Iron Guardists. The old Communist style had "spontaneously" reasserted itself. In rising defiance of the regime, a small city of tents appeared, and University Square was declared a "neo-Communist Free Zone." Students occupied the square day and night, right under the windows of the Inter-Continental Hotel, where Western reporters and international observers who had come to monitor the elections were staying. The walls around the university sported anti-Communist, anti-NSF, and anti-Iliescu slogans. Unfortunately the Bucharest rebellion found little support in the country at large—with the exception of Timişoara and within intellectual circles. This situation arose partly because radio and television were completely pro-front and did their best to minimize, ridicule, and ignore the legitimacy of the demands of those in the square and because the opposition was fragmented, insecure, and unable to agree on a plan of action. Iliescu, who had been seen on television through the crucial hours of the revolution, was a hero. His mild smile played well with the inexperienced electorate, which was having its first taste of (controlled) media politics.

Rising nationalism also played its part. An ethnic bloodbath occurred in the Transylvanian city of Tîrgu Mureş between Romanians and Hungarians. Hungarians had been demanding rights long denied under Ceauşescu, including higher education in Hungarian. The nationalist Vatra Românească ("Romanian hearth") came into being in opposition to these demands and in general opposition to "foreign" elements, a category both vague and specific enough to include Jews, Germans, Gypsies, Serbs, and anyone else unfortunate enough not to be Romanian. Trucks full of Vatra members *wielding steel pipes and sticks* attacked Hungarians in Tîrgu Mureş. Vatra later claimed that the Hungarians attacked *them*. But more curiously, the trucks and the weapons resembled very much the trucks and weapons with which Iliescu's "workers" had gone to work on the demonstrators of Bucharest. It was no coincidence.

On May 20 the National Salvation Front, headed by Ion Iliescu, won an overwhelming 83 percent of the vote, a kind of percentage eerily reminiscent of the "unanimous votes" for Ceauşescu. International observers agreed that despite a number of irregularities, the Romanian electorate had spoken. Romania became the only country in Eastern Europe freely to elect another Communist government. A good case can be made that the Romanian people did not know that they were electing a Communist government. After all, Iliescu *said* that he wasn't a Communist. But that is hard to believe. Most likely, the subtle and not-so-subtle hints with the lead pipe and the stick had kept alive the fear instilled by forty-five years of police terror that three months could not erase.

After the victory of the front, the demoralized intellectuals and the dispirited opposition settled for airing their discontents in the (still) free press. Most of the demonstrators in the square went home. Two dozen hunger strikers stayed on. Speeches still went on in the "neo-Communist Free Zone," but this stage of the protest appeared to be at an end. In its first flush of victory the government even agreed to the protesters' demand for an independent television station. On June 13 there was a predawn raid by riot police, who cleared the square, beat up the people who refused to leave, and arrested several students. Sanitation trucks hosed down the tent city and ripped down the slogans of the rebellion.

Later that day, when the news of the arrests spread, a new demonstration began gathering strength. Unlike the previous demonstrations, however, here there was a feeling of violence. The young men leading the demonstration were not familiar to the observers, according to NPR reporter Kathleen Hunt, who observed the events at close range from the Inter-Continental Hotel. "They looked like drifters, and they looked violent," she writes. When riot-ready police arrived with shields and helmets, the demonstrators attacked them with rocks and Molotov cocktails. This behavior was clearly against the students' nonviolent beliefs until that point. I watched a videotape shot by a student that clearly shows that the first Molotov cocktail was not even thrown by a student but had ignited rather conveniently behind a police barricade.

Battles between the mob and police lasted all day, becoming increasingly more violent. The police barricades were formed of buses that were blocking intersections. Curiously these buses appeared to have had no gasoline in their tanks because they did not explode when they were set on fire. Inexplicably, at a certain point during the afternoon, the riot police suddenly abandoned their posts and retired inside their barracks. The streets were left to the demonstrators, who became jubilant and delirious. Their ranks, which had increased by several thousands, attacked the Ministry of the Interior, the building that had been the Securitate headquarters. They set it on fire. Oddly the firemen watching from one street away did not intervene to put it out. The crowd went to the television station next. The building was surrounded by cordons of soldiers and police. A newscaster inside announced that programming was being interrupted by demonstrators. But according to numerous eyewitnesses, there were no demonstrators in the building at that time. Amazingly then Romanian television, which had *never stopped broadcasting during the Revolution in December when it was under "heavy attack,"* stopped its operations because of student demonstrators. After that announcement had been made and when the station was off the air, "workers" armed with pipes and nightsticks attacked the crowd and brutally clubbed several dozen people. That evening Iliescu went on television (which had been miraculously "liberated") and said that a "Fascist," "Iron Guardist" coup was being attempted. He called on "democratic forces" to come to the capital to "liquidate" the Fascists. General Victor Stănculescu, the defense minister, mysteriously failed to restore order with his troops. President Iliescu claimed that he was unable to find his defense minister for a full six hours on June 13. The general had an image problem. He did not want the "People's Army," which had "come to the side of the revolution" in December, to look bad by killing people on television. Let Iliescu solve his own problem.

The "democratic forces," armed with pipes and sticks, arrived in trucks in the early morning. They wore blue miners' helmets with lit miners' lamps, their faces streaked with coal, looking as if they had come directly from the underworld. Iliescu greeted the first five thousand "miners" with a speech, thanking them for their prompt response. Food, drink, and dormitories had, in fact, been prepared for a full week before their arrival. Inspired by their leader, the "miners" took to the streets. For the next two days the horrified reporters at the Inter-Continental, and the world through them, watched as rampaging gangs of burly men beat hundreds, perhaps thousands of citizens, including women and children. While the nightmare beatings went on, some of the inhabitants gathered on the sidewalks to cheer. After kicking to a bloody pulp most people who looked even vaguely like students and intellectuals, or simply readers of books, the miners left for the Gypsy suburbs, where they attacked Gypsies in their homes. Several reporters attempting to cover the events were beaten, had their cameras destroyed and their notes ripped up. Small groups of these "miners," led by men with lists of intellectual opponents of the regime, began making "home visits." Some of my friends, by sheer luck, barely escaped being beaten either because they had been warned or because they happened to be away. The listholders were, of course, Securitate agents. And so were the so-called miners. According to Radu Tudoran, a poet who knew well the area of Jiul Valley where the mines are, these miners were not miners at all. They were Securitate-trained soldiers who had replaced the real miners of Jiul Valley in the seventies, when there were labor strikes against Ceauşescu. Since that time there had been few real miners in the coal region. All the mining was done by the Army.

The violent actions of Iliescu's shock troops were received with revulsion around the world. All the sympathy Romania had garnered during the overthrow of the Ceauşescu regime was lost. It was clear now that one dictatorship had replaced another. The spokesmen for the opposition, which had had its headquarters devastated by the "miners" (who also destroyed the school of architecture building), protested before international bodies. Romania's imminent observer status in the European Conference—an immensely helpful step toward rebuilding its devastated economy—was suspended. Most favored nation status, which had been withdrawn by the United States because of Ceauşescu's human rights abuses, was held up in Congress. Iliescu's victorious government had made a major blunder with grave consequences. The worst part of it—at least from the front's point of view—is that it was unnecessary. With a clear mandate to rule, the front could have ignored the protests and gotten on with its job of rebuilding. But old habits—especially police mentalities—die hard, if ever. And the big questions remained.

13

The Big Questions

A group of students, professors, and artists in Timişoara constituted themselves into the December 21 Association, with the purpose of finding out the truth about the events in December that were being distorted and lied about by the government. These "Decembrists" asked a cluster of extremely troubling questions that began with the dead of the revolution and ended with the men leading the country. They questioned the entire story of the revolution as told by the government.

Who fired at the demonstrators in Timişoara from December 15 to 17 and then at unarmed people everywhere in the country on December 22 and 23? What were the roles of the Army and Securitate in the killings?

The Army has maintained that the soldiers who fired on the crowds in Timişoara, Sibiu, and elsewhere were really Securitate officers in Army uniforms. These Securitate officers also led disobeying soldiers away and, barely out of sight of the crowds, shot them in the head. The Army now admits that orders to fire were given and obeyed by regular soldiers and that many of the killings were the work of the "People's Army." It is not clear why the Army fired on the people since its commanders had already decided, long before December, that they would back any popular uprising against Ceauşescu. A conspiracy to overthrow Ceauşescu had been in existence since 1981; it was centered on generals. General Nicolae Militaru revealed its work in some detail in the August 23, 1990, issue of the front newspaper *Adevărul*. General Iulian Topliceanu conceded in an interview on February 6, 1990, that weeks before Timişoara the Army's chiefs had been secretly analyzing and discussing the so-called curve of unfolding of social opposition, according to which it took only ten days for a Communist regime to fall from the moment that "destabilization" began. This analysis was based on the events in the rest of Eastern Europe and was made ostensibly for the purpose of pinpointing the correct time for the Army to pass to the "side of the people." On December 21 the Army did side with the people. But on December 22 the Army opened fire on the people. Why? The original explanation was that the Army that opened fire on the people was not the "People's Army," but the dreaded Securitate, small units of which fired invisibly at crowds from house roofs and basements. Securitate units loyal to Ceauşescu also fought in the Square of the Republic in Bucharest. In order to smash Securitate, the Army used tanks, cannons, and extraordinary quantities of ammunition. An Army shell destroyed the library of the University of Bucharest, where Securitate "terrorists" were hiding. One million bullets were fired by the Army at (or over) the neighborhood where many of my friends live in the city of Sibiu in Transylvania, ostensibly in response to the invisible Securitate. But according to Silviu Brucan—interviewed in conversation with General Militaru in *Adevărul*—Securitate was also part of the conspiracy against Ceauşescu. Brucan identified four Securitate units that remained loyal to the dictator: the Securitate school at Băneasa (2,000 men), USLA (Special Unit for Antiterrorist Action, 800 men), Section Five (450 men), and the Bucharest Defense Unit (600 men). According to Brucan, the reason why they remained invisible and why fighting in Bucharest took place only at night is that all the men in these units were trained as sharpshooters and had nightscopes on their rifles. This did not explain why these loyalists held their fire on the night of December 21, when the National Salvation Front was taking charge of the country in the Communist party headquarters in Bucharest. Nor did Brucan explain who fired on the people in all the other Romanian cities. Above all, what kinds of loyalists were these? They had abandoned the objects of their loyalty, Nicolae and Elena Ceauşescu, to hitchhike aimlessly with one bodyguard until captured by an unarmed country bumpkin. Asked about what happened to these "terrorists" after the shooting had stopped, Brucan said that they were captured by the Army but were then released by unknown people and allowed to "melt away" into Hungary and other foreign countries. Who were those responsible for letting them get away? Why weren't they punished?

After strong popular demands for trials of "terrorists," the NSF produced a number of laughable show trials. These trials of former high-ranking Ceauşescu officials, which had been expected to yield all sorts of revelations, were conducted with great restraints. A five-man military tribunal condemned four former ministers—Emil Bobu, Manea Mănescu, Ion Dincu, and Tudor Postelnicu—to life in prison. The verdict was hastily announced after two hours of deliberations. Other trials, of low-ranking Securitate men dressed in prison uniforms reminiscent of concentration camp inmates, with their heads shaved, were likewise conducted in secrecy and haste. The much publicized trial of Nicu Ceauşescu, the dictator's son, was interrupted and delayed several times because Nicu embarrassed the prosecutors by maintaining that no one in his entourage had fired either at the Army or at the people and that he hadn't ordered anybody to do so. Evidence bore him out. Nonetheless, he received twenty years in prison, mostly because of his name. The question, then, of who fired on the people in December remains open. The best guess is still that of my literary friend who surmised that a struggle for power between two rival Army or Securitate gangs claimed many innocent lives. And the awful truth is that the winning faction is in power in Romania today.

How many people really died?

The events of December 16, 17, and 18 in Timişoara were reported early by the Yugoslav news agency Tanjug, Hungarian radio, and TASS. Everyone praised these formerly inert news organizations for getting their journalistic feet wet in Romania, for reporting with such vividness and alacrity the extraordinary slaughter going on in a twentieth-century European country. Less than a year before, these news agencies could not have reported the truth if their lives depended on it. Their sole job had been to read pieces of paper handed to them by the "appropriate organs." Their young reporters were now able to report from a scene that Western reporters could not get to. They were able also to describe horrors unheard of since the Holocaust and to describe them in almost the same language used to describe Nazi horrors. Western news agencies soon joined the chorus by distributing the news from their Eastern European colleagues verbatim, even adding adjectives to drive the horror home. Before long, counts of the dead in Timişoara reached a horrific 10,000 with many more wounded. Through obsessively repeated broadcasts on Radio Free Europe, BBC, and the Voice of America, Romanians heard about the massacres taking place in their own country. Subsequent reports wildly inflated that figure to 64,000 until the world believed that genocide on an unprecedented scale was occurring. Even after Western reporters had reached the areas where the purported battles raged, the news continued to present the situation in the same way. A seasoned French reporter, Michel Castéx, who had covered the civil war in Lebanon, admits to having been completely taken in, in spite of his experience. Two decades of war in Lebanon had not produced as many victims as were claimed for Romania, yet he did not—for an unconscionably long time—question these reports. The original figure of 60,000 to 80,000 dead and twice as many wounded, uncritically accepted around the world, today stands—in the official government figure released on February 2, 1990—at 682 dead and 1,200 wounded in the entire country.

How was such discrepancy possible?

Castéx concludes that a process of mass hypnosis was going on, aided in part by the desire on the part of the world to believe that communism had finally come to an end in a spectacular and definitive way. The Romanian Revolution *would* have been a neat closure to the stunning collapse of Communist bureaucracies. The only trouble is that it wasn't a closure. More troubling than that, it was a skillfully staged play.

Staged by whom?

The Brucan-Militaru interview in the front newspaper *Adevărul* on August 23, 1990—the anniversary of the Soviet "liberation" of Romania in World War II, a highly significant date in the annals of Romanian communism—is an extraordinary, though partial and self-serving, admission that plans for a coup d'état to topple Ceaușescu had been in existence since 1981. The two men, Silviu Brucan and Nicolae Militaru, had been, respectively, heads of the political and military branches of the three-branched conspiracy. The third branch was Securitate. Plans were drawn to eliminate the Ceaușescus in 1984. The original attempt failed because the conspirators were partially betrayed. Several Army generals were placed under arrest. The three nuclei of the conspiracy functioned independently from one another so that any betrayal would affect only their immediate circles. The original nucleus came entirely from inside the Army and consisted of Generals Militaru, Ionița, and Kostyal. General Stefan Kostyal took the fall for the failure of the 1984 plot. According to General Militaru, the conspirators, who had gone so far as to purchase silencer pistols with hard currency from Turkey, looked for another opportunity to kill Ceauşescu, but none presented itself for several years. Exceedingly interesting is Militaru's assertion that he originally approached the Soviet Embassy to obtain the silencer pistols but that the KGB turned him down. He nonetheless surmises that the Soviets knew every move being made. Of course, they did. He does not say this in the interview, but General Militaru was a KGB agent. Furthermore, he was well known by the Ceauşescus to be one. A videotape of a prolonged tryst in a motel with his Soviet contact was used for entertainment at Ceauşescu parties. Silviu Brucan admits in the interview that Securitate knew about his role in the conspiracy as well but did not arrest him because he, too, was under the protection of Moscow. While confined to house arrest, he received regular visits from the Soviet ambassador—but also, he hastens to add, from the American and the British ambassadors.

What is the National Salvation Front?

All those who witnessed the "spontaneous" birth of the National Salvation Front on television believed that the front was the gift of the revolution on the streets. Bit by bit the biographical profiles of Romania's new leaders began to emerge, leading one to the inescapable conclusion that links between them had been forged in the deepest recesses of the Communist party and that many of them were connected directly to the mother party in Moscow. The front was unable to explain its origin. The Decembrists of Timişoara wanted to know if the NSF and its "revolution" had appropriated the revolt on the streets to use for its own ends. They were worried by the front leaders: Iliescu, Moscow party school chum of Mikhail Gorbachev's; Petre Roman, son of Valter Roman, cofounder of the Romanian Communist party; General Nicolae Militaru, KGB agent. . . . They remembered that Ion Iliescu, an engineer who had headed the State Technical Publishing House, had been also one of Ceauşescu's most trusted advisers until 1981, when he'd been accused of heresy. Iliescu's language, including his famous line about "the hydra" having been "decapitated," was familiar to those used to Communist phraseology. The young Petre Roman was also just the kind of new face this revolution of the young seemed to have spontaneously birthed, a young engineer, educated in Paris, who spoke three languages fluently. On the other hand, his Communist blue blood was unimpeachable. The more familiar face of Silviu Brucan, one of the pre-Ceauşescu ideologues of Stalinist Gheorghiu-Dej, was mitigated by his having been a "dissident," the author of the famous letter of the six addressed to Ceauşescu demanding democratic reform. A videotape (another one—note the multiplication of illusions) made only hours after the Ceauşescus had fled in the helicopter showed a meeting attended by many of these future leaders of Romania. They have drafted a proclamation and are looking for a good name to characterize their coalition. The Democratic Council and the Popular Unity Front are suggested. General Militaru interjects, "Why not the National Salvation Front? After all, it's been in existence for six months!" But according to the same General Militaru, the conspiracy against Ceauşescu led by senior members of the NSF began as far back as 1981. We are now approaching the eerie and unsteady ground where illusion meets reality, lies meet other lies, and nothing is generally what it seems. As for videotapes, it is worth noting that the chief producer of videotapes in Romania for all the years of the Ceauşescu regime was Securitate! It is known, for instance, that General Militaru and Ion Iliescu had been filmed and recorded in conspiratorial conversations by Securitate many months before December but were not arrested. In fact, they were protected. By whom? Securitate, at the request of Elena Ceauşescu, made many "blue movies" of government and party officials, including Elena's favorite: General Militaru's all-night party with his KGB honey. It appears though that like everything else in Romania, there were two Securitate, a "good" one and an "evil" one. The "good" protected the conspirators. The two "scholars" who executed the Ceauşescus—Colonel Măgureanu, the philosophy professor, and Voiculescu-Voican, the amateur astrologer—are believed to have been part of a super securitate unit, "the meta-Securitate," as poet Dorin Tudoran calls it. As befits a mystery that hovers continually among the sublime, the ridiculous, and the occult, the Ceauşescus' trial and execution appear to have been carried out by a philosopher and an astrologer.

What about the Ceauşescu flight and trial?

Never explained to anyone's satisfaction, the flight of the Ceauşescus remains one of the most pathetic stories of December.

One imagines the couple alone on the national highway, cold and disoriented, trying to understand where their thousands of expensively trained and armed "children" were.

How long before their arrest were the Ceauşescus abandoned? French secret services learned from the KGB that Ceauşescu was due for a fall in December. And then there was the TASS correspondent whose vodka I'd drunk and who told me that he had been in Timişoara waiting for something to happen since December 10. The events that sparked the revolution did not begin until December 15. For more than a decade there had been a slow erosion of support for the couple that became total on December 22. In the end, they were left absolutely alone, without a single friend. Was this the payoff for boundless arrogance or merely the extremely successful work of the conspiracy? Both, no doubt. At some point, a modicum of compassion for the couple was still operative. It is possible that the ill-timed visit to Iran after Timişoara had already exploded was in fact an attempt to get the Ceauşescus out of the way without killing them.

The ironies of the ultimate loneliness surrounding the end of the dictator did not stop with his physical death. A French pathologist who viewed the videotape of the dead Ceauşescus concluded that they had been executed at least one day before the videotape was made. His evidence suggests that the bodies were rearranged for filming. Given all the other staged dramas of this most showy "revolution," I am not surprised. But one must ask why? What purpose was served by the delay? Were there signs of torture that had to be cosmetically erased? We still do not have an official explanation.

What took place during the mysterious days of December 22 and 23—when the Ceauşescus were in custody but their capture had not yet been officially announced? Why were the arrests not announced until the twenty-fourth? Crucial days were either squandered, lost, or deliberately withheld. During these days many people died in fighting between still-mysterious factions. If any of them were indeed loyalists fighting for their leader, they might have laid down their weapons if they had known that their leader had been captured. Most likely, however, during these two "blank" days, various interests were negotiating for power in the post-Ceauşescu era. The faction holding the dictator and his wife was holding the best hand. Precisely who was holding them, what was being negotiated, and what personalities were involved are a subject of intense debate in Romania today.

The melodramatic story of the couple's useless attempt to escape, and the enthusiasm of the execution squad turned out to be lies. Why add such baroque detail? One is tempted to attribute some of the extra color to the dramatic enthusiasm of the scriptwriters, who like all artists, needed to show off with extra flourishes, perhaps leaving stylistic clues of their identities.

After the image of the two crumpled bodies was released, there was a storm of emotional controversy about the execution. Those who opposed the swift disposal claimed that Romania was off to a bad, undemocratic start. A public trial should have been held. Those who approved said that the execution had been necessary in order to stop the dictator's loyalists from still waging fierce resistance in the cities and in the mountains. The debate was international, and it involved many people and issues. President Bush said that he would have preferred a public trial but he could understand the need to act decisively. But others, who would have had plenty of cause to rejoice at the demise of the tyrants, were not so sanguine. Virgil Tănase, a dissident Romanian writer who had been the victim of a Ceauşescu-ordered assassination attempt, said unequivocally on December 28 in Bucharest (where he'd returned after thirteen years in exile): "The trial was the shameless farce of an incompetent court. . . . The tribunal did not have any proof of guilt. . . . I would have preferred to see a public trial taking place even after the abolition of the death penalty. To my great surprise, the Ceauşescu regime has managed to continue, thanks to this trial. . . ."

Originally, the National Salvation Front had promised a public trial of the Ceauşescus. When it executed the couple instead, its explanations were confusing. The interim president of the provisional government, Ion Iliescu, announced the execution by saying that the "hydra had been decapitated," a hackneyed phrase plucked right out of old Communist party jargon. Iliescu said that thousands of lives were saved by the prompt execution. He was supported by some of the country's officials. "After telling us for years that 'dead is better than red,' " a Romanian writer told an American reporter, "we give you a dead red and you complain?" And the poet Mircea Dinescu, on television, looked the world in the eyes: "A dead dictator is better than a live one." One whole month later, Silviu Brucan looked an interviewer in the eyes and mused: "Perhaps it would have been better to conduct a public trial. . . . Seeing the dimensions of the disaster they had wrought . . . it would have been a lot worse than death. . . ."

Clearly, those who executed the Ceauşescus feared the revelations a public trial would bring. But the truly disquieting aspect for a student of language is that the prosecution and the accused were like mirrors of each other. They spoke the same language, one filled with mutually understood bureaucratic buzz words, the simulacrum language of the professional *apparachik*. Asked if they understood that they have been condemned to death, the Ceauşescus nodded yes. Asked whether they objected, they shook their heads no. Under Romanian law, an objection is considered sufficient reason for a new trial. Yet they did *not* object. Why? Perhaps because they did not recognize the authority of the tribunal, and thus no sentence passed by this unrecognized tribunal could be valid. But the tribunal that condemned them, whether valid or not, was clearly going to subject them to a very real death. A real death by an unreal tribunal is still death. Therefore, they ought to have objected. It was almost as if we were watching a play by Eugène Ionesco, the Romanian playwright who understood the absurdity of life in the Balkans better than anyone. To deepen further the unreality of the terrible reality, the Ceauşescus were mockingly given medical exams before they were executed. One wonders if they would still have been shot if the doctor had found something wrong with them.

To answer the whys by means of how, how was the revolution stolen?
    The television station was said to be under constant siege by Securitate "terrorists," but it never went off the air. Couldn't these "crack troops" of snipers take out the transmission tower? The unfolding of the military situation as reported by Romanian television was a dramatic backdrop to the birth of the National Salvation Front out of political chaos. The Romanian "Revolution" was *entirely* televised, and all those of us who believed for years with Gil Scott-Heron that "the revolution will not be televised" were shaken by it.
    In truth, there were two revolutions: a real revolution that was not televised and that continues, particularly in Timişoara, and a studio revolution that fooled the entire world. Who could ever forget the piles of corpses stacked like cordwood in front of the Timişoara cathedral? Or the slaughter of children holding candles on the steps of the Timişoara cathedral? Or the image of the mother and child shot with a single bullet, lying in the arms of death? Watching these images in New Orleans via CNN, I was moved and enraged, along with millions of others around the world. We now know. The mass graves discovered in Timişoara and presented to the world as proof of the Hitlerite insanity of Securitate were in fact bodies dug out of a pauper's cemetery with autopsy scars visible. Many of them were in an advanced state of decay.

Ted Koppel found out that the dead children on the steps of the Timi-şoara cathedral were a fabrication. An independent videotape taken seconds later at the spot showed no bodies at all. And the extraordinary picture of the mother and her baby killed with the same bullet, seen thousand of times on all the world's TV screens, was a gross collage. A woman who had died of alcoholism had had an unrelated dead baby placed on her chest for video purposes. Someone made a neat bullet hole in both bodies.

There were other fabrications presented on Romanian TV. The poisoned water in Sibiu was never poisoned. There is no proof that a single Arab, whether Libyan or Palestinian, shot at anybody anywhere in Romania. It was discovered that much of the gunfire we heard in the Square of the Republic was simulated, using the same loudspeakers Ceauşescu used to amplify his speeches. Many other spontaneous images begin to look suspect. The extraordinarily articulate peasant from Maramureş who called in December for a shorter workweek and better pay for "our brothers the miners" got immediate satisfaction. The miners were given a shorter workweek, and their salaries were doubled. In June "our brothers the miners" came to Bucharest and went on a bloody rampage against the enemies of the National Salvation Front. Was anything what it looked like?

The mystery of the videotape made of the Ceauşescu "trial" is significant in this regard. Besides the "doctored" section showing the bodies, we know that there were two versions of this tape: a crudely edited short one, shown first, and a longer one, shown later, which led to the suicide of Major General Georgică Popa, the head of the "tribunal." But by the time Romanian television broadcast the edited tape of the trial on December 27, complete copies of the longer, unedited tape were already in wide circulation. A French news agency received one. A professor in Tennessee called to tell me that a famous Romanian athlete had given her one. Who was distributing the tape, and why?

If a certain eeriness begins to creep in right now alongside the genuine emotional power of the events, it is as it should be. The Romanian revolution was a complex affair. It was a dramatic triumph that had the whole world for its audience, a world that keeps wondering long after the final curtain how much of what it saw was real. If I hadn't lost my normally skeptical head to the euphoria of December, I would have questioned the single most evident source of news about the revolution: television. But it was precisely television that seduced me during my visit and made me lose sight of things I already knew. I have raged enough against TV to know that the medium is eminently manipulatable. But even though I knew that the extraordinary figure of sixty-five thousand dead (used as an accusation against Ceauşescu at his "trial") was considerably lower, I did not ask anyone at the time what caused such astounding discrepancy. I had seen the bodies on television, but only a few and *always the same bodies*. I didn't ask how such thing could be possible.

Imagine the shock and dismay of our newsmakers and our idealists—including myself—when most of these horrible events we saw with our own eyes on television turned out not to have happened at all. How could the grizzled, experienced Western journalists who are sworn to hard facts have missed the many clues and glaring contradictions that pointed to artifice? The astounding truth of the matter is that much of the glorious Romanian "revolution" was, in fact, a staged play, a revolution between quotation marks. Let me also say that for all that, there were heroes, martyrs, and true revolutionaries. A mass uprising did take place, but it was skillfully manipulated by the men who run Romania today. It could also be true that for a few glorious moments the first rebels to arrive at the television station created a free atmosphere unparalleled in the history of the country, an atmosphere in which all ideas of "taste" and "propriety" lost meaning. Whatever could be put on the screen was, whether it was a one-legged beggar with a delirious story or a rock video brought out of a secret drawer. But it couldn't have been long after, however, the young revolutionaries (if that's who they were) started becoming "responsible," and the "spontaneous" provisional government showed up with its own TV script. The television station then became the headquarters of the new government, which, as far as most people were concerned, was born out of video like Venus out of the seashell. And hats must be off to the producers of the exceedingly realistic docu-drama of the strategic military center from where, in a charged atmosphere reminiscent of *Reds* or *Dr. Zhivago*, generals with telephones on both ears shouted orders at troops on vast invisible battlefields in every part of the country.

Today I stand abashed by my naiveté. Much of that Romanian "spontaneity" was as slick and scripted as a Hollywood movie. If I were in charge of the Emmys, I'd give one to the Romanian directors of December 1989. Many aspects of the televised drama remain extremely mysterious. I still do not understand Secretary of State Baker's offer to allow the Soviets to intervene on the side of the "revolutionaries." He must have known at least in outline the true shape of the Romanian situation. I cannot believe that the CIA was as taken in by the exaggerated reports of massacres and fighting from East European news agencies as the more naive press organizations were. The administration must have had reasons for going along with the hysteria of the press, in part because it distracted from the U.S. invasion of Panama but also because a deal must have been made with the Soviets, a deal that, I am sorry to say, leaves Romania where it always was: in the Soviet sphere of influence. Many people now believe—in the face of mounting evidence—that the mastermind of the Romania operation was the KGB, that the Romanian revolution was a beautifully orchestrated piece of Kremlin music conducted by Maestro Gorbachev. What's more, the operation had the full cooperation of the CIA. I recently bought a T-shirt in Washington, D.C., that says: "TOGETHER AT LAST! THE KGB & THE CIA. NOW WE ARE EVERYWHERE." Even one T-shirt can sometimes be smarter than all the news media.

Many weeks after I returned from Romania, I was not prepared to entertain the increasingly obvious scenarios of deceit. I wanted to preserve the euphoria of my visit. But innocence is hard to preserve.

On March 16, 1990, in Houston, Texas, exactly three months after the demonstrations in Timişoara that sparked the Romanian Revolution, I met the man responsible for setting off that spark: Reverend László Tökes of the Reformed Lutheran Church in Transylvania, Romania.

"He is younger than I thought," commented one of the Houstonians gathered for the occasion at the house of Arvàd Téléké, a Hungarian-born businessman. Indeed. A young-looking thirty-six, the average-built man with dark hair and modest manners before us seemed hardly the type to start a revolution. I had come at the invitation of Peter Kurz, president of the American-Hungarian Association, and I was the only Romanian there, a fact that didn't escape the guest of honor. He insisted on speaking Romanian to me. He also insisted, in the face of various nationalist sentiments expressed later by Hungarians, that solidarity between various nationalities in Transylvania is essential to the survival of the region. A member of the National Salvation Front, Bishop Tökes defended the new government and said that he was suspicious of the so-called historical parties of Romania, resurrected for the upcoming elections, which made little mention of minorities. When a violently anti-Communist Hungarian remarked that "the only good Communist is a dead Communist," Reverend Tökes said gently, "It is easy to say such things from abroad."

The Télékés' living room with its immense fireplace gave onto a well-tended Japanese garden. The portly men of a certain age and their elegant wives wearing expensive jewelry were for the most part refugees from the Hungarian Revolution of 1956. They had done well in America. Among those in attendance was Madame de Menil, the fabulously rich art patron. After a modest speech in which he mentioned the need for reconciliation in Transylvania and the plight of orphans, Reverend Tökes was presented with a check. He held it awkwardly and said, "Thirty thousand dollars, thank you!" The embarrassed host looked at the check and whispered in Reverend Tökes's ear. "Ah, three thousand!" he corrected himself. Everyone laughed. The host also took the opportunity to announce at this moment that Reverend Tökes had been just named bishop of the Reformed Lutheran Church of Transylvania, an announcement that drew warm applause. The old bishop, whom Bishop Tökes was replacing, had been the man who had ordered the young minister to evacuate his house and move to a small congregation in a remote village. When Tökes refused, the bishop sued and Romanian authorities were called upon to enforce the eviction, the famous human chain was formed, and Timişoara exploded (as reported by members of Eastern European and Soviet news agencies).

In the Télékés' dining room, a sumptuous display of national Hungarian dishes, with little Hungarian flags sticking out of the stuffed cabbage, had been laid for the guests. Amid all the opulence the minister emanated modesty and a kind of moral force that was delightfully evident. I spoke to the chief doctor of a Houston hospital, a man obviously moved by the events in his native region. "I will do anything to help," he said. "I can offer medicine, a complete clinic, medical equipment. . . ." I took his card, hoping to pass it to someone on my next trip to Romania. I had the distinct impression that the generosity of those present could be multiplied by many well-meaning Americans, but I sensed also that one had to act quickly before the sympathy aroused by the Romanian revolution could evaporate.

Next day Reverend Tökes held a trilingual service at Madame de Menil's Rothko chapel in Houston. Rothko's large black canvases dominating the famous interdenominational room were charged with the spiritual vibrations of the many religious and spiritual leaders who'd held services and meetings here. I felt their power the moment I entered the room, and felt, too—quite physically—the added force of the Hungarian-Romanian minister who was a symbol of the revolution. "I am sorry," he said, "that so many died. Let's pray for them." After the memorial service to the dead of the Romanian revolution, small groups formed, discussing the events. There were quite a few Romanians here. Several people were greatly animated, and I approached them. I wanted to ask them what they thought of Bishop Tökes's conciliatory speech, but I was stopped cold in my tracks when I heard a man say: "It won't help us with the kikes. . . . The goddamn Prime Minister Roman is a kike . . . and the Hungarians are right behind him. . . ." The speaker was a rotund man in his fifties with an expression of virulent contempt on his face.

"At this late date, with so many dead, how can you go about spreading hate?" I said indignantly and, no doubt, loudly. "How can you say 'kike'?" He turned to me as if I had just complimented him on the design of his obnoxious flowery tie and introduced himself: "Georgescu. I own a travel agency here and I'm a member of Vatra Românească!" I'd heard of Vatra Românească, the ultranationalist organization whose only platform, as far as I could discern it, was hatred for minorities.

"Then you're in the wrong place," I said.

"Not really. We have to see what *they* are up to."

It chilled my blood. Georgescu had been out of Romania since the end of World War II. He had been, no doubt, a member of the Nazi Iron Guard. Here he was, unrepentant. For a moment Mark Rothko's large black paintings seemed to project a whole spiritual drama of shame and futility instead of hope and transcendence. It wasn't going to be easy. I prayed that Georgescu here would somehow disappear in the smoke of his own hatred. But I knew that he wouldn't. Today Vatra Românească has grown immensely. Its platform hasn't grown any more sophisticated.

Listening to Tökes, I had the feeling that great events are sometimes possible because of the unadorned moral force of a single human. That is, of course, a Christian belief, and Christianity may, in spite of Georgescu and in spite of the church's own dark past, be a force for the good in Romania. There is an unavoidable religious dimension to the Central-Eastern European revolutions of 1989. From the Roman Catholic Church in Poland to Bishop Tőkes's small ministry, Christianity played a major role. That said, it should be noted that the administration of the Romanian Orthodox Church, as well as Rabbi Rosen, leader of the Jews in Romania, were cynical servants of the Ceauşescu regime, responsible for terror, not faith. The leaders of these churches were criminals, who not only kept silent when people were killed for their beliefs but actively denounced and betrayed activist believers. The sinister Ministry of Cults, which oversaw the churches in Romania, was an arm of Securitate. The Romanian Orthodox Church has an evil past that precedes communism. In the 1940s its priests were active Nazi sympathizers who blessed and sometimes participated directly in pogroms against Jews. Next to Ceauşescu's monstrous palace in Bucharest stands the Church of Ilie Gorgani, where the founder of the Iron Guard, Corneliu Zelea Codreanu, was canonized as a saint in 1940. The religious story must be told, uncomfortable as it may make people. For all their positive work during the recent events, the Polish and Czech churches also have checkered pasts. It will not do to ignore this problem as does *The New York Times*, for instance, which printed excerpts from Václav Havel's speech before the United States Congress, but left out all references to God and miracles.

Nonetheless, I fancied that I could see why Reverend Tőkes had been the impetus for the popular revolt that sparked the revolution. The quiet man dressed in a well-worn black suit emanated calm confidence. He seemed to be simply *decent*. His sermons, preaching nonviolence and resistance, were only the considered thoughts of a man who decided to speak out. There was a Gandhi-like simplicity about him, a frugality, too, that contrasted most pointedly with Georgescu's rolls of fat. The day before, Tőkes had met President Bush in Washington, had spoken in New York, and was now on his way to Los Angeles. Bishop Tőkes bore his notoriety and exhaustion with good humor. "I wonder what's more exhausting," one of the Houstonians murmured, "persecution or fame. . . ."

I asked Bishop Tőkes what he saw outside his window on December 15, the day of the human chain. "People," he said simply, "a lot of people."

But these "people" were many people. They were by no means united in a multinational human chain any longer. After the "miners" beat up the students and intellectuals asking to know the truth on June 14 and 15, 1990, it became next to impossible for even the most tolerant well-wisher to support the Romanian National Salvation Front. I decided to go back to Romania to observe the situation at close range. I was afraid that the temporary liberty (or illusion of liberty) that had been won in December was about to vanish. I had the perfect pretext for returning: my twenty-fifth high school reunion.

14

Return to Bucharest

Otopeni Airport on this hot July day was an ugly idea of a police state antechamber. It looked like a movie director's idea of a set for a grade B thriller. The walls dripped a kind of fifties substance. Hawaiian glass beads were embedded in it. Travelers passed through unvarnished wooden cubicles ringed by soldiers. On the other side waited an unsavory assortment of cabdrivers, porters, money changers, black marketeers. Faded posters advertising Romania's wonder drug Gerovital and the delights of Black Sea casino gambling hung in dusty disarray around the filthy baggage terminal. I had noticed last December how creepy the place was, but it took a hot, muggy Bucharest summer day to bring out the highlights. I had spent three cramped hours from Paris listening to an obnoxious professor from Brooklyn College who was writing a book on the Romanian Communist Lucian Goldmann. He was going to Bucharest to talk to Goldmann's old Communist pals, some of whom had only recently been put to pasture by the revolution. Others were former honchos of Ana Pauker and Gheorghe Gheorghiu-Dej's regimes. "Doesn't it strike you as ironic," I asked him, "that the only Marxists left now are American academics?" He launched into some spiel about good intentions thwarted, misread Marx, and so on. I tuned him out, so he continued riffing in French to a young guy who was going to Bucharest to buy cheap Romanian shoes for resale in France. *There you have it*, I thought. *Between these two clowns lies the whole story.*

Happily Bucharest is not Otopeni. I looked out the window of the taxi and decided to take everything in with an open mind, simply smell and feel my way around. I wanted to walk the little streets, sit on park benches, and go to museums. That meant, of course, holding off my work-crazy colleague Mr. Michael Sullivan of NPR, who was coming along once more. This time he claimed to be on vacation. Or so he said. The trouble with Mr. Sullivan is that he is a member of his generation, a thirtysomething that can't take it easy. He had a list of notables to interview, beginning with the president and the prime minister. Also on his list was Colonel Virgil Măgureanu, the mysterious Securitate philosophy professor who was rumored to run the country. General Stănculescu was also rumored to run the country. Quite possibly everyone was rumored to run the country. My money was on the one-eyed Gypsy with the shiny suit who hung out on the corner by Hotel Bucharest with a stack of English-language picture books called *Scenes from the Romanian Revolution*.

Hotel Bucharest, where we put up, is a new hotel, guaranteed, according to ever-knowledgeable sources, to have been built with bugs already installed in the walls like the American Embassy in Moscow. The reception was crystal clear, and the equipment Sony. There *was* something in the walls because when I recorded a few impressions later that evening, Michael heard a distinct electronic sound in his earphones. He pinpointed the probable source of the buzz and fed some high-pitched sound into it. If anyone was listening, he's probably seeing an ear specialist now. From that time on, we put Bruce Springsteen in the cassette deck whenever we discussed Romanian personalities. Discussing Colonel Măgureanu between the lines of "Dancing in the Dark" seemed appropriate somehow. Personally I was hoping that Michael wouldn't get any of his interviews so I wouldn't feel guilty when I refused to go along and translate. Unfortunately it was July 1, two weeks after the awful beating of students by "miners," and Romania was trying awfully hard to repair its damaged image. There were not many Western reporters in the country. Michael got all his interviews, with the significant exceptions of President Iliescu, colonel Măgureanu, and the arrested student leader Marian Munteanu, who had been taken to prison directly from his hospital bed, where he lay after a severe beating by the "miners." Both Prime Minister Petre Roman and General Victor Stănculescu had agreed to talk. In addition, there was Culture Minister Andrei Pleşu, Anton Uncu, the editor of Romania's only serious and trustworthy newspaper, *România Liberă*; the student leader Mihai Gheorghiu, who was leading a National Students Congress to discuss action for freeing Marian Munteanu; and Foreign Minister Adrian Năs-tase. The postelection Iliescu government was composed mostly of young technocrats who had studied abroad. Very few ministers were over forty-five years of age, but significantly, they were the minister of defense, General Stănculescu, and Victor Babiuc, the minister of justice. I wished Michael good luck.

I went out onto the streets, expecting to see a nervous city that had recently been at war. But something didn't add up. Bucharest was no Beirut. If anything, it was narcotically peaceful, in a deep green mid-summer way. People strolled lazily in the warm evening. The cinemas were doing brisk business. Two theaters, one specializing in musical comedy, the other in satire, had their doors wide open. On one of their posters a wit had added the name of Romania's prime minister, Petre Roman, to those of the actors. In Cişmigiu Park lovers on benches were wrapped obliviously about each other. On other benches, ladies and gents of a certain age murmured and nodded in the twilight, their gestures unhurried. Children played soccer on the grass. A dog lying lazily on the path of cars on a traveled street got up only when a Romanian Dacia was *this* close to his cur's head.

Around University Square, where only days before coal-striped miners had beaten students and bystanders with lead pipes, the Gypsies were doing a lively business selling the latest papers, some of them like *Ro-mânul* ("The Romanian") born that day. I bought: *Papagalul* ("The Parrot"), a satirical weekly; *Sărutul* ("The Kiss"), Romania's first erotic publication, with pictures so fuzzy it's hard to say whether they are nudes or distant space blots; *Opus*, which calls itself a "semi-independent weekly" and explains the "semi" by claiming that "in a world of mutual dependencies" it is "dependent on truth and humor"; *Phoenix*, another weekly, which proclaims in bold letters that it is "melting in the flames of its own dream . . . only to luminously reappear out of it. . . ." There are, in fact, elements of exuberant silliness and touching humor to the mushrooming and, amazingly, still free press of Romania. But the chief opposition newspaper, *România Liberă*, was not easy to find; a vendor pulled it from under his box when I handed him twice the cover price. Later, when we interviewed its editor, Anton Uncu, he complained bitterly about government sabotage of his newspaper. Under the pretext of a "paper shortage" (a ploy known since the days of Ceauşescu) his run had been cut from a million and a half to just under half a million. There were no ways of verifying the accuracy of the runs since all the printers were front supporters. The bundles of papers headed by train to the provinces never got there. This was true. In Sibiu I stood in line for the papers, and the woman in front of me asked for *România Liberă*. "I don't have it," the vendor replied. "Why not?" the woman insisted.

"You know why not." He shrugged impatiently.

And she did know. The trouble with having been such a closed society is that everyone knows everything, unfortunately. And what is not known is assumed. And what is assumed is that certain things are better left unspoken. But then here was *România Liberă* saying all the unspeakable things. For that reason, it was unavailable. Clearly, whoever ran the country wanted things left unsaid.

"What paper do you read?" I asked several people, including my cabdriver.

"*România Liberă*," they all said.

"Why?"

"Because it tells the truth."

We asked Uncu if there was a split in the government on the action of the "miners" in June. He believed that there was indeed a split between the old politics of Ion Iliescu and the slicker new style of Petre Roman. "When there is a crisis, Iliescu calls the miners. Roman calls the technocrats."

Not far from the raucous street vendors, by the fountain in University Square, a crowd was arguing politics. All about them were reminders of the June violence, mostly on the graffiti-scarred walls. I read: "ILIESCU-CEAUŞESCU, FREE MARIAN MUNTEANUŞ" "ILIESCU THE NIGHT-STICK, THERE IS NO DEMOCRACY WITHOUT PLURALISM," "DOWN WITH THE DICTATORSHIP." But there were no demonstrators here now, and the police presence was minimal. Gypsies had appointed themselves keepers of the candles still lit at the sites commemorating the dead of December. Last winter they had burned dramatically in the ice-covered snow. Now they seemed makeshift, like campfires, blackening the university walls. I stepped carefully over streamlets of infernal black goo, watching for my pockets. It seems that the Romanian government, so proud of its December "revolution," would have built some sort of heroes' monument here instead of allowing this unsightly barbecue pit to smolder in the heart of the capital. Something definitely didn't add up. I asked a Gypsy man if he'd had any trouble with the miners. He gave a wide gold-toothed grin. "We have swords now, this big." He gestured, his palms about three feet apart. "We are waiting for the miners now!"

Bucharest, its old fin de siècle buildings peeling melancholically in the twilight, had plenty of monuments to heroes of other revolutions. As I looked at the university library, now enclosed in scaffolding, and saw people back in their slow summer Balkan rhythms, I found it hard to match this city to the crisis-racked, snow-covered revolutionary Bucharest in my mind. And yet this *was* the place I had visited during the terrible winter of 1989, burying its dead under the snow, the place most recently torn by an earthquake and ripped apart by violence. The facade of every building was still pockmarked by bullets from first to last floor. Only weeks ago these sidewalks had seen new blood. Still, I couldn't help feeling—and what can you do about feeling? it cares nothing about facts—that it was safer here than in certain parts of Washington, D.C., or New Orleans at this hour. Back at the Bucharest I put through a call to America. The operator said, "All the circuits are disturbed." They sure were.

The hotel had two restaurants and a lobby bar. The obvious restaurant was a crowded and smoky joint that served the basic burned gristle steak and motor-oil french fries and cheap wine. We ignored it and headed for the other through the bar lounge. Reclining on the vinyl settees were a dozen hookers with their pimps, sipping delicately at overpriced Pepsis and smoking ostentatious Kents. They batted extremely long eyelashes as we passed, shifting nylons in miniskirts. One of them whispered to me between clenched teeth, "A dollar for a condom!" I felt for them. All the outward signs of their well-being were dearly bought. Romanian women had been long deprived of even the most elementary beauty aids. Nylons could be had only on the black market. The same was true for cosmetics. Even absolutely essential articles of feminine hygene were lacking. One foreigner was offered an heirloom icon in a silver frame for a box of Tampax.

The other restaurant had no sign above the door. A Napoleon-like creature guarded the front. I slipped him the required dollar bill and entered a grand salon. Under the sparkling chandeliers diners in evening clothes supped on a stunning variety of dishes. Fifteen different salads sat on a white linened buffet table. Viennese puff pastry on silver dishes circulated on noiseless carts. The popping corks of champagne bottles punctuated the throaty laughter of women wrapped in revealing haute couture and Italian shoes. We could have been in Paris and Rome. "Where did this world come from?" I asked Michael. He had no idea. But he ordered two entrées, just in case we had to return to reality. This was clearly the favorite place of the *nomenklatura*. All the men were partly bald and in their forties, and many of the women, only few of whom were wives, were in their twenties and thirties. An air of insouciance reigned as the fat tuxedoed waiters rushed to refill champagne and wine glasses. The place was not as much decadent as possessed by a desire to live high, to show off, to be grand in some imaginary European manner of the last fin de siècle. I ordered two soups, a sweet one and a sour one, trout with vegetables, and mămăligă (cornmeal mush) with sour cream on the side. We had several bottles of vintage wine. A tall man with fierce dark mustaches, accompanied by a beautiful barefoot Gypsy in several colorful skirts, appeared in the doorway. The couple stood there in erect splendor, perfectly aware of the sensation they were creating. The maître d', followed closely by two subalterns, rushed toward them. "Do you have a reservation?"

"Yes," the man said proudly, "Cioaba."

The three men of dining bowed simultaneously halfway to the floor. "Right this way!"

The couple were seated at a table right in front of the Gypsy orchestra, which also bowed when they sat down, broke off whatever sentimental air they were worrying, and began playing something that resembled "Hail to the Chief."

"Who's that?" I asked the waiter.

"Cioaba, king of the Gypsies. He's a member of the front. Owes the government twenty million marks." Between courses our waiter told us the whole story. Cioaba, the *boulibasha* ("king") of the Romanian gypsies, was a very rich man who had persuaded the new government to return to the Gypsies two ounces of gold each in payment for the gold confiscated from them by the Communists in 1947. He pledged to reimburse the government for the difference in the cost of gold at current market value, which came to twenty million deutsche marks. But as of now Cioaba hadn't paid the government a red cent, so everyone treated him very well. "When he pays," said the waiter, "he'll never eat in a restaurant like this again!"

Next morning, while Michael went to interview General Stănculescu, I strolled leisurely through Bucharest and talked to ordinary people. I honestly did not want to have anything to do with that man whose picture I had seen and who made my gorge rise. I have never been able to abide either authority or bureaucrats. That is why I'm a poet. When Michael insisted that I come, I told him, "You're a journalist, so guys like that may be your business; but I'm a poet and I hate snakes, and I don't have to pet them if I don't want to." To his credit, he understood me perfectly. I think he hates snakes, too, but he wanted me to come along so he wouldn't have to suffer alone. Some peoples' ideas of vacation are most amazing.

I sat down on a kind of windowsill that was actually a bench at an open-air beer garden. A guy with bulging muscles under a thin shirt knocked back three quick beers in a row as I watched. His elbow rested on a soggy copy of the front newspaper, *Adevărul* ("The Truth"). "What's the government saying?" I asked him.

"The government is lying," he said. "That's what governments do," he added.

(At that very moment Michael was being lied to by General Stănculescu. The way he tells it, the general received him in an extremely ornate hall. There were ten telephones on his desk. Prime Minister Petre Roman had only eight. "You have ten telephones and the prime minister has only eight. What are those phones for?" Michael asked. "That's for city troops; that's a Warsaw Pact phone; that's a red line. . . ." The general recited all his phones in measured tones. When he finished, two men dressed in coat and tails came in, bent at the waist, bearing two delicate porcelain cups of steaming espresso. They set these in front of the two men, and still bent at the waist, they walked backward out the door. "Where were you for six hours on June thirteenth when President Iliescu needed help in University Square?" The general did not answer for a long time. Clearly the time had come either to liquidate this news provocateur or to bite the bullet. The general looked up. In an instant a man appeared carrying a cigarette on a small platter. Following closely behind him was another man with a lighter. The general took the cigarette, accepted a light, took a long drag. The two men disappeared. "I was . . . at a Warsaw Pact meeting," he said, very slowly, puffing on every word, which came out with a little smoke cloud around it like a cartoon. "Still," insisted Michael in American faux innocence, "it seems that the president of the country ought to be able to find his defense chief anytime." Stănculescu answered: "Yes." At that moment Michael knew that he stood before the true ruler of Romania. The man was no longer a rumor but a very scary fact.)

I bought the guy a beer. "This country is sick; everyone in it is sick. . . . If we don't get the truth, we all are going to die," he said. When I told him that we have the same feeling about Romania in the West, he turned on me. "You have no right," he said. "We need help. We are men, not animals. You sent us ripped clothes in December, used pajamas. You do not punish sick people; you help them. But now you stand smugly by, refusing to help." He was in a belligerent five-beer mood now and insisted on telling me how he sees it: "This country's being sold piecemeal by Gypsy speculators, torn apart by Hungarians and émigrés, cheated by Jews . . . the government is bankrupt!" he shouted, putting all his peeves together in no apparent order.

As I walked on, the trees, so peaceful-looking only yesterday, now seemed rather sad and underwatered. Those lovers sitting on the benches under them probably had had little to eat since yesterday. If they made the mistake of marrying and trying to live on something more than love, they'd be hopelessly navigating Bucharest's empty "food complexes," after long workdays, in search of something other than rusty cans of congealed fat and sausages that are better left unpictured.

There was a market next to the store where tomatoes and peaches at exorbitant prices lay unattended under swarms of flies. It wasn't a great start for free enterprise. Starved for fresh fruit, I bought a kilo of peaches, which I carried in my shirt because paper bags were nonexistent. I bit greedily into one, juice running down my shirt. The old people on benches eyed me hungrily but politely, looking at me from a great distance, as if we were still an ocean apart. And I was—an ocean of worthless local money obtained for a few dollars, a rich émigré trailing pricey peach juice behind me like gold dust. . . .

The blossoming free press of Romania, so quaint only yesterday, was, in fact, full of dire economic news, angry antigovernment invective, and, above all, the Chief Subject in Romania Today: the Big Plot, with its little plots, subplots, supersubplots. Were the events of December a real revolution or only a vast dramatic play staged by a few men who took power behind a curtain of blood? Always the same question. And by now everyone knew that yes, in December 1989 the Army and the secret police gave a revolution and the people came—to be slaughtered, on live television. One of the greatest staged media events of the twentieth century happened here, using these starving people's bodies, a true theater director's dream: a play with *real* bodies. Romanians are, after all, descendants of the Romans.

The group schmoozing by the fountain in University Square was not the crowd at the Free Speech Alley at LSU. It was an embittered gathering. Some of them had been recently beaten up for protesting. The bloody shell and mirror games of December and June were inscribed on their bodies. The students, looking for all the world like students of 1968, blue-jeaned and bearded, stood in small groups, passing papers around. Others were obviously of another class, the socialist unemployed, the never-acknowledged but ever-present city lumpenproletariat. "It was better under Ceauşescu!" shouted one of them. "We had no black-market speculators, uppity Gypsies, and émigrés!"

Another one agreed. "Democracy . . . pshaw! A democracy takes at most two months to put food on the table!" he said, emphatically confusing things.

"Yeah," said the first one. "And what did Nicu Ceauşescu ever do? He fed his people in Sibiu . . . and liked the things that matter: women and wine."

A goodly number of them also hated intellectuals for "spouting off," overlooking the obvious fact that if it weren't for "spouting off," they might not even be talking about it. The one thing that Romania produced in abundance these days was free speech. But everyone was angry, from poets to beer-guzzling proles. Anton Uncu said that "government by miners cannot be tolerated."

Back at the Bucharest I met with Michael over a drink. I was impatient to get on to Sibiu for my high school reunion a few days hence on July 8. We were waiting for the ABC News team to arrive so that we all could travel together. They were going to do a piece on the reunion for *Nightline*, a follow-up to the piece I had done in December. They were due to arrive next day.

We had been invited to the house of Nicolae Prelipceanu, an old poet friend, now vice-president of the Writers' Union. His wife, Denisa Comănescu, is the best translator of modern English and American poetry into Romanian. I was hoping to persuade her to translate my poems into Romanian, an operation I am surely incapable of. When we arrived at Nicolae and Denisa's apartment, it was already past ten in the evening. There was a full moon out. Ana Blandiana was also visiting. I was very happy to see her again. The subject this time was poetry,

but very soon it changed to politics. Ana, who had been recently denounced in the official front newspaper *Azi* ("Today") for betraying her
country (the newspaper demanded that she, Doina Cornea, and several
other dissidents be brought before the court for slander against Romania
in the foreign press), said, "Until the government tells the truth, we
cannot move forward." She is among a handful of intellectuals in postrevolutionary Romania who refuse to put on blinders. The visit lasted a
good long while, long enough for Michael to become enamored of
Blandiana. That wasn't very difficult. Blandiana, I believe, is the true
Miss Liberty of Romania. While Denisa and I became involved in an
obsessive discussion about the multiple meanings of the word "brass" in
English, Michael and Ana argued passionately about the future of Romania. Neither one of them noticed that they were not speaking the
same language.

  The streets were deserted on our way back, and all was peaceful.
Across the street from the Bucharest, however, a noisy mob of men in
suits, many of whom looked like gigolos, were gathered in front of the
Athenée Palace, the famous locale of intrigue described in *The Balkan
Trilogy* among others. Half its floors had been blasted away by cannon
fire, but the basement was still operational. It was a hard-currency
nightclub, just opening at 2:00 A.M. A hostess with a flashlight directed
us to the foot of the stage. When I began to make things out in the dim
light, I saw a silver bucket with a champagne bottle to my left. We were
seated on some kind of low revolving stools. Immediately to our right
was a beautiful sphynxlike woman flanked by two effeminate boys wrapped
in silk scarves. The rest of the clientele looked like extras in a Werner
Fassbinder nightmare. I did not have much time to reflect on my neighbors. The stage lit brilliantly up, and a sequined grande dame with a
grande décolletage attacked an oversize microphone with the ruined voice
of Piaf. She was immediately followed by a drunk comic who fired rapid
volleys of incomprehensible slang at the largely immobile crowd. Nobody laughed. Maybe nobody spoke Romanian. Or, most likely, nobody knew how to laugh. I ordered a second champagne bottle and
studied the Sphynx, who smiled a thin smile and beckoned me over. I
ambled casually to her table, just as the stage was taken by a fifteen-
year-old girl in a blue sequined bikini with a tiny fringed top. Behind
her, standing erectly at attention, was a creased and pale vampire in
evening dress holding a whip. I introduced myself to the Sphynx, who
was French and who introduced me in turn to her two companions,

Maurice and Armand. The little girl onstage was a contortionist. At the sound of the whip, backed by a drumroll, she made a ball out of herself, then extended one leg into the air. Her master deposited his top hat on her foot. Maurice and Armand turned out to be saints of capitalism. I motioned Michael over. He came, bringing his tape recorder. While the little girl spun the hat, rested it between her legs, picked it up with her toe, and sat it first on her head, then on her buttocks, Maurice and Armand explained to us that they had come to Romania to spread the doctrine of capitalism. They had traveled to every country in Eastern Europe with their doctrine. I asked them what they were selling. "We are not selling anything!" they replied impatiently. I was not quite sure what this religion was, but I was getting bored, and the Sphynx wasn't talking. "Where are you staying?" I asked her.

"Room two twenty-three at the Bucharest," Armand replied for her.

Amazing! That was next door to me. The contortionist rolled off the stage to thunderous applause, which Michael and I took to be our cue that we'd had enough champagne. We went back to the hotel.

I stayed awake for a while, listening for the Sphynx and the two saints of capitalism. Nobody came. I fell asleep and had a complicated dream in which a contortionist called Romania tried her best before an audience of capitalist saints seated on puffy pink clouds of champagne. Next day I found out at the desk that no one was occupying room 223 and that it had been vacant for a week. Postrevolutionary Bucharest was not an entirely real place.

15

My High School Reunion

If Bucharest simmered deeply in the summer of its discontents, Sibiu was cool, high in the mountains. Children played on the cobblestones in the square just as they had last winter; only now they weren't slipping all over the ice. A little Gypsy beggar girl ran up to me when I got out of the car and poured forth a tragic lament belied by her ruddy good looks. "My mother is dead," she cried, "and my father, too, and my brother has no legs, and my sister's a baby! They robbed us, they beat me, and my dirty little hand's all that keeps them living and the family name still in the world!" She said this, with variations, over and over. Watching the little girl with an air of seeming unconcern, a Gypsy man with a black hat pulled low over his eyes leaned, smoking, against a wall. Three older females of his tribe squatted like multicolored onions on the ground, playing cards. The government had given the Gypsies certain minority rights (to the dismay of most other citizens), including representation in parliament and the right to their national dress. They now walked the streets dressed proudly, the men in black suits with red or yellow silk kerchiefs around their necks, the barefoot women wrapped in bright fabrics with gold coin necklaces between their barely covered breasts.

At the martyrs' shrine at the center of the square not much had changed since December. The names of those killed in the revolution were inscribed in two handwritten rows on a plaque leaning against the

223

statue of Gheorghe Lazăr. An old man with a face carved out of Carpathian rock was laying a flower on top of the mounds of dried weeds piled at the shrine.

The new graduates of Sibiu high schools stared out of store windows at me. From the window of my father's photo shop the group portrait of the 1990 graduates of Lyceum Gh. Lazăr looked out. But they hadn't been photographed by my father, and there were bolts of fabric in the window, the future dresses and suits of the college-bound soon-to-be new technocrats of Romania. My graduation suit, made for me by Mr. Fischer, came to America with me and saw use for years until I couldn't fit in it anymore, or maybe I didn't fit *with* it anymore because I'd gone over irrevocably to the jeans generation. Ready-made clothes still hadn't invaded Romania—though it exported shirts, pants, and even suits—and this was a good thing, as far as I was concerned, because people still looked as if their clothes and their bodies had made an effort to know one another.

Seized by nostalgia, which is stronger and more childlike in the summer, I went to the Bruckenthal Museum, the wonderful dark oasis where Marinella and I conducted prolonged and timeless amorous struggles behind statues of bygone Romans and new bronze Communists until they closed the place in the evening and put us out dizzy into the linden-tree–perfumed dusk of the Middle Ages. The Dutch paintings of my childhood were just where I left them, still dark, blissfully unrestored into those cartoon colors now popular in well-heeled Western museums. Several Rembrandt people, sensible, well-rounded, stared with some recognition at me. But clearly it was the swarm of creatures in the background of Van Eyck's landscapes that knew me the most. I had watched them many times change shape with the rise and fall of my own shape wrapped around the changing shape of Marinella. We'd changed shape together! That's hard to forget. The Bruckenthal was not as solitary as I would have liked. I am often drowned by an erotic wave in an empty museum. And this was the museum where I'd first set foot in the waters of Eros. But roving gangs of children—among whom I glimpsed myself—swarmed by on clouds of self-importance in summer camp splendor, led by well-turned young teachers with huge twinkles in their eyes. All these children, born partly out of the dictator's draconian edicts . . . I liked them. I half expected to see my Hungarian nanny, my German Fräulein, and our Romanian housekeeper coming out from the shady tunnel under the clock tower calling my name.

When I finally put up at the "Emperor," it was already afternoon. Ion had been waiting impatiently for me for the better part of three hours.

"So let the reunion begin. Where is Marinella?"

"Well, there's been a hitch . . ." said Ion.

"No. She's married."

"I will have to explain about the reunion—"

That wasn't very reassuring. The twentieth reunion was in 1985. Nobody had invited me to it. I'm even amazed that my name was on the officially published reunion list. It must have taken some courage to type it. Until December 1989 my name was on the shortest blacklist of Securitate. The still-classified decree stated that names on this list could not be publicly pronounced, "not even in crossword puzzles," an injunction so fearsome I trembled at the thought of some overwrought young poet attempting to foment revolution with 3 Across: "Lives in New Orleans. Graduated from the Lyceum Gheorghe Lazăr in Sibiu, Transylvania, in 1965."

I did get my invitation to the twenty-fifth now, on July 6, 1990. Ion Vidrighin handed it to me personally in the lobby of the "Emperor of the Romans." "We sent it to you!" swore my best high school friend with all the sincerity he could never muster, not even back then, when he was only eighteen. He had changed a little since winter, or maybe it was just my imagination that became overstimulated in the place of its origin. Last December he had been fat, but now he seemed even larger, a porcine figure of some development, a prime example of desperate eating, weighty authority, and survival under the Ceauşescu regime. He still knew all the girls behind the desk at the mighty "Emperor of the Romans" Hotel because they had not changed. Neither had the "Emperor." But something *had* changed. One of the girls behind the desk was a lissome bottle blonde with dark Gypsy looks who laughed when I explained that I wanted the room without the microphones. My friend Vidrighin laughed, too, and winked at her. The net result of these laughs cum wink was that she exchanged the room key she had just given me for another. I winked, too, not sure what it meant. I wasn't sure if the room I now had was the one with or without the microphones. One thing I did know was that I was back in the land of winks and hand signals. Two fingers drawn across the shoulder signified epaulets and rank in the secret police. The signal was used to warn you silently that someone was a Securitate agent, and that's just what my friend did when the elevator door closed behind us. In a well-practiced dramatic whisper he also let me know that the pretty receptionist was famous for walking up to Nicu Ceauşescu, the late dictator's heir, two days before, during his trial, to hand him a bouquet of flowers. The gesture was on national TV. I wasn't too sure whether my best friend from high school was himself two-fingers-across-the-shoulder.

I wasn't entirely without shadows myself. I was a hell of a lot skinnier than Ion, but I had a secret agenda as well—namely, writing, taping, and filming the story of this reunion of my post–iron curtain school chums in the chaotic days of postrevolutionary Romania. He didn't know it yet, but Michael of NPR and Reed, Fabrice, and Dennis of ABC News were close by. I wasn't sure whether I had come foremost as a steely-gazed observer-journalist or as a sentimental friend eager to recapture the past. A bit of both, I suppose, though the journalist in me was worried because at this late date I still did not know whether an official reunion was going to take place or not or whether I even remembered my friends.

After I had dropped my two bags on the bed, I opened the window. There it was, my beautiful medieval burg, Sibiu, slanted roofs, windows opened like eyes in them, Gothic church towers, twisty cobblestone streets, stairways, shady plazas, and tunnels between towers. Sibiu had escaped Ceauşescu's plan to raze it and have "agroindustrial complexes" built over it. "We can thank Nicu Ceauşescu for that," Vidrighin explained, echoing the odd sympathy for the ex-dictator's son that was widespread in his former fiefdom. In addition to preserving the town, Nicu, who liked "women and wine," made sure that there was bread and salami in the stores.

There were whiskey, Kents, ibuprofen, and Madonna's "Breathless" in my bag. I put her on the Sony. (Later, when we went out, there was Madonna, in the elevator! "I didn't know you had 'Breathless' in elevators already," I said to Ion. "We have everything in Romania," he replied, "except dollars.")

"So what's the plan?" I asked my pal. There was no plan. There was no official reunion; most people were on vacation. Check one off for the journalist. It was going to be just our old gang getting together to see what twenty-five years had done to our senses of humor. Vidrighin's sense of humor was about the same. On our way back down, he told me that the reason he was fat was that his girl friend "blows instead of sucking."

Ion was probably the skinniest kid in class. The two of us used to play hooky at the Hungarian café across from school, with our collars raised rebelliously up, drinking defiant coffee and cognac while our teachers passed by, withering under our scorn. Occasionally we were brought before Comrade Sausage, who dispensed justice by slapping everyone equally across the face, no matter who started what or what the offense. His stinging fingers echoed in my resentful head for years, giving birth to complex fantasies of revenge visible in detail within the smoke of my cigarette. My gaze would wander in those days with the smoke, past the spiral stairway passages, towers, and spires of my beautiful Gothic town, past the blue-green and often snowy Carpathian mountain peaks surrounding us, past the fishlike shape of Romania, across the Black Sea, past the Bosphorus, across the Mediterranean, straight into the future, which was hazy but had a rock 'n' roll beat like what we were listening to now. We spoke French and German in the café, never Romanian, of which we had plenty in school. We could get by in Hungarian, especially when it came to communicating with the paprika red Marishka behind the counter, who resembled and, no doubt, tasted, like one of her whipped cream carrot cakes. We also had Russian in school, a language everyone made an effort not to learn, as a political statement, although for me it was a matter of our teacher, Comrade Papadopolu, who wore the first miniskirt in Europe. I never heard a word she said. She wasn't coming to the reunion. A pity. Vidrighin's main job back then was to listen to me hold forth. His other job was to defend me against the kids from the Tech School who were in the habit of sweeping our elevated haunts whenever their team lost a soccer match and beating up everyone with glasses. On those occasions Vidrighin's knife and the pleasure he took in pounding flesh were extremely satisfying. Once I had to stop him from utterly destroying a young mechanic who was lying on his face in the alley under the clock tower while Vidrighin jumped on him over and over from the top of a stairway. I distracted him by pointing out two young factory girls who were passing arm in arm on the bridge over our heads, their billowing skirts poised like bells above us. Vidrighin had an interesting problem, having to do with a generous and inordinate amount of male flesh that was a legend among our classmates, many of whom paid one *leu* to see it. One doctor had advised tying it with a belt around the knee, but it was too painful a thing, so Vidrighin took the occasionally embarrassing chance of appearing in public with what looked like a stolen Sibiu salami in his pants.

For intellectual stimulation, I had other friends: Alex, mentioned earlier, one of the three Jews in my class (besides myself and Max Fischer), with whom I discussed philosophical problems after school on a street corner in talmudic detail even in the dead of winter, when we had to jump from one foot to another to keep from freezing to death, and Aurelia, my girl friend, with whom I engaged in protracted bouts of wrestling that always led to a reading of Baudelaire in lieu of sex. And happily there was Marinella. Baudelaire bored her. But sex was her poetry, and after having sex with her, I inevitably wrote poetry, which was infinitely more gratifying than just reading it. I even had the pleasure of defending her honor once when an older kid surrounded by a clump of ruffians suggested in the schoolyard that "Marinella would do this and that to all of them in no time flat." I decked him. They all jumped me. Vidrighin showed up. We all were slapped by Comrade Sausage.

Alex lived rather reclusively in New York now; Aurelia moved to Canada with Max. In the first two or three years after I emigrated to the States I used to put on the suit Mr. Fischer made for me just to feel the "good fabric" on my skin emanating a piercingly sweet effluvium of nostalgia for my lost girl, my adolescence—a possible life.

There were a few others in our immediate entourage, notably Ancuţa, who was a good kid, but not above frequenting a late-night dive called the Golden Barrel, a catacomb dug beneath the old city wall. It had Gypsy fiddlers who rent the smoke with their violent melancholy. We slapped money on their sweaty foreheads when they came near. There was a whole art to slapping a nonchalant tip at just the right spot on the fiddler's head. It was a disgrace to miss. The cavernous round brick rooms with the roughhewn wooden tables could have been there at the time François Villon entertained his companions in the middle of the fifteenth century. Many functioning establishments and houses in Sibiu dated from the twelfth century. The Golden Barrel was a new joint by comparison, and the wine was obscenely cheap. The tramps and floozies who lived in there never saw the light of day, and there was enough cigarette smoke to keep day out forever. Sometimes Ory came with us because she loved poetry. Sometimes Bucur came, a blue boy who died our last year in high school from the blood ailment that made him blue. When Ory got drunk, she got on the table and sang with the fiddlers. Every cross-eyed amputee in the joint wept in the sour brew at those times.

Marinella ran off with the ticket taker at the Corso Cinema. Everyone applied to universities in different towns: Vidrighin and Ancuţa to Cluj; Ory to Timişoara; Aurelia to Bucharest. After the final exams my mother and I received the passports for which we had secretly applied two years before. In the fall of 1965 I said my good-byes to my high school chums, my beautiful Sibiu, and Romania.

Ancuţa was a portly fellow, too, the king of a domestic realm that included his wife, a history teacher, two graceful and self-possessed daughters, Laura and Livia, educated partly, as it turned out, in Vienna, and an ancient mother with a stern look on her black babushka-framed face. He was a veterinarian, keeper and caretaker of five thousand of the state's pigs, one of which was succulently giving up his juices for us at this very moment. His house had modern amenities I have yet to attain: a satellite dish for his TV, an outdoor barbecue grill, a wine cellar. I remembered the quick-witted boy who sat in front of me and smirked in sympathy when our history teacher picked on me—and tried hard to see his outline in the man before me.

Ory had filled out, too, but she was clearly still in possession of that sexy spark of long ago, a fact outlined with rouge and mascara. She was a country doctor in a town near Sibiu, where she dispensed mostly advice; medicines are hard to come by. Amazingly she remembered poetry I wrote in high school, silly verses that I had long forgotten. She began reciting these with abandon, to the visible distress of a giant brute with a bandaged hand who lurked awkwardly at her left. He was her husband, a famed Romanian soccer player long retired who was chain-smoking himself into an early grave.

"Goddamn Gypsies!" he shouted, apropos of nothing.

"You go home if you don't behave!" said Ory.

On my right was Marcel, a quiet boy I recalled liking very much for what was an unruffled calm in the face of constant adolescent agitation. He was still calm, an engineer at the Olt waterworks, where he measured the rise and fall of the old river, which, like Romania, is both seasonal and unpredictable.

Romanians are an affectionate people. We hugged and kissed and toasted our reunion with Ancuța's strong plum brandy. The thick, fresh steaks cooked on the grill, and the first cool stars appeared over the mountain.

"I almost didn't come," I told them, "because of the violence of the miners beating up students in the square." I said this only half-jokingly, referring to the violent events of two weeks ago.

But they became unexpectedly serious.

"Those bastards got what they deserved!" shouted the ballplayer to the dismay of his wife, who agreed with the sentiment but found him crude.

"There were few students there," she said, "There were mostly Gypsies, speculators, foreigners. . . ."

"I was ready to go to the square to beat up the scum myself!" Ancuța said vehemently. "There weren't just miners there . . . there were all kinds of workers. . . ."

At the mention of "miners" they all began to speak at once. They were speaking well and persuasively, but there was something awfully familiar about their articulateness, it was the articulateness of rostrums, plenary meetings, party conferences. . . . Amid the sudden din of their voices I had a sudden and rather chilling revelation. My friends here were . . . the "miners." I had been afraid to come back to Romania because . . . of my friends!

I felt suddenly remote in time and place, no more remote perhaps than I once felt back in high school, where I was also in a minority: a poet, a Jew. My friends here all were solid Salvation Front supporters, but I wondered about those who were not present: the Germans and the Jews who had emigrated, the ones who hated school and everything about it and were never going to return, the ones who were sent to prison for trying to escape, the ones who faded away, unable to play the system as well as my friends here. . . .

The women had laid out a long table covered with clean hand-woven cloths. Large dishes full of fresh and pickled cucumbers, toma-toes, eggplants, as well as hams and cheeses, were arrayed splendidly before us next to large wineglasses and small ones full of brandy. Almost everything was homemade: the wine, a five-year-old white from the cel-lar of the country house, the brandy, the cheese, the salamis, and even the pots. After the hors d'oeuvres the women served a delicious chicken dumpling soup with large ladles from big ceramic pots with flowers on them. All through the meal, which proceeded festively and almost without politics until the very end, I noticed that none of the women—with the exception of Ory—had yet sat down to eat or talk. When I remarked on this to her, she said: "Yeah, that's the next revolution. . . . We learned how to make one now. . . ."

There was irony going every which way here, so I asked Ory about the way the December revolution unfolded in Sibiu. According to early news accounts, Sibiu had been the site of fierce battles between Ceau-șescu's Securitate troops and the Army, which had gone to the side of the people demonstrating against the tyrant. Early casualty figures men-tioned tens of thousand of dead people. The water had been allegedly poisoned. Ceaușescu "terrorists" of the Securitate had burst into hospi-tals and killed the wounded. All those reports were quickly revised. Eighty-nine people had been killed. The water was fine. Nobody had killed anybody in any hospital.

"The Army just fired at the people," Ory told me. "One day in December there were posters calling people to the square to protest Ceaușescu. When they showed up, Army sharpshooters fired at them from the rooftops. Later they pumped one million rounds into our neighborhoods. We hid under tables, in bathtubs. When everything stopped, there were dead people everywhere. Everyone knows somebody who died."

To my surprise everyone at the table agreed. No one believed the official accounts of the "revolution." In their opinion, Ceaușescu had been overthrown by a coup d'état backed by the people. Not sure how or if their coup would succeed, the conspirators—which included the chiefs of Army and Securitate—had created mass hysteria by showing piles of bodies on TV. The whole world had been taken in.

It was a strange thing. Here in the middle of this sumptuous feast, I experienced the eeriness of another (hardly new) revelation: They all were blaming the Army for the shootings; no one mentioned Securitate, the secret police. . . . Clearly the official line of the government, which they all defended passionately, was that Securitate—not the Army—massacred all those people who were undeniably massacred in Bucha-rest, Sibiu, and elsewhere. Could my friends have also been . . . ? I felt like drawing two strips across my shoulder with two fingers, but I had no one to do it for. . . . In any case, the point that they were making, and that is being corroborated everywhere these days, is that very few shots had been fired in defense of Ceaușescu. He had been betrayed by everyone. Even his son, who'd been in charge at Sibiu, hadn't ordered anybody to fire at demonstrators or at soldiers. All the shooting came from the "People's Army" at the same time that the Army was officially coming over to the "side of the people." Romania's TV revolution had only *one side.* Everyone had been on it. . . .

For the next ten or twelve hours we flickered in and out of our past selves in clouds of smoke. There were snatches of song, gales and ripples of laughter. I caught now and then the wide-open sober eyes of Ancuța's beautiful daughters, staring at the proceedings with a combination of curiosity and disbelief. "What the hell's with the new generation?" their father asked.

"They don't have our talents," said Vidrighin, meaning, no doubt, something obscene.

"And what's so special about *us?*" I asked.

Ory leaned forward, drunkenly confident. Her husband had passed out in his chair. "Optimism!" she said.

A quarter of a century had passed. It sat between us like a dark, unconscious mass, lit only now and then by an odd remark. In addition to time, we were separated by languages, politics, a sea (the Black Sea), and an ocean (the Atlantic). My Romanian was still rusty, having been practiced mostly on the phone with my mother (with whom I have an accent-maintenance contract for the purpose of keeping my R's rolling) or in formal interview situations in which the translation can be as wooden as what is being proffered. My whole adult life had taken place in America in the American language. My Romanian was frozen in that eighteen-year-old curl of existential and sexual melancholy smoke at Marishka's café. I barely got their jokes, and I was no doubt missing all the subtleties, where the real story was. Here came another revelation, just as eerie as, if not eerier than, the rest: I was missing *the story!* The journalist in me slapped me soundly once across my unstudious cheek. But there was also hardly any way I could have made them see my story, the ecstatic madness of an American poet's life lived in several cities on the coasts of two different oceans, a life, I might add, in complete sympathy with rebellious students of all causes. So have another brandy, and another wine! And roll on, tape!

To tell you the truth, they scared me, my friends, these supporters of the National Salvation Front, applauders of brutal drunken miners who beat up students and Gypsies. But maybe I scared them, too, a grown-up journalist, part of those powerful and mythic media that run the world they've never seen. And yet all of us felt quite clearly an affection that the years had not dimmed. I recognized under the layers of a mean time the hopeful adolescents we had once been. Another brandy now, and age would drop off altogether, with all its flesh and compromises.

Next day, after an hour or so of agitated sleep, during which the eyes in the rooftops of Sibiu blinked without surcease under the full Gothic moon and the microphones in the wall picked up my every muttering, I rose to see how bad it would feel to stand. Surprisingly I felt little pain. The pork buffers between drinks had done their job. There was a knock at the door. Here was Vidrighin, his countenance lit by a lascivious grin caused, no doubt, by some salacious exchange with the girls at the front desk.

We were going to the mountaintop. The car lurched through brilliant pastures. We passed peasant carts full of hay with children waving from the top. At some point we disembarked, and here was the whole gang, looking as fresh as if the politics of darkness and last night's drinks had never washed over them. They were carrying picnic baskets full of cooked meats, wines, and apéritifs. There was some kind of decaying sculpture park nestled between crags. We hiked up there. Laura and Livia, joined by their mother, sang in German. At the crest we stopped to take in the breathtaking view and to toast ourselves with fluted glasses of brandy. Everyone was singing now, except me. I never could sing. Up above us somewhere was Ion's father's sheep farm, where I once spent a magic summer. We were in a beautiful place where I forgot for a moment the ever-present politics of Romania.

This day, too, turned into evening, and evening turned into night at Ancuța's country house in the beautiful village of Săliște, not far from where we were. The cellar of the country house was well stocked. Every gorgeous chunk of rolled ham and pickled tomato stood in Technicolor splendor on its dish, posing for Fabrice's video camera.

The state of festive exhilaration and profoundly bewildering alienation deepened the next evening, when my friends, their spouses, and their children came to a dinner I gave in their honor at the hotel restaurant. They hired a singer and panpiper for the occasion, "a famous professor of music," a man who looked me directly in the eyes and in the dulcet tones that make "one's soul flow out," as the Romanians say, asked me why I had left home, my mother country, my hearth. Just as I began to wonder myself, awash as I was in sentiment and brandy, the tenor of his songs changed. He began singing nationalist Transylvanian songs, and the whole table joined in. The Hungarians, Germans, Jews, and even people from Bucharest cringed at their tables. Songs forbidden during Ceaușescu's era, Fascist Iron Guard anthems poured out, directed against foreigners, of which clearly I was one—though forgiven for the moment—and against émigrés, and I was forgiven for that, too. . . .

Next day I stood hung over and bewildered on the balcony of my hotel room and pondered the deeply troubled soul of my birth country. I could see all along the central street the portraits of the graduates of the year 1990 displayed in store windows. Among them were the 1990 graduates of the Lyceum Gheorghe Lazăr including Ory's daughter Cosmina, looking innocently at year 2000 or 2005. I felt for them. It will be tough.

16

Bucharest: The End

It was my last day in Romania. We had returned to Bucharest, Michael and I, feeling every twist and turn of the mountain road in our feast-weary bones. I would have liked to be able to draw some conclusions from the long days and sleepless nights spent talking, talking, talking. Romania is a country of voices, long-suppressed voices, speculating, debating, shouting, wondering. I closed my eyes and listened to them; they lurched like the road, filling my head with all the forgotten charge of sound of my childhood and adolescence. The main product of this country now was theory; there was little else. My good friends of yore had made safe lives for themselves that were now coming under anxious questioning both from within themselves and from others. They feared their own obsolescence. I still had no idea how much of their affection was genuine and how much of it had to do with clutching at a Western straw through which they might be able to glimpse their lives in the future. But I wasn't a very good straw; I do not value stability as highly as my friends. Through me they would glimpse only trouble, uncertainty, constant movement, defiance for order. "All we want in this country," Ancuța said at one point, "is peace and quiet." In other words, just like before, when the peace and quiet of the dictator gave life, their life, an illusion of permanence. But I'm afraid that nothing will be the same ever again, and my friends know it. A long period of unrest, violence, suppressed strains, and unpleasant truths awaits them. They know it, too. Unfortunately they are rallying about the obsolete facts of their imaginary national identity, which is mostly a fairy tale.

Michael and I were drinking a beer at the Inter-Continental Hotel in Bucharest, a few hours before leaving. This ugly, looming monster of cement and corruption, where all the news reporters stayed, was the only place to get cold beer in Bucharest. The slime of this country sloshed against the police beige walls. I spotted liver-colored vampires of both sexes who stood ready to spread infection under the ghastly neon. I saw the money changers, now paying 150 lei to the dollar, up from three days ago. I saw people dealing in anything foreign from disposable lighters to condoms. Was this the beginning of the famous change to the market economy touted by everyone from government ministers to street corner philosophers? If so, there was little to sing about.

Everyone I spoke to wanted to leave Romania. Paradoxically, now that it was possible to have some freedom, the only freedom anyone wanted was to get out. As I listened to the voices in my head, I saw little reason to hope. Communism had torn up people's souls. There was hatred, resentment, and despair everywhere. "We've got to do something about the Hungarians, the Gypsies, and the others" was the recurring refrain that played lento over every encounter. This "others" chilled the Jewish blood in my veins to a temperature, alas, only too familiar throughout history. In Sibiu, while I sipped a glass of wine with Ion, we were approached by a city slick, a friend of his, who said, when we were introduced; "You talk just like the kikes who are coming back." His use of "kike" was casual, like Georgescu's in Houston.

"And your mother," I asked him, "was she Hitler's dentist?" He was offended.

During my whole stay it proved impossible to talk reasonably to my Romanian Transylvanian friends about their Hungarian neighbors. "They didn't tell you," one of them raged, "that the Hungarians played football with the head of a Romanian priest and that they paraded an impaled Romanian child through villages. . . ." When I asked for proof, they just shook their heads, disbelieving my disbelief. Did I know my friends? My original fear had been that I would not recognize them. But I'd had no trouble. The flesh hadn't changed as much as the spirit. On the other hand, there were islands of darkness big enough to be seen with the naked eye. About these I knew little.

My great fear for our generation was that the "nationalist" urge, this need for hate and "purification," was a way to assuage the guilt for getting on so well during the Ceauşescu years. One way to deal with such guilt would be to burn in the flames of nationalism, a collective death wish too horrendous to contemplate. On the face of it, my cheerful drinking buddies did not seem ready for suicide. But I had my suspicions.

At Otopeni Airport I clutched my Air France ticket tightly, happy to be leaving. I experienced, in an attenuated form, the same mixture of intoxicated elation and fear that I had experienced when I first left Romania in that faraway year 1965, sure that I would never return. I was brought suddenly to my senses by the barking of the immigration officer holding my passport. *"Where is your exit form?"* I didn't know.

"I don't have it," I told her.

She glanced at my visa. *"Journalist?"* Her voice dripped with contempt.

"Yes," I said. "Have something against journalists?"

"Codrescu?" she said, with the same hatred. I saw myself suddenly in her eyes: a journalist out to bad-mouth her country and an émigré. How she wished for the old days! *"I am an immigration officer!"* she shouted. *"I can ask you to the next room!"* I could imagine the next room well: a small green chamber with rusty flakes of blood all over it. But she refrained, and I was glad.

This would be the end of the story if life were as neat as stories. But no sooner had I gotten out of the clutches of the Romanian police apparatus than it was announced that Air France had canceled the flight. Used to the endemic paranoia of Romanians, I immediately assumed that a crisis was at hand. In fact, the airplane needed repairs, and it would not be ready until next day.

Going once more through the routine of retrieving luggage and getting a taxi back to Bucharest, I saw little to look forward to. I was wrong.

Massed by thousands in University Square, students from all the universities in the capital were marching toward the Justice Ministry.

They were demanding the release of their imprisoned leader, Marian Munteanu. FREE MARIAN MUNTEANU! The students carried flowers; their slogans echoed throughout Bucharest. They chanted, *"Dormiţi uşor, dormiţi uşor, aţi ales un dictator!"* ("Sleep well, sleep well, you've elected a dictator!") and *"Jos comunismul!"* ("Down with communism!")

I joined the demonstration, not as a reporter or as an older supporter but as a body, feeling at once that there was hope yet. As the crowd rounded the corner to Opera Square to listen to Mihai Gheorghiu, the vice president of the Student League, speak, I knew why my high school friends seemed so much older than I did. They were against the young just as the older generation had been against the young of America during the student demonstrations in 1968. They were the people the young wanted out of power. Time had stood still in Romania. Until recently. A revolution did take place in December and then in June. It was not the staged revolution that we saw on television and that was most likely a play scripted by the KGB and acted by the Army and Securitate with the innocent help of a cast of millions. It was a revolution in people's souls when they suddenly felt no more fear. This revolution is going on still. Whoever let the tiger out of its cage is in no position to put it back again.

Index

239